THE BEAUTY OF
SOUTHERN ENGLAND

THE BEAUTY

OF

SOUTHERN

ENGLAND

Published by The Reader's Digest Association Limited

LONDON • NEW YORK • SYDNEY • MONTREAL

THE BEAUTY OF SOUTHERN ENGLAND explores east Dorset, Hampshire and the Isle of Wight, Sussex, Surrey and Kent. Although the southern part of London overlaps Surrey and Kent, most of Greater London is covered by *The Splendours of London*, another book in this series. The region is densely populated, but it includes areas of unspoilt countryside such as the New Forest and parts of the North and South Downs. Tourists crowd the resorts of the south coast, and pass through the area to airports and ferry terminals. The strategic importance of the region is also clear, with museums and defensive sites bearing witness to a less peaceful past.

The Road to Canterbury, by Shirley du Boulay, is a personal record of the author's walk from Winchester to Canterbury, following the path taken by pilgrims travelling to the shrine of Thomas Becket in Canterbury Cathedral during the medieval period. Specially commissioned features and photographs complement the text and an introduction gives an overview of the area. The 'Highlights' section of the book has a small selection of the many attractions in this large region.

THE BEAUTY OF SOUTHERN ENGLAND was edited and designed by Tetra Publishing Limited, The Barley Mow Centre, 10 Barley Mow Passage, Chiswick, London, W4 4PH, for The Reader's Digest Association Limited, 11 Westferry Circus, Canary Wharf, London E14 4HE

The Road to Canterbury Original full-length version by Shirley du Boulay, first published by HarperCollins Publishers, 1994
© Shirley du Boulay 1994
British condensed version © The Reader's Digest Association Limited, 2000

FOR TETRA PUBLISHING LIMITED

Art Directors Eddie Poulton, Paul Wilkinson

Editorial Director Louise Tucker

Volume Editor Elizabeth Tatham

Consultant Dr Robert Dunning

Associate Editors David Blomfield, Hugo de Klee

Copy Editor Barbara Roby

Additional material by Malcolm Day, James Harpur, Elizabeth Tatham

Cartography Anthony Sidwell (pages 8–9), Malcolm Porter (pages 150–51)

Index Brian Amos

FOR READER'S DIGEST ASSOCIATION LIMITED

Series Editor Steve Savage

Art Editor Karen Stewart

FRONT COVER *The verdant greenery of Scotney Castle Garden overspills into the moat of the ruined castle.*
BACK COVER (TOP) *Bluebells are a lovely sight in many parts of the South where they thrive in woodlands.*
BACK COVER (BOTTOM) *Two occupants of the sheltered accommodation at St Cross Hospital, Winchester.*
TITLE PAGE *Oast-houses, once used for hop processing, remain an intrinsic part of the Kent countryside.*

THIS PAGE *An angel and maze are part of the fine carvings on the walls of the Watts Chapel, Compton.*
PAGES 6–7 *A shaft of sunlight illuminates a path in a densely wooded area of the New Forest.*
PAGES 24–5 *The fields and woods of the North Downs, viewed from the vantage point of Reigate Hill.*
PAGES 148–9 *Beachy Head's lighthouse is dwarfed by the mighty chalk cliff itself.*

CONTENTS

EXPLORING

SOUTHERN
ENGLAND

with Malcolm Day

SOUTHERN ENGLAND

with Malcolm Day

SOUTHERN ENGLAND, with its long coastline and mainly green landscape, is an area rich in contrasts. Its gently rolling downlands, fertile pastures, cornfields, orchards, vineyards and hop gardens are many people's idea of the epitome of English country life, and the term the 'Garden of England', often used in association with Kent, aptly describes much of the region. Other areas seem to reveal different aspects of life in the South. The rugged chalk coastline, especially the White Cliffs of Dover, has featured in key events in England's history and is seen as the gateway to the nation. The seaside resorts of the South and the great racecourses, golf and cricket clubs evoke the region's role as a playground for all.

The South is all of this and more, but if there is perhaps one characteristic that defines the region, it is the fact that it is a landscape that has been largely shaped and moulded by humankind. Much of it, though it may appear untouched, has been cleared, tilled, cultivated and built upon over the centuries. For all this, there is a sense of harmony which, along with the region's location, and the notable absence of large-scale manufacturing industry, continues to attract a variety of people: day-trippers wishing to escape London, those wishing to retire to the country, or to combine working in the city with living in the country, and holiday-makers, bringing to the region an affluence that supports a thriving leisure industry and helps to maintain the attractiveness that is the enduring appeal of the South.

THE LIE OF THE LAND

Southern England, from Poole Harbour in the west to the North Foreland in the east, and from the Isle of Wight in the south to the outskirts of London in the north, contains some of the most prosperous and fertile areas of the country. The counties comprising the area—east Dorset, Hampshire and the Isle of Wight, Sussex, Surrey and Kent—can also be defined by their proximity to the coast and London. In physical terms, most of the area is united by the North and South Downs, part of a geological unit that has played a major role in the history

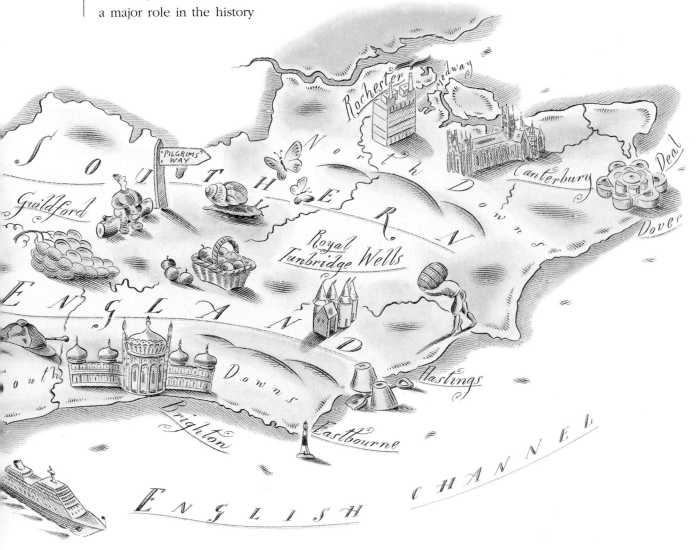

ABOVE *Dusk falls over the South Downs, creating a dramatic silhouette behind the green fields of Sussex. The poor chalk soil has meant that much of the Downs is uncultivated and wild flowers thrive in the grassland.*

and land use of the South, as well as determining its appearance. The chalk hills of the Downs are arranged in an elongated horseshoe shape: the North Downs curve westwards from the cliffs of Dover right round to Winchester, where they turn to the east, becoming the South Downs, and run eastwards until they reach the imposing chalk cliffs at Beachy Head on the Sussex coast, reappearing briefly on the Isle of Wight. Lying between the two ridges of the Downs is the Weald, whose clays and sands provide a sharp contrast with the chalky Downs. At the open end of the horseshoe are two areas of marshy coast, the Pevensey Levels and Romney Marsh; a third area of marsh, the North Kent Marshes, lies north of the North Downs in the Swale Estuary, which connects to the Thames. West of the chalk cliffs at Beachy Head are the mainly shingle beaches and small natural harbours that characterise the south coast.

The chalk downs and cliffs, the marshes, the Weald and the beaches each have their own character, making this region extremely varied in terms of appearance, and the flora, fauna and activities it supports. The Downs, for example, have since ancient times provided east–west pathways on high, dry land above the Weald, once densely wooded. These pathways have been revived today by the Countryside Commission, which has created an official walk across each of the Downs. The walks offer magnificent views that seem to stretch into infinity over hill upon hill of patchwork fields, once grazed only by sheep but in recent times turned over to arable farming. The chalk of the Downs also supports

a range of wild flowers, including some rare orchids, and the vegetation attracts butterflies, both natives and migrants from the Continent.

Many of the butterflies and birds that migrate between the British Isles and the Continent make their journey through the southern counties. The spectacular chalk cliffs along the coast provide staging posts for birds gathering before they leave the country, and a more permanent home to sea birds. The cliffs at Dover are one of the best-known landmarks of the British Isles, making a spectacular sight, best seen from a boat, as they rise almost sheer out of the sea. Beauty spots such as St Margaret's Bay and Beachy Head offer the walker an invigorating, if terrifying, experience of this dramatic drop to the sea. One of the most unusual outcrops of the chalk cliffs forms the Needles on the Isle of Wight, whose amazing white jagged pinnacles apparently darting out of the sea have been both a danger to ships and an attraction for tourists.

In contrast to these rugged cliffs are the low-lying stretches of marsh that punctuate the area. The marshes are remote, eerie places, shrouded in mist and tales of ghost ships stranded on the sandbanks. It is easy to see how such stories evolved as you look across the North Kent Marshes and see Thames sailing barges travelling so close to the water's edge that they appear to be sailing on the fields. It is in the North Kent Marshes that the sinister opening scene of Dickens's novel *Great Expectations* takes place, when the young boy, Pip, comes across a convict, recently escaped from a hulk, or prison ship, moored in the Medway, and still in

ABOVE *Fairfield Church stands alone in the reclaimed pastureland of Romney Marsh. The medieval church that originally stood on this site was once surrounded by water and sometimes accessible only by boat or on horseback. The present church, whose design follows that of its predecessor, was built in 1912.*

chains, hiding out on the misty flatlands. Although now largely drained and farmed, the marshes retain their bleak demeanour, as can be seen at Romney Marsh, in southeast Kent, where Dungeness power station and lighthouse loom out of the plain. Dungeness itself is a large shingle beach protruding beyond Romney Marsh into the English Channel, and is home to one of the area's most important breeding colonies of gulls and terns.

The shingle coastline extending west from Beachy Head, with the rolling South Downs providing a backdrop, is punctuated by a series of natural harbours that have served not only fishing and trading, but also smuggling, for which this coast was notorious. The smugglers have largely been eradicated, seaside resorts have sprung up out of the fishing villages, and yachts have replaced many of the fishing boats. The coast is now dominated by the leisure industry: hotels line the seafronts, watersports of all kinds take place in the bays, and the warm climate attracts day-trippers, holiday-makers and people wishing to retire.

A quite different landscape is to be found on the Weald, inland of the South Downs. Much of this once-dense woodland has been cleared, its timber used for shipbuilding in centuries past. Nevertheless, many forests remain. The trees in these forests are periodically cut back, or coppiced, yielding timber and encouraging growth, and a freshly coppiced area of woodland is a wonderful sight in spring. This is the traditional season for woodland flowers, which bloom early before the leaves of the trees above them unfurl and create the dense canopy that blocks out most of the sun in summer. Coppicing creates even more light and many plants flower in greater profusion. Carpets of bluebells, for example, are one of the loveliest features of the Wealden forests. The trees of the Weald vary with the types of soil that make up its various parts, with Wadhurst Clay producing what are reputedly the best oaks in England. Similarly fertile soil is found on much of the Weald, and where the forest has been cleared, the area has become prime agricultural land. This fertile soil, along with a mild climate, has been exploited by generations of farmers in Kent and Sussex, making agriculture one of the area's main industries and giving Kent its reputation as the 'Garden of England'.

A GREEN AND PLEASANT LAND

Both Kent and West Sussex make ideal fruit-growing country. In the orchards of the region the apple is the main fruit, but pear, plum and cherry are also plentiful. The trees are kept to a low level, allowing for easy picking, and sheep often graze beneath the spreading branches, keeping the grass in check. Like the forests, the orchards look their best in spring, when the trees blossom with their pink and white blooms and lambs gambol among the falling petals. It is with good reason that H. E. Bates's affectionate tale of life in the Kent countryside is called *The Darling Buds of May*. Soft fruit such as strawberries, raspberries and gooseberries grow well too, as do Kentish cobnuts and vines.

Kent's most distinctive crop is not a fruit, however, but a flower, the hop, which is the ingredient that gives beer its distinctive bitter flavour. Through the summer, the hop gardens produce their delicate, yellow-green, papery, cone-shaped flowers. They sprout from stems that twine around 'cages' of string and wire supported by upright hop poles, and by late August these structures are transformed into a wonderful forest of dense green foliage and flowers. Hop-picking machinery has now replaced the gangs of casual labourers who, in days gone by, swarmed the fields at harvest time. Often from London, these workers would make hop-picking a working holiday, and whole families would decamp to Kent. Although the hop-pickers have gone and the hops are no longer dried out in oast-houses, these lovely symbols of Kentish agriculture, with their distinctive pointed roofs and white cowls, are still scattered about the landscape, mostly as an unusual style of housing. The area under hop cultivation is declining, but the harvest is still celebrated in such brewing centres as Maidstone and Faversham, and hop bines, the long stems with hops and leaves attached, still decorate the local pubs at harvest time.

Such fertility is not typical of the southwestern part of our region, home of the New Forest. Though the area appears no less rural, it has poor, sandy soil, a factor that must have contributed to the forest's preservation. A royal hunting

LEFT *A hop-picker cuts the hop bine from the hop pole by hand in the traditional way. Hops (above) are usually harvested in late August.*

ABOVE *A red deer suckles her young in a New Forest clearing. The forest was originally created as a royal hunting ground by William the Conqueror, and it was there that two of his sons were killed in hunting accidents.*

ground in medieval times, it is still largely owned by the Crown, and is managed by the Forestry Commission. Covering an area of some 145 square miles, the forest comprises sizable mixed conifer and broad-leaved plantations and great expanses of heath and grassland that not only provide wonderful views, making the New Forest good walking and riding country, but are also of great ecological importance, making up the largest expanses of semi-natural vegetation in lowland Britain. Ponies, donkeys and cattle have rights to roam freely.

Some parts of the forest are still quite remote, being far enough away from the more urban surrounding districts to retain a distinct, unspoilt character, enhanced by the forest's proximity to the sea. These qualities attract about 8 million tourists annually and a leisure industry has developed around the forest, providing walking and riding trips as well as specific attractions. One such attraction is the fine collection of vintage cars at the National Motor Museum, situated in the grounds of Palace House, Beaulieu, home of the Montagu family. The picturesque village of Buckler's Hard was built by the Montagus in the 18th century on the banks of Beaulieu River, and developed into a shipbuilding village, where three of the ships that formed part of Nelson's fleet at the Battle of Trafalgar were built. Little more than two rows of cottages running down to the river, the village is in a lovely setting and has been preserved, with some houses open to the public. The history of the village is traced in its maritime museum. Shipbuilding was an important industry in many of the towns and villages in southern England, where there was access to plentiful supplies of wood from the New Forest and the Weald. The decline of wooden ships, especially those required for battle, has meant that much of the industry has disappeared, but the great maritime bases of the south coast, Dover, Portsmouth and Southampton, remain.

GATEWAY TO THE NATION

Dover, in particular, with its impressive fortress castle and the vast sprawl of its trade and passenger port, encapsulates the great forces that have shaped the southern coast—defence, trade and leisure. One of the shortest routes to the Continent is between Calais and Dover, today providing a major trade and day-trip passage, but these towns once stood on hostile shores. Then, Dover was Britain's first line of defence, and its castle, standing proud on a steep hill above the town and the famous white cliffs that stretch from Folkestone to Deal, embodies many layers of the country's military history. Roman invaders recognised the strategic importance of the site when they built a fort and a pair of lighthouses here, the remains of one of which still stand. Raids by Saxons, Vikings and Jutes followed the collapse of the Roman Empire. The last major invasion of Britain took

place at Hastings in 1066, led by William the Conqueror, and one of the new king's first actions was to strengthen Dover. Continued threats from the Continent ensured Dover's ongoing importance; although much of the present-day castle was built in the 12th century. At the turn of the 19th century, when much of Europe was controlled by Napoleon, tunnels built in the hill in medieval times were extended to accommodate troops, and were reused in the Second World War, when Britain stood alone against occupied Europe once more. At this time Dover became one of the most powerful symbols of Winston Churchill's island fortress, the white cliffs providing a natural defence and the castle evoking Britain's historic military capabilities and defiance. Today, Dover Castle is a major tourist attraction, with thousands of visitors flocking to walk the battlements and tunnels, take in presentations of medieval siege warfare, or simply enjoy the view of France.

Other remnants along Britain's defensive coast are also impressive. Rochester Castle, for example, originally built by the Normans as a classic square fortress, still dominates the River Medway. Deal Castle, ideally viewed from the air, is a perfectly preserved example of Tudor military engineering, its circular keep surrounded by two rings of defence forming a shape that resembles a flower. Other military installations that stand out in their now-peaceful surroundings are the Martello towers, built between 1805 and 1812 to defend the Southeast from the threat of Napoleonic invasion. The region's coastal scenery is littered with these little circular forts, of which there are seventy-four between Folkestone and Seaford. Some, like the one that has been restored at Eastbourne, are open to the public and hold exhibitions on coastal defences. More recent traces of Britain's military history can be found at Tangmere Museum near Chichester, situated at the famous Battle of Britain airfield, which documents the history of flying.

ABOVE *A cross-Channel ferry carries tourists between France and Britain. As the journey takes less than two hours, the coastal towns of both countries are regularly filled with day-trippers.*

TOP LEFT *The White Cliffs of Dover provide the famous first view of Britain's shores on the Channel crossing.*

TOP RIGHT *Dover Castle, one of the most popular tourist attractions in the Southeast, was still being used for defence as recently as the Second World War.*

The ships that defended Britain at sea were once provided by the Cinque Ports at Dover, Hastings, Hythe, New Romney and Sandwich, and later at Winchelsea and Rye, which were contracted to provide ships and sailors. The silting up of many of these ports, and the establishment of a permanent Royal Navy, resulted in their falling into disuse, and today Dover is the only one of the original seven that is still a major port. It was Henry VIII who established the beginnings of the Royal Navy—at Portsmouth, which was strategically positioned on the narrow peninsula of Portsea Island and is still England's chief naval station. The naval base, occupying over 300 acres, is almost a town in itself, and the busy harbour teems with vessels including naval frigates, tugs, and ferries serving the Continent and the Isle of Wight. The salvaged wreck of Henry VIII's warship, the *Mary Rose*, is on display in the dry dock in which she was built, and in the oldest part of the dockyard can be seen Horatio Nelson's flagship HMS *Victory*.

ABOVE *HMS* Victory, *now in dry dock at the Royal Naval Dockyard at Portsmouth, was Admiral Viscount Nelson's flagship during the Battle of Trafalgar in 1805. Nelson died on board, but the battle marked Britain's triumph over Napoleon's Franco-Spanish fleet.*

Comparable in strategic maritime importance is Southampton, situated west of Portsmouth on a peninsula where the Itchen and Test rivers flow into the Solent. With its fine natural harbour, Southampton has a nautical heritage dating back for over 1,000 years. Southampton was Britain's leading port for passenger ships, particularly for transatlantic voyages, and, like its neighbour, has been both a point of departure for English armies and a tempting target for foreign invaders. The port saw one of its finest hours as a departure point for the Normandy invasion, and part of the flotilla of landing craft needed for the invasion occupied most of the boat-builders of the Solent in 1944. Now the Solent is renowned for its lively yachting community. Southampton's role as a transatlantic passenger port has changed since the decline of travel by ocean liner, but the port is still a busy centre frequented by a variety of vessels, including container ships, car ferries bound for the Isle of Wight, liners setting sail for the Mediterranean, and huge commercial tankers.

LEFT *The vast complex of Gatwick Airport is set on the outskirts of London in the lovely Surrey countryside.*

A TRANSPORT REVOLUTION

Britain's ancient maritime tradition has in many ways shaped the coast of southern England, but it was the advent of the railways in the 19th century that spelled the beginning of a transformation of the inland South into a well-connected unit. This fast and reasonably efficient method of transport across the region, and in more recent years a network of motorways, has made the South one of the most densely populated parts of the country, bringing to it a measure of prosperity and securing its position at the heart of communications between England and mainland Europe.

While railways and motorways have created a transport network across the South, London's second-largest airport at Gatwick and the Channel Tunnel, have improved communications with international destinations further afield. Hotels, restaurants and road and rail links have grown up to serve Gatwick, and it has its own police, fire stations and chapels, making it a small community, and provides about 25,000 jobs for people in the area. Over 24,000,000 passengers travel through Gatwick every year and, as a result, congestion on the ground and noise in the skies of the South have become increasing problems. Serving a growing number of passengers each year is the Channel Tunnel. Opened in 1994, the tunnel takes passenger trains and vehicle-carrying shuttles, it has helped to boost the South's expanding leisure industry, and is seen by many as a symbol of closer links between Britain and the Continent.

SOUTH COAST SEASIDES

Brighton, one of the main cities of the south coast and its most famous seaside area, is one of the focuses of the leisure industry in the South. A destination favoured by day-trippers, holidaymakers and commuters, Brighton first became popular in the 18th century, after a local doctor set up in practice there, proclaiming the wonderful healing powers of sea water. A craze for sea-bathing spread round the south coast and fishing villages everywhere were transformed into resorts.

Much of Brighton's Regency architecture, with its elegant balconies and bow windows, remains today, and the town has one of the most impressive promenades

ABOVE *The spectacular Royal Pavilion at Brighton, built for the pleasure-seeking Prince Regent in the early 19th century, epitomised the spirit of the age. The Chinese-inspired interiors match the opulence of the Indian-style domes and minarets of the exterior.*

on the south coast. The town's crowning spectacle is the Royal Pavilion, an Oriental extravaganza with spires and onion domes, much of which was built by John Nash between 1815 and 1822 for the Prince Regent to use for entertaining. Brighton still has a reputation for a lively nightlife, as seen in the illuminated Palace Pier. Behind the stucco-fronted hotels and boarding houses lies the old quarter, known as 'the Lanes', where narrow, twisting passages take you past antique shops and cafés.

One could say that the craze for sea-bathing has never ceased, though now it is primarily for pleasure instead of for health. Any hot day in August will be accompanied by a blaze of holidaymakers along the beaches of the south coast, swimming, paddling at the water's edge, playing or just sunning themselves in deck chairs. A continuous ribbon of promenades and seaside culture stretches from Bognor Regis to Seaford.

To the east of Seaford is Beachy Head, and beyond lies Eastbourne, an established resort, where one can listen to military music playing from the

LEFT *Palace Pier, opened in 1899, is one of two piers extending into the sea from Brighton's shingle beachfront. The other, the West Pier, which opened in 1866, was closed for many years, but is currently being restored.*

turquoise-topped bandstand or walk along the three-tier promenade and enjoy the brightly coloured Carpet Gardens. The town's Devonshire Park has some of the best grass tennis courts in the world which, along with the clement weather, makes the town second only to Wimbledon for tennis enthusiasts. Eastbourne is also a favourite among retired folk, as is Bournemouth at the extreme western end of the south coast of our region. During the summer months, tourists sunbathe on the seven miles of sandy beach or explore the chines, the natural pine-clad valleys that run inland from the coast, and provide a desirable setting for avenues of salubrious residences.

Resorts of the north Kent coast have long been a favourite with Londoners, who could reach the area quickly by river boats, even before the railways brought greater numbers. A gentle, refined place that has retained some of its old-world charm is Broadstairs, at the most easterly point of Kent. Here, a breakwater shelters a scalloped sandy bay, where fishing boats can land their catch, and over-looking all looms the castle-like Bleak House, where Charles Dickens wrote his

RIGHT *The seaside resort of Broadstairs, seen here on a perfect summer's day, was a favourite resort of Charles Dickens. In the background on the left is the castellated Bleak House, where he used to write.*

novel *David Copperfield* and planned *Bleak House*. Round the headland is Margate, as old as Broadstairs, but with quite a different atmosphere. A seafront of amusement arcades, gift shops and ice-cream parlours provides side attractions to the popular theme park, which lies at its heart, while nine miles of beaches, caves and grottos offer recreation when the sun shines. Further along the north Kent coast are Herne Bay and Whitstable, the latter famed for its oysters.

Poole Harbour, back on the south coast, is one of Europe's largest natural harbours. In the harbour proper lies Brownsea Island, a bird sanctuary that also has an open-air theatre in summer, to which spectators are conveyed by launch. When the conditions are suitably windy, this expanse of water is a haven for windsurfers, whose scudding sails and flying spume make a fantastic sight.

PLAYGROUND OF THE SOUTH

Windsurfing is one of many outlets in the South for enthusiasts of watersports. The coast is dotted with yacht clubs, especially along the Solent, which has several inlets, and the Isle of Wight. When August comes, it is Cowes Week, a sailing regatta where the most popular event is the Round-the-Island Race. It is the largest boat race in the world, well over 1,700 boats of all classes pitch in to circle the Isle of Wight, putting their navigational skills to the most strenuous of tests. The finale of the week, run every second year, is the Fastnet Race, in which competitors set off from Cowes on a 605-mile course, sail round the Fastnet Rock off Southwest Ireland, and return to Plymouth.

Cowes is also famed for its yacht club, the first English club, which was founded in 1815 and later became the Royal Yachting Club. Royal patronage in the area continued when Queen Victoria made the nearby Osborne House one of her country homes. The South in general has a rich heritage of stately houses and gardens, where many have made country homes close to London. Rudyard Kipling lived at Bateman's, a Jacobean house in East Sussex, where his love of the East is reflected in the decor, featuring Oriental rugs and artefacts. Winston Churchill bought a house called Chartwell in 1922 and lived there until his death, the gardens there provided inspiration for his hobby of painting. Some houses, such as Sissinghurst, where Vita Sackville-West and Sir Harold Nicolson created their famous gardens in the grounds of an Elizabethan manor house, have become especially noted for their gardens. These houses and gardens, like many others in the South, are open to the public and have become popular destinations for day-trips. Gardens are of particular interest for those living in the suburbs and towns of the South, who often have quite large gardens of their own. Also of interest to keen gardeners is Wisley in Surrey, the base for the Royal Horticultural Society, and visitors flock there to see the gardens and buy plants from the garden centre.

Goodwood House, home to the Dukes of Richmond since 1697, is where visiting kings and queens have traditionally stayed when enjoying the horseracing at 'Glorious Goodwood'. The mansion overlooks the entire scene, its commanding setting among the gracious, rolling South Downs rivalling any to be had in England, and galloping steeds have delighted race-goers here for two centuries. The Epsom Downs is another famous venue for race meetings. Two classic races dating from the 18th century take place every June at Epsom racecourse, they are the Derby, known as the 'scurry over Surrey', and the Oaks.

Elsewhere in the South, other prestigious sporting events take place, such as the world's oldest golf championship, the Open, which has been held at Sandwich several times. That very epitome of the image of southern suburban life, the golf club, is found throughout the area, enhancing its reputation for being green. Cricket greens, too, are found in many villages, and Hampshire, Surrey, Sussex and Kent all have First Class county teams. One Hampshire village, Hambledon, is renowned as the cradle of cricket, as it is here that cricket grew and was promoted by the landlords of The Bat and Ball pub.

Some parts of the South have not been cultivated or developed, and have been preserved in a more natural state, to provide sheltered habitats for flora and fauna. Many are close to the walks that crisscross the region and can be visited. Box Hill, for example, is one of Surrey's most popular beauty spots, and is one of the few natural habitats for box in the country. Nearby runs the North Downs Way, and close to it the less scenic Pilgrims' Way, which links the great cathedral cities of Winchester, Rochester and Canterbury.

ABOVE *With the rolling South Downs stretching away behind them, racehorses thunder towards the finish line at Goodwood.*

PILGRIM CITIES

Canterbury was the destination for medieval pilgrims walking from either Winchester or London, via Rochester, to the shrine of the martyred St Thomas Becket. Canterbury still celebrates this ancient role in an annual festival focusing on Chaucer's poem *The Canterbury Tales*, which has immortalised so much of medieval life, and the act of going on pilgrimage, for later generations. Many of the city's museums and visitor attractions also use the poem as a starting point for reconstructing medieval Canterbury and others use finds such as a Roman pavement as a basis for interpretation. Remnants of the city's past can still be seen all around Canterbury: the wonderful medieval walls and gate that stand on Roman foundations, for example, are an impressive sight. Much of the city retains its medieval atmosphere, with the jettied top storeys of timbered shops almost meeting across the narrow streets. Visitors making their way through these crowded streets may be taken by surprise by the view of the cathedral entrance that suddenly greets them at the Christ Church Gate. Defended by angels carrying shields, and a large figure of Christ, the gate stands in a line of shops facing a favourite spot for buskers, often in medieval dress. In summer this entrance is full of tourists, the sound of many languages and excitement re-creating the impression that many medieval pilgrims must have felt when they arrived at their destination.

The cathedral itself has some fine examples of Gothic and Norman architecture, with beautiful stained glass and many interesting tombs, including that of the famous Black Prince, eldest son of Edward III, whose life-size effigy is surmounted by his 'achievements', items of personal armour. Tourists are guided through the cathedral by official guides, who ensure that nothing disturbs the regular services that take place in this, the mother church of the Anglican Communion. Canterbury was the first church to be founded by St Augustine, who reintroduced Christianity to southeastern Britain in the late 6th century; the second was Rochester.

Set on the banks of the River Medway, the historic city of Rochester was founded by the Romans on the site of an Iron Age settlement. Although the Roman walls and Norman castle were added to in later centuries, they both still form a magnificent site on a hill overlooking the river on one side and the town on the other. Rochester Cathedral, at the base of the hill, is part Norman and part Gothic, and inspired the last lines ever written by Charles Dickens, in *The Mystery of Edwin Drood*, which describe the cathedral in the changing morning light. One of Rochester's most famous inhabitants, Dickens lived just outside the town and used many of the old buildings of the town in his novels. These locations are now identified for visitors to the Charles Dickens Centre, where they can see tableaux from scenes in Dickens's novels and visit the Swiss chalet that once stood in his garden and served as his study. The town's quaint, crooked medieval shops and houses and more dignified later buildings combine to give Rochester a unique flavour, enhanced by special events such as the Sweep's Festival in April or May, which features morris dancers, and the Dickens festivals held in summer and in winter, when Dickensian characters parade through the town centre, attracting visitors from across the country and abroad.

ABOVE *Canterbury's Christ Church Gate, completed in 1517, is a fine example of a late Gothic building, although much of its stonework dates from later periods. The central figure of Christ, missing from this picture, had been taken away for restoration.*

Even more popular among tourists is Winchester, where many medieval pilgrims began their journey to Canterbury. The city is dominated by its magnificent cathedral, begun in 1079, which, at 556 feet from east to west, is the second-longest church in Europe, after St Peter's in Rome. One of the city's most famous visitors, Jane Austen, who lived the last few weeks of her life in a house in College Street, is buried in the cathedral. Winchester became the chief town of Saxon Wessex in the 9th century under King Alfred the Great, whose bronze statue now presides over the Broadway. Today an agricultural market centre, Winchester contains some fine relics of its ancient history from every period since the 12th century, including medieval gateways, well-preserved 16th-century timber-framed houses and Wolvesey Castle. Apart from some excavated foundations, the Great Hall is all that remains of Winchester Castle, once one of the finest in the country, where King Arthur's Round Table, made in the late 13th century, has hung for over 600 years. Winchester is also home to Winchester College, the oldest public school in the country.

INTRODUCING *THE ROAD TO CANTERBURY*

Winchester is the start of the Pilgrims' Way to Canterbury, the route followed by Shirley du Boulay, author of *The Road to Canterbury: A Modern Pilgrimage*. Her journey took her along what is, in all likelihood, the path taken by medieval pilgrims visiting the shrine of St Thomas Becket in Canterbury Cathedral, as an act of devotion, penance or thanks, or simply as a contemplative holiday. Shirley du Boulay's modern-day pilgrimage, told in the pages that follow, is both a spiritual journey and a celebration of the lovely countryside of southern England.

ABOVE *Rochester Castle, whose brooding presence for centuries defended the passage of the Medway, looms out of the evening mist.*

THE ROAD TO CANTERBURY

A condensation of the book by Shirley du Boulay

CHAPTER ONE

THE FIRST STEP

ABOVE *Author and former TV and radio producer Shirley du Boulay in her study. Her walk from Winchester to Canterbury retraced the Pilgrims' Way.*

I MOVED SLOWLY AND SILENTLY. I was walking the Mizmaze, an ancient turf labyrinth on Winchester's St Catherine's Hill. It stretches comfortably across part of the top of the hill, near the side of a chapel, and is roughly square, measuring 86 by 90 feet. I set foot on it apprehensively, wondering what I would experience, wondering whether I would experience anything at all. It is a unicursal maze, in other words, there are no choices—just keep going and you must reach the centre. Almost immediately I was filled with a great sense of trust. I knew that this simple track would not mislead me: if I followed it faithfully I would arrive where I wished to be. To and fro, crisscrossing the holy hill, I covered quite a distance and was aware that I was becoming intimately acquainted with the terrain, feeling at home in this intricate weaving. Often, as is the way with the labyrinthine pattern, the path took me away from the centre, but this did not diminish the sense of trust I felt as I went on, almost hypnotically...

Then, so suddenly that it was with a sense of shock, I was there, standing in the centre, a rough log my only company. Did I feel any different, having accomplished this small feat? I did. But why? And how? I could not lay claim to any great achievement—it was not far, nor was it hard—but the tortuous path had honoured my trust and led me to the centre. I was filled with a sense of security and wholeness. I stood there in thrall. Time was suspended. I could hardly tell how long I stayed thus, but it was probably only a matter of minutes. Then some children arrived at the periphery of the maze; at the edge of consciousness I heard them laughing and talking as I remained separate, sealed off in my safe, womb-like little world. Suddenly, one of the children, spurning the long, winding path, scampered straight across the maze and jumped into my pool of quiet, shouting, 'I've won!' I was jerked back into the competitive world.

The Christian tradition has long seen the maze as a symbol of pilgrimage, and in the Middle Ages to tread a maze was to make a symbolic pilgrimage to Jerusalem. In a few months' time I would be walking the Pilgrims' Way from

Winchester to Canterbury, and this pilgrimage in miniature, around St Catherine's Hill, was, as it were, an aperitif before the meal.

QUESTIONS

The idea of making a pilgrimage had been suggested by a friend, some two years after my husband's death; it was one of those moments of illumination that can appear when life is at its bleakest. After months and months of apathy and indifference I was immediately excited, curious, expectant. It was as if a light had been switched on.

My excitement lay in the symbolism of the journey—the search. When I was about fifteen I had one of those experiences of union, a sense of oneness with nature and with God, that (although I did not realise it at the time) set me on the path of the searcher. Since then I have been pursued by what the poet Francis Thompson called the 'Hound of Heaven', and though I have sometimes

ABOVE *The turf maze on St Catherine's Hill is the only surviving ancient turf maze that is square in shape.*

blessed him, sometimes wished he would go away, he refuses to give up the chase. Perhaps it would be possible, I thought, by making a pilgrimage, by trudging the long miles from departure to destination, to learn more about the universal pilgrimage, the journey we all make from birth to death. Perhaps this physical re-enactment of the inner search might shed some light on my own doubts and questions, might even heal my wounds.

I was intrigued by the interest pilgrimage aroused in my friends. 'Are you a keen walker?' they asked. 'What made you choose Canterbury?' The idea of pilgrimage struck a deep resonance and their questions forced me to examine my own motivation.

I have never been a particularly keen walker. However, I was attracted by the thought of the physical activity and the challenge to complete an undertaking. I was drawn to the idea of travelling through beautiful scenery and the deep satisfaction of going slowly, able to feel the earth under my feet, savour my surroundings.

As for Canterbury, there were many reasons for my choice. I was keen to be anchored in the tradition of the Middle Ages, the golden age of pilgrimage.

THE CANTERBURY TALES

ONE OF THE GREAT POEMS of English literature, *The Canterbury Tales* by Geoffrey Chaucer (*c.*1343–1400) is a series of 24 stories told by a group of pilgrims as they journey from London to Canterbury to visit the shrine of Thomas Becket. In the famous 'Prologue', Chaucer starts his book by describing the scene in the Tabard Inn, Southwark, with brilliant cameos of his fellow pilgrims—ranging from a monk with a passion for hunting to a five-times-married widow from Bath and a 16-stone miller with a beard as red as 'any sow or fox'. The Host of the Tabard proposes that each of the 30 pilgrims, including Chaucer himself, tells two stories on the way to Canterbury and two on the return journey—in fact Chaucer wrote only 24 of the projected 120 tales before he died—and that the best storyteller should be dined at the expense of his companions.

Agreeing to this plan, they set off and begin to tell their stories, which are by turns bawdy, satirical, romantic and moralising. Drawing on legends, fables and folk tales and probably on his own pilgrimage to Canterbury in 1388, Chaucer weaves a rich tapestry of medieval life, giving insights into such subjects as marriage, Church corruption and medicine. 'The Knight's Tale', for example, tells of love and chivalry, while 'The Nun's Priest's Tale' uses a fable about

LEFT, BELOW AND RIGHT *Illustrations from William Caxton's second edition of* The Canterbury Tales *show some of the pilgrims enjoying a meal (left), the Wife of Bath (below) and the Knight (right).*

a cock and a fox to warn against the dangers of flattery. The book ends on a serious note, with the Parson's sermon, which covers the Seven Deadly Sins.

Chaucer was well equipped to comment on society's foibles. His colourful career included spells as a page, a diplomat, a customs official, an MP, a JP, and the Clerk of the King's Works—experiences that his

For over 300 years after the murder of Thomas Becket in 1170 his shrine in Canterbury Cathedral was one of the most popular in the whole of Europe. What better route could I take if I wanted to share the experience of the medieval pilgrims? Further, the story is one of the best known in British history: it has been immortalised in Chaucer's *Canterbury Tales* and T. S. Eliot's *Murder in the Cathedral*, and the pilgrimage has left its legacy in everyday language: 'Canterbury bells', whose flowers resemble the bells worn on pilgrims' horses, the word 'canter' from the 'Canterbury-gallop' (the easy pace at which the pilgrims moved); even the word 'Canterbury' is sometimes used as an epithet for a long and tedious story.

It is also a pilgrimage that not only has an end, but a beginning, at Winchester. Though Chaucer's pilgrims travelled from London, there is also a route from Winchester to Canterbury traditionally taken by pilgrims. Though this has been argued, even dismissed as modern fantasy, there is a case in its favour, strong enough to ensure that this route is inscribed in memory, even marked on modern maps as 'The Pilgrims' Way'. Further,

poetic talent transformed with humour and perception into the panoramic vision of the tales. Also, influenced by French and Italian writers, he helped to establish the supremacy in England of verse based on regular syllables and rhymes over the older English tradition of alliterative poetry. And at a time when many different dialects existed in England it was his work that made the dialect of the Southeast dominate subsequent English literature.

RIGHT *Pilgrims on the road, with the city of Canterbury in the background. The picture is from a 15th-century book of poetry by John Lydgate.*

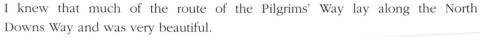

ABOVE *The year 2000 was marked by a series of events staged by local dioceses along the Pilgrims' Way.*

ABOVE *The author, Shirley du Boulay, walking through an avenue of poplars on the Pilgrims' Way.*

I knew that much of the route of the Pilgrims' Way lay along the North Downs Way and was very beautiful.

I became a Roman Catholic in 1989, but am too late a convert for relationships with saints and reverence for relics and shrines to come naturally, and cannot claim to have chosen this route out of a particular devotion to St Thomas Becket; I was drawn more by the thought of those who had walked before. The idea that this could have been the route taken by the medieval pilgrims appealed to me; but even if it were proved to be fantasy, I could take comfort in the fact that there is no doubt that the Pilgrims' Way from Winchester to Canterbury is an ancient way, used by mankind for thousands of years. However changed it might now be, I would be following in the footsteps of men, women and animals who had trodden the same path, sharing the experience of pagans and Christians, of Neolithic man and 20th-century backpackers. It was, above all, this primal, atavistic, aspect to the Pilgrims' Way that excited me.

Pilgrimage concerns the body as much as the mind and spirit, so it seems fitting to answer some of the eager questions my friends asked about the practicalities involved in a long walk.

Would I go alone? I had considered it. In medieval times, travelling alone was thought to be especially virtuous. Why it should have been so raises a hornet's nest of questions. Solitude brought risks, there was no question about that. Travelling in those days was a dangerous business and, despite the special protection given to pilgrims, their regular passing was too great a temptation to the professional robber bands, villagers and innkeepers who constantly chanced their luck and flouted the law. Murders were commonplace. So the pilgrim who walked alone must receive high marks for courage.

For the medieval mind, suffering, even to the point of masochism, was one of the ways to speed the climb to Heaven. So the merits of the journey were assessed according to the pain and inconvenience endured. Thus it was thought better to go on foot than on horseback, better still to go alone on foot, even better not to wear shoes at all. There are even recorded cases of an exceptionally ascetic, extravagantly humble pilgrim (although even in the Middle Ages they were rare) arriving at the shrine alone, barefoot and stark naked.

My attitude would not have earned me high marks. I verge towards hedonism rather than masochism and, apart from my almost fanatical wish to walk every inch of the way, I saw no reason not to be as comfortable as possible—and that included walking with friends. I suspect in this I was a fairly typical child of my time.

Though I enjoy solitude in small doses, I knew that over a long period I would become bored and lonely, yearning to talk and to share experiences, jokes, a bottle of wine. Also, I was constantly reminded that nowadays there are risks for a woman walking alone and, though I was put to shame by hearing of solitary adventures undertaken by braver women than I, I had no wish to walk in fear. Medieval thieves and bandits have their modern equivalents.

So I was delighted to find others keen to come and willing to spare the time. As my companions wish to remain in misty anonymity, I shall simply say that one, Jane, is a very close friend whom I have known for over thirty years. Eileen is an Oxford friend, and although we have not known each other for long, she became very involved with the whole venture, helping to plan the route and braving wind and weather as we took regular exercise together, in preparation for the trip. The third, Barbara, did not want to walk, but preferred to drive, spending the day painting and drawing along the route and meeting us in the evenings. So there would be three of us walking and four for friendly evenings and meals. It was a good balance.

The wish of one of our number to drive solved the problem of what to do with our luggage. Of course there are the doughty hikers who travel with all their needs on their backs, but it was unrealistic to think that three middle-aged women could do that. Our luggage would stay in Barbara's car and we would meet up with her and it in the evenings.

The use of a car and a driver would also solve the problem of reaching our night's lodgings without adding tiring miles to our day's travel. As we were planning to complete the journey in about twelve days, we needed to average thirteen miles a day. (Although the Pilgrims' Way is said to be about 120 miles, with diversions for lunches and visiting sites just off the route, not to mention getting lost, we eventually covered at least 150 miles.) The other side of the pleasure of walking mostly in woods, over fields and downs, and on river banks, we were to discover, was that it was seldom possible to find bed-and-breakfast accommodation—which in any case would have had to be booked in advance— without diverting from our route. Three or four miles more is three miles or four miles too much at the end of a long day's walk, but it is nothing by car, so we shamelessly asked Barbara to pick us up and drive us to wherever we were staying. I say shamelessly, but we were also scrupulous. If not exactly marking our last steps each evening with chalk, we would at least the next morning go back to exactly the point where we had left off the night before.

Another question I was sometimes asked was whether we prayed together. Two of us were Roman Catholics, one an Anglican and one calls herself a lapsed Catholic, but there was far more that united us than divided us, and we had no problem in finding a way to come together most evenings and sit quietly for a while. We had intended to discuss thoughts that had come to us during the day, but when the time came we were usually too tired, sometimes too taken up with the practicalities of the journey. So usually we would meditate in silence for a while, then one of us would read a prayer or a poem.

RIGHT *Languid water meadows bordered by wild flowers line the River Itchen outside Winchester. In the distance is St Catherine's Hill, which affords good views of the city.*

PREPARATION

Before I donned my walking boots and set out along the banks of the Itchen River, there was much to do. First I had to get physically fit. To a serious walker a journey of 120 miles is quite a leisurely stroll, but I had not walked any distance for three decades; also, I had had three operations in the previous eighteen months. I began to take regular exercise. Bike and car stood idle as I seized every excuse to walk—to the shops, to visit friends, to think, to talk. I walked on Oxfordshire towpaths, over muddy fields, on tarmac roads and, when I could find them, up hills. I was determined to be fit enough to enjoy the walk, which would leave my mind free to absorb the experience and encounter fully whatever might happen along the way.

I went to libraries to read about pilgrimage. I wanted to learn something about the tradition of the pilgrims in whose footsteps I would be following. I needed to understand something of medieval piety and the way medieval people regarded pilgrimage, relics, saints and martyrs; to know about the practicalities of their journeys—how they travelled, what they wore, how they relaxed, where they slept. I wanted to enter, at every level, into the nature of pilgrimage and to share and understand the passion that animated those who had travelled before me.

Less pressured by time than their 20th-century successors, the medieval pilgrims spent at least four weeks walking from Winchester to Canterbury. They would not have had to plan their day's travel or make long detours to find bed and board: in those days, hospices, inns and monasteries could be found along the route and they would simply have stopped when they were tired. Some, if they could afford it, travelled by coach or on horseback.

On our journey, there would be constant reminders of how different the landscape would have been in medieval times, how different from us the pilgrims would have looked. While we, wearing trousers and anoraks, rucksacks on our backs, guidebook in hand, were indistinguishable from other walkers, the pilgrim of the Middle Ages demonstrated his new, if temporary, way of life by wearing what was virtually a uniform, a declaration of his special status. He would have worn a *sclavein*, a long, coarse, russet-coloured tunic with large sleeves, occasionally patched with crosses. A leather belt was suspended round his shoulders and from it hung a soft pouch known as a scrip, in which he would keep his money. A rosary of large beads hung from his neck or arm and, most distinctively of all, he would carry a staff, a tough wooden stick with a metal toe, and wear a large, broad-brimmed hat, attached at the back to a long scarf. The hat might be decorated with scallop shells or lead images of the Mother of God and the saints. As the old ballad about the girl seeking her lover reminds us, those on pilgrimage and clothed in 'pilgrim's weedes', would have been easily recognisable.

> *And how should I your true love know*
> *From many another one?*
> *O by his cockle hat and staff*
> *And by his sandal shoone.*

BADGES OF PILGRIMAGE

WHEN VISITING A SHRINE medieval pilgrims almost always bought a badge or a miniature flask called an ampulla. These 'signs', as they were called, were not just souvenirs: they were proof that the pilgrim had reached his destination—crucial if he had been sent by a priest as an act of penance. They also distinguished genuine pilgrims from vagabonds and outlaws and entitled the bearer to protection from warring armies and to practical help from fellow Christians.

Millions of badges were mass-produced between the 12th and the 16th centuries and each shrine had its own symbol, such as the scallop shell associated with Santiago de Compostela in Spain—an image that became so well known that it was used as a symbol of pilgrimage in general. In England, the

LEFT *The scallop shell badge, originally worn by pilgrims visiting the shrine of St James in Santiago de Compostela, has become a well-known symbol of pilgrimage.*

FAR LEFT *A pilgrim's ampulla, bought at St Thomas's shrine at Canterbury, bears images of the saint's murder* (top) *and burial* (bottom).

greatest producer of signs was Canterbury, home of the shrine of Thomas Becket. Motifs of Becket on badges and ampullae varied, covering aspects of his life and death, and shrines dedicated to the saint. The ampullae were filled with what was known as 'Canterbury water'—water supposedly mixed with drops of Becket's blood, which was believed to cure ailments. Badges, too, were accredited with

miraculous powers. This was because pilgrims pressed them onto the shrines' relics to 'absorb' their spiritual power. Once badges had been endowed with sacred energy they could be used to ward off the ever-present dangers of the road or taken home to cure a sick relative. Back home, they were often attached to houses, cattlesheds and wells for their positive influence, or buried in fields to ensure good crops.

As with so many objects of medieval times, the pilgrim's apparel was invested with an elaborate symbolism. The pouch was usually small, too small to hold much money and thus showing the pilgrim's dependence on charity. The staff was used to fend off wolves and wild dogs, who represented the snares of the devil, but also for support, thus becoming the pilgrim's third leg and symbolic of the Trinity. Sometimes the tunic, not unlike the garments Christ might have worn, represented his humanity. This imagery often finds poetic expression, most famously in Sir Walter Raleigh's poem.

> *Give me my scallop shell of quiet*
> *My staff of faith to walk upon;*
> *My scrip of joy, immortal diet;*
> *My bottle of salvation;*
> *My gown of glory, hope's true gage,*
> *And thus I'll take my pilgrimage.*

WINCHESTER

By the time May 3 arrived, and we were set to start, my excitement had turned to panic. I couldn't understand it. I was only going for a fortnight's walk, in gentle English countryside with three good friends, yet I was in a state only a few shakes from terror.

Perhaps it was not totally inappropriate. The unexpected is part and parcel of travel. And, if to make a pilgrimage is to mirror life in microcosm, then it is fitting to embark on it with a degree of apprehension. It wasn't that I expected anything dreadful to happen outwardly; my anxiety was more over what I would experience inwardly. Would I encounter depths in which I would rather not swim, meet buried emotions I would rather not unearth? Then there was the fear that I would experience nothing at all, and the thought of that blank emptiness was even worse. There was no pleasing me. On the one hand, all I wanted to do was to curl up in bed, hidden deep in warmth, while on the other, I knew that I would feel deeply disappointed—and deeply ashamed—if I turned back before I had even started.

I had been consoled by the words of a wise friend, who had written to me saying: 'Just give yourself to the pilgrimage and don't think about anything except what's going on from moment to moment.' Yet the peace arising from my resolution to live in the present was disturbed again. The phrase 'It is only the first step that counts' haunted me. If it is only the first step that counts, what a world of significance would be invested in that step. In any case, when would it be taken, when does a pilgrimage begin? I imagined myself pinioned to the ground outside Winchester Cathedral, too fearful of the implications of that first step to move, looking longingly back at the life I was temporarily leaving behind and, like Lot's wife, turned into a pillar of salt, a new curiosity for passers-by. I decided to forget the proverb and remember the wise words of my friend.

OPPOSITE *The bright sunlight of a summer's day illuminates the delicate tracery on the west front of Winchester Cathedral. The front was built in the Perpendicular style during the 14th century.*

ABOVE *A street sign for Beggars Lane, which retains its old name in today's Winchester.*

RIGHT *The tower and part of the Church of St John, Winchester, where the author received a blessing before starting her pilgrimage.*

Our journey was to start at the cathedral, but first, following the tradition of the medieval pilgrims, we went to St John's, the oldest surviving parish church in Winchester. Here, the vicar, Canon Robert Teare, read a short and ancient service, the *Itinerarium for Pilgrims.*

The medieval pilgrim would, before his departure, seek the permission of his wife, his parish priest and his feudal lord; he would make his will, set his affairs in order and, most importantly, make amends to anyone he had wronged. He would probably have attended Mass, and then, at either a public or a private ceremony, would have received a formal blessing (such as the *Itinerarium*), in which his clothes, his wallet and mantle, his emblems and staff, would have been blessed as well. If he then made his confession, his penance, the expiation of his sins, lay in the pilgrimage itself.

When the short service was over, Canon Teare showed us the 'squints' close to the altar, through which the medieval pilgrims would have seen Mass being celebrated, and Beggars Lane, to the north of the church, so called because the beggars used to collect there, hoping to take advantage of the pious state of the pilgrims as they started out on their journey. Then we modern pilgrims, blessed in this ancient tradition, walked to the cathedral as Canon Teare regaled us with some of the less familiar facts about Winchester. He told us that in the Middle Ages there were fifty-five parish churches within the city walls; that the grounds of Winchester College boast the longest avenue of Siberian Wing-nuts in the world;

BELOW *Winchester College is one of the oldest and most famous public schools in England. Founded in the 1380s by Bishop William of Wykeham, its pupils are called Wykehamists.*

that the grass within the Bishop's Palace is the only piece of lawn in the city not fouled by dogs; that the large and imposing house, Number One, The Close, was once the home of Mary Sumner, founder of the Mothers' Union. Having just left the vicarage at Old Alresford, so large that it is now the diocesan retreat house, she complained that her new Winchester mansion was too small.

My only personal connection with the city is that one of the houses of Winchester College was founded in 1862 by the Reverend James du Boulay,

a schoolmaster, who was, I believe, a first cousin twice removed. I knew that for many years it had been known as 'Cook's', so when I went to see it I was amazed to find 'DU BOULAY'S', my own maiden name, still emblazoned on its stone walls. It gave me a warm sense of belonging.

Winchester is not a place for driving. But to wander on foot round the streets is to find that it is still a beautiful city, filled with the ghosts from centuries of English history—the Celts, for whom it was *Caer Gwent*, 'the white town'; Roman soldiers walking the long roads they had built connecting the city with Southampton, Dorchester, Cirencester and Silchester; the Saxons who, tempted by Winchester's position at the centre of this network, challenged and conquered. Under them Winchester became the chief town of Wessex, and when the kings of Wessex became kings of all England, the city for a time rivalled London itself. The Danish invasion brought King Canute, most vividly remembered for deflating his flattering courtiers by showing them that the sea would not retreat at his command.

One of Winchester's most prized possessions is the Round Table of King Arthur, which has hung in the Great Hall of Winchester Castle since the 13th century. It is made from 121 separate pieces of oak, measures 18 feet across, and weighs well over a ton. In 1522 King Henry VIII proudly took the Holy Roman Emperor Charles V to see it, claiming it was one of the most interesting sights in the kingdom. Henry had had it painted in the Tudor colours of green and white, with the Tudor Rose in the centre, a picture of King Arthur at the top, and the names of twenty-four of Arthur's favourite knights round the edge. No doubt Henry's pride owed something to the fact that the figure of Arthur bears an extraordinary likeness to the Tudor king himself.

ABOVE *The Great Hall is all that remains of Winchester Castle. It was rebuilt in the 13th century by Henry III on the site of William the Conqueror's earlier castle. It is one of the finest medieval buildings in Britain and is still used for some important ceremonial occasions.*

Once in the cathedral we visited the catafalque of one of Winchester's most famous citizens, St Swithun, the saintly bishop believed to have been tutor to the great King Alfred. Many legends surround this humble and good man. I was charmed to learn that he so disliked the cheers with which he was greeted as he walked round the streets, that he took to travelling by night. Another story tells of how he once saw a poor woman drop and break all the eggs she was carrying home. Concerned at her distress, he restored the eggs, miraculously whole, to the basket. By popular consent rather than Roman decree he had already, during his lifetime, come to be regarded as a saint, but the most famous legend associated with him arose after his death. The story is that when he was dying, his humility led him to ask to be buried in the common graveyard 'under the feet of passers-by and rains from the eaves'. A hundred years later, on July 15, when his body was moved from its modest grave to a shrine within the early cathedral, there was a downpour, and it continued for forty days. Were these

ABOVE *Banners by Thetis Blacker line the nave of Winchester Cathedral. The banners on the north side represent the Old Creation and the Fall, and those on the south side represent the New Creation, Christ's life, death, resurrection and the second coming.*

showers the tears of the saint, dismayed at being moved from the grave of his choice? Thus began the legend concerning his effect on the weather—that if it rains on July 15, St Swithun's Day, it will rain for forty days; if it is fine on that day, it will be fine for forty days.

For 300 years after his death, until it was superseded by Thomas Becket, his shrine was the object of the most popular pilgrimage in England. Although he is best known for his effect on the weather, he has also left more lasting memorials: he not only built the bridge at the East Gate of the city and enlarged the cathedral, but was cosignatory to the legislation that set aside tithes, a tenth of all yearly profits, to support the Church.

Having paid homage to St Swithun, I lit a candle for John, my husband. I don't understand what it is about lighting candles, but somehow that ephemeral light carries a deep symbolism and it was something I felt compelled to do. Then we were engulfed in another sort of light as we went down to the west door and were greeted by sixteen banners representing the Creation, splendid wings of colour floating down the length of the nave. They are the work of that great religious artist Thetis Blacker, and are displayed regularly in the cathedral. She would, no doubt, have been pleased at the reaction of a young man beside me. 'Wow!' he said: 'Wild!'

ABOVE *A modern icon depicting St Swithun, the patron saint of Winchester, is on display in Winchester Cathedral.*

RIGHT *A candlelit canopy protects the site of St Swithun's shrine in Winchester Cathedral. The shrine stood in this place, the centre of the retrochoir, from 1476 until 1538 when it was destroyed by agents of Henry VIII during the Reformation, and the saint's remains were removed from the cathedral.*

THE CONTENTED RIVER

Blessed, touched by symbols of healing, love and creation—surely these were auspicious conditions in which to take that first step? Yet as we set off on that May morning, the weather as muted and grey as the quiet bank-holiday streets, I felt irritable and nervous. If it was only the first step that counted, then I was not doing well.

As we crossed the pedestrian section of the High Street, I was amused to see a white upright piano, and sitting at it a young man playing Chopin. I felt as if I had strayed inadvertently into a surrealist painting and my mood temporarily lightened, only to darken once more as we passed all that remains of the 12th-century Hyde Abbey, dissolved, stripped and wrecked in 1538 by Henry VIII's commissioner, Thomas Wriothesley. Wriothesley not only took the gold from the shrine of St Josse, the lead from the roofs and much of the stone, but then had the temerity and hypocrisy to tell his king: 'We intend to sweep away all the rotten bones that be called relics; which we may not omit, lest it be thought that we came more for the treasure than for the avoiding of the abomination of idolatry.'

Some of the stone taken from Hyde Abbey was used in local walls where a stone inscribed 'Alfred Rex DCCCLXXXI' was found, suggesting that King Alfred was buried there. But the truth is that nothing remains of the

WINCHESTER BIBLE

Of ALL THE BIBLES produced in England in the 1100s none is bigger or more magnificent than the one made by the monks of Winchester Cathedral's priory of St Swithun. Originally bound in two volumes, the Winchester Bible has pages that measure almost two feet in height and more than fifteen inches in width, and illuminations that represent the zenith of 12th-century book art: on page after page, large initial letters—brilliantly coloured with reds, blues, greens and shimmering gold leaf—are filled with dramatic biblical scenes, such as the death of King Saul, David killing a lion, or Jesus Christ exorcising a boy.

Created between about 1160 and 1175, the Winchester Bible has resided at the cathedral, almost uninterruptedly, up to the present. The inspiration behind the making of the book is thought to have come from Henry of Blois, bishop of Winchester (1129–71), an energetic patron of the arts.

Bibles played a crucial role in monastic life, providing the basis for services and study, and every monastery was expected to have a complete copy of St Jerome's Latin version of the Bible, known as the Vulgate. The Winchester Bible displays this Latin text in an elegant hand, or script, written mostly by a single scribe. The writing was done on vellum—

prepared calfskin—and it is thought that the book's 468 folios required the hides of as many as 250 animals. Copying the text was a slow process and would have taken about four years. The illuminations may have taken as long as 15 years.

Walter Oakeshott, a 20th-century scholar, reckoned the book had six illuminators, whom he described according to their most typical traits—for example, the Master of the Leaping Figures. Five of these illuminators may have been itinerant professionals who travelled to monasteries across Europe practising the skills that give the Winchester Bible the distinctive quality still in evidence today.

ABOVE *Illuminations for Psalm 6:1 show, on the left, David killing a lion and bear; Christ curing a possessed boy, top right, and, at the bottom right, Christ releasing the righteous souls held in hell. They are probably the work of two artists.*

RIGHT *Depictions of scenes from the Book of Genesis begin with the Creation of Eve at the top, then the Flood, the testing of Abraham, Moses receiving the Ten Commandments, David being anointed, the birth of Christ, and the Last Judgment.*

LEFT *These pages from the Winchester Bible feature the Epistle of St Jude on the left-hand page, and the Prologue to the Epistles of St Paul on the right. The unfinished work is attributed to the Master of the Leaping Figures, who is thought to have been the Bible's main designer.*

tomb of the great king who made Winchester a seat of learning and who himself translated Bede's *Ecclesiastical History of the English People* and Boethius's *The Consolation of Philosophy*, who inspired the compilation of the national year-by-year record known as the *Anglo-Saxon Chronicle*.

As we looked sadly at the ruins of Hyde Abbey, we were faced with the first of many decisions about which route to take. It can be argued that the medieval pilgrims would have continued north to Headbourne Worthy. In favour of this choice is the fact that it was a fragment of the Roman road to Silchester and would have been known to the pilgrims coming from the north into Winchester to visit the shrine of St Swithun. Even more telling is the village's Saxon church, dedicated to St Swithun and famous for its great rood of the crucified Christ above the west door. Just as the pilgrims to the shrine of St Swithun must have prayed before it as they neared the end of their journey, so too might the pilgrims to Thomas Becket's shrine have drawn inspiration as they started on their long trek.

The argument for the alternative riverside route is that it is close to water and yet, at least in summer, dry. Also, it is the more direct. There can rarely be certainty over the exact path trodden by the pilgrims, or that they all used the same route. We, drawn by the river, chose to take this first opportunity to follow its winding ways.

We were rewarded for this choice by meeting some friends who live in an idyllic cottage by the river, waiting to greet us as we passed their home. Feeling slightly like a royal procession, we joined the route from Headbourne Worthy at Kings Worthy church, where we couldn't resist telling a man tending the church-yard of our destination and were gratified at his admiring response: 'Canterbury? Rather you than me.'

Here the ancient track passes what was the first post office in Britain, becoming a modern high road; so we followed the way suggested by our guidebook and were soon on a narrow path, walking through cow parsley and comfrey along the banks of the Itchen. Then we passed a huge patch of wild onions, remembering, as we sampled them, that they were a regular part of the diet of our medieval predecessors.

Already we were deep in history; indeed, the writer and poet Hilaire Belloc observed that here 'We were walking these few miles upon earth beaten (to quote recorded history alone) by the flight of Saxons from the battle of Alton, and by the conquering march of Swegen which was the preliminary to the rule of the Danes over England.'

Of all who have written about the Pilgrims' Way, pride of place must go to this prolific and versatile writer. Belloc set out one cold winter's day over ninety years ago and mapped out, yard by yard, all that could be recovered of what is now known as 'The Pilgrims' Way'. His book, *The Old Road*, first published in 1904, is essential reading for anyone wanting to exercise their minds as well as their legs. Although he has been dismissed as 'an incurable old romantic', I do not share this view and feel he should be taken seriously, for not only did he, for the most part, take infinite pains to question and check every detail, but, more crucially, he did so with a real sensitivity to the habits and inclinations of travellers, entering into their minds and souls. As I recalled his theories and conclusions, he became almost a fourth companion on the walk.

Soon our peaceful walking was disrupted by the need to negotiate the A33. I had been revelling in the quiet, yet on this first day was surprised to find that my reaction when we came to a busy road was ambivalent, initial resentment at the intrusion of noise and speed being swiftly followed by a feeling of reassurance that life was streaming on and that help was at hand if needed. (This ambivalence was short-lived: after a day or two, as I became accustomed to the quiet—indeed, as it became the norm—quiet was all that I wanted.) The next few miles were pure delight and, although I was feeling more like a bank-holiday walker than a pilgrim, my mood was softened by the beauty surrounding us. The river was full, meandering gently along its path through the luxuriant vegetation.

The Itchen is a contented river and it breeds content, even in irritable walkers. I wished I had brought field glasses, for I had read that the river's chalky waters attract a miscellany of wildlife. Nonetheless, I saw trout, coots, moorhens and swans, eternally elegant, drifting along its surface. I heard blackbirds, thrushes and warblers but could not identify the long-eared, short-eared and pipistrelle bats that can, I had been assured, be seen there.

The water meadows bordering the Itchen are famous for their fertility. The river is perplexing in its divisions and meanderings, but questions about which is the main stream and which the tributary, even the distraction of the constant hum of the M3 and the A33, took second place to sheer delight in the fact that, in this stretch at least, the countryside bears some resemblance to the road walked by the poet Edward Thomas before the First World War.

> That road, in its winding course from Winchester to Canterbury, through Hampshire, Surrey and Kent, sums up the qualities of roads except those of the straight highway. It is a cart-way from farm to farm; or a foot-path only, or a sheaf of half a dozen footpaths worn side by side; or, no longer needed except by the curious, it is buried under nettle and burdock and barricaded by thorns and traveller's joy and bryony bines; it has been converted into a white country road for a few miles of its length, until an ascent over the Downs or a descent into a valley has to be made, and then once more it is left to footsteps upon grass and bird's foot trefoil or to rude wheels over flints. Sometimes it is hidden among untended hazels or among chalk banks topped with beech and yew, and the kestrel plucks the chaffinch there undisturbed. Or it goes free and hedgeless, like a long balcony half-way up the Downs, and unespied it beholds half the South Country between ash tree boles. Church and inn and farm and cottage and tramp's fire it passes like a wandering wraith of a road.

It was too much to hope that, all these years later, nature would be allowed such freedom along the whole Way. We would enjoy it while we could.

THE WATERCRESS WAY

The Pilgrims' Way passes close to two more 'Worthies'—Abbots Worthy and Martyr Worthy. 'Worthy' is derived from the Saxon *wordie*, a place or hamlet. While Abbots Worthy was once the property of an abbot and Kings Worthy that of the Crown, the logic does not extend to Martyr Worthy: it was not a site of martyrdom, but belonged, in the 13th century, to the Norman Henricus de la Martre, whose name is derived from the Old French name for a weasel.

There are still sheep here, a reminder that once the villagers' prosperity was measured by the number of sheep they owned. The village flock was cared for by the churchwardens, whose vestments were made from the wool, and it was the sheep, not the parishioners, who were referred to as the 'parish flock'. Wool was shipped to Venice and Genoa, and in the 17th century the industry brought the area even more prosperity, for, in order to encourage the wool trade, an Act of Parliament declared that shrouds must be made only of wool or fine plaid. Anyone who dared bury a relative in any other cloth was compelled to pay a fine.

LIVING WATERS

THE CHALK that underlies much of southern England, filled with rainwater, forms a reservoir that feeds many of the region's rivers. Known as chalk rivers or streams, they contain water that is clear and pure, having been filtered through the chalk, and provide a wide range of habitats—in the rivers themselves, on their banks and in the surrounding valleys—for fish, birds and mammals. Human activity over the centuries has had drastic effects on the populations of many native species, however, and with a view to their protection, certain chalk rivers have been designated Sites of Special Scientific Interest. Among them are the Itchen and the Test.

The Rivers Itchen and Test vary greatly during their respective courses, providing a variety of habitat conditions for fish at different stages in their life cycle. Species native to chalk streams include the brown trout, pike, eel, stone loach, bullhead and lamprey. Migratory species like salmon also visit the Itchen and the Test, although populations of these fish have declined in recent years.

These rivers, and the adjoining valleys and meadows, are home to a myriad bird species, including kingfishers, grey

LEFT *A stretch of the River Itchen exemplifies one of the many habitats provided by this important chalk river.*

wagtails, grasshopper warblers, mute swans, and common waterfowl such as moorhens and mallards. Watercress beds, unique to chalk river systems, support many water birds during the winter months, when other food sources are scarce, including water pipits and rare water-rails.

Watercress beds are also favoured by water shrews, as are shallow waters in which short dives can be made to forage for food. Other mammals to be found living near chalk rivers include the water vole and the otter, the latter mainly in the upper and lower reaches of the Itchen, where calm waters and plentiful fish provide opportunities for feeding.

ABOVE *A sign outside The Trout Inn, where the author made her first stop on the journey.*

When we reached Martyr Worthy church we chatted briefly with the verger, who was sitting quietly in the sun after cleaning the church, and passed the village hall, proudly displaying a sign advertising *The Pirates of Penzance* the following week, and continued along fields and through Chilland to our first stop, Itchen Abbas.

We arrived in time to meet some friends at The Trout for an early lunch. We tackled two huge plates of sandwiches, drank shandy and chatted for an hour. This pub (then called by a different name) was made famous by Charles Kingsley, who stayed here in 1862 while he was writing the final chapters of his novel *The Water Babies*.

Itchen Abbas is one of many villages along the Pilgrims' Way where there is still tangible proof of ancient generations that lived and died there. The discovery of flint arrowheads suggests the presence of Neolithic man; chalk coffins found in a vault under the church indicate that the site had religious significance before the stone building was built in the 11th century; it was the site of a Roman villa, and in the 20th century Lord Grey, the Liberal Foreign Secretary, had a home here, where he used to entertain the famous naturalist W. H. Hudson.

But for me the spirit of this ancient place comes even more vividly to life in a legend: on moonlit nights a headless woman is said to walk up and down the avenue of trees leading to the 17th-century rectory. This, the locals affirm,

ABOVE *Avington Park is set in beautiful grounds near the River Itchen.*

cannot be just fancy, for one night in the 19th century she was seen clearly by Peter Bignell, the village carpenter, 'a big, burly man with a grey beard, unlikely to tell untruths'.

From Itchen Abbas the Pilgrims' Way would have continued along the highroad to Itchen Stoke; to avoid the highroad, we crossed the river by the church, passing Avington Park, owned for a while by King Charles II, who brought Nell Gwyn to stay here when Thomas Ken, a canon of Winchester Cathedral 'refused to give poor Nelly a lodging', and met the old road again at Ovington. There was a deep ford ahead and for a moment I hoped that crossing it might present a challenge and earn us pilgrim status, but a footbridge rendered it distressingly easy. So, slightly deflated, we came to the first of many watercress beds that give yet another use to the waters of the Itchen.

Watercress is unique in that it is a crop grown in running water. In Victorian times, farms were established where springs emerged through faults in the clay, releasing pure, relatively warm, water from the deep layers of chalk beneath. Today, each bed contains some 6 million plants; when all the sowing, transplanting, picking and bunching was done by hand it must have been one of the coldest and

wettest of jobs. Now rice-planting machines have been adapted to Western use and electric pumps raise the half-million gallons of water needed every day for each acre. This local crop provides nearly a third of the watercress consumed in this country, and has given its name to the Watercress Line, ten miles of track from Alresford to Alton, which runs parallel to the Pilgrims' Way and where it is still possible to travel on some of the few remaining steam trains in the country.

Soon we were on Tichborne Down, less than a mile from Tichborne village. So far it had been easy walking, but I had not yet found a rhythm and was beginning to tire. There is no reason to believe that the pilgrims would have strayed from their course to visit Tichborne, and nor did we, but the stories associated with it cannot be left untold.

The Tichborne family have lived in the village since the 12th century, and though during the Reformation they were persecuted and many were killed (notably Chidiock Tichborne, executed for his part in the Babington Plot against Elizabeth I), theirs is one of the few families to have remained continuously faithful to the Roman Catholic Church. Tichborne House has its own chapel, but the family also had the use of the parish church, a rare example of an Anglican church in which a part, the north aisle, is officially allowed to be used as a Roman Catholic chapel.

One spring I was visiting a friend who lives in Tichborne, who showed me a great bag of flour that she had just been given and told me the legend of the Tichborne Dole. In 1150, Lady Mabella, wife of Sir Roger Tichborne, was dying. As her last wish she asked her husband to allow her the money to leave a bequest granting flour to all who should come to the house asking for it on March 25,

ABOVE *A steam train recalls a bygone era as it rolls along the Watercress Line* (above left). *A signalman at work along the line* (top right) *that runs between Alton and Alresford* (above).

ABOVE *An advertisement for the town of Alton on the Watercress Line.*

Lady Day. His callous response was to offer corn from all the land round which she could walk in the time that it took a blazing brand to burn. Too ill to walk, she managed to crawl round twenty-three acres. The field is still called 'The Crawls' and the dole—six pounds of flour for every adult, three for every child—is still distributed every March by the head of the Tichborne family.

But this tale born of charity and cruelty does not end here. Lady Mabella had laid a curse on any Tichborne who failed to distribute the dole; should this happen, the next generation would consist of seven daughters, the family would die out and the house would fall down. In 1796 the dole was not distributed, and in 1803 part of the house fell down, and the successor to the baronetcy went on to produce seven daughters and no son. So the huge estates came to a nephew, another Roger Tichborne, and thus to the tale of the Tichborne Claimant.

In 1854, when Roger Tichborne was only twenty-five, he was thought to have been drowned at sea. His mother, refusing to believe it, advertised widely, offering a reward to anyone who could find her beloved son. Eventually, a large, middle-aged man came forward to claim his inheritance. Although he was recognised by his mother as her son and was supported by some of the locals, the rest of the family declared him an impostor. A great deal of money was at stake and the affair caused an international sensation: there was a civil lawsuit lasting 103 days, followed in 1871 by a criminal action lasting ten months (one of the longest trials ever held in this country), in which the Tichborne Claimant was tried for perjury. He was found guilty and sentenced to fourteen years' penal servitude. The controversy did not end and the truth will probably never now be known.

The Itchen had now left us, turning south at Tichborne to find its source near New Cheriton. The day was close and warm and the last few miles of this first day's walk, through Bishop's Sutton to Ropley Dean, though pleasant enough, were an anticlimax after the beauty of the river bank. My irritability and nervousness had gone, but by the time we reached our goal for the first day, after about fifteen miles' walk, a feverish cold that had threatened as we left Winchester had emerged, and was doing its best to deprive me of hearing in one ear. My legs were aching and a muscular spasm in my back left me wanting no position other than the horizontal. I came to regard these aches and pains as 'the battle with the body' and they were to overshadow most of the next few days—in fact, to be a continual problem, until I learned simply to accept them.

Our meeting place, picked at random from Ropley's pubs, far from providing a warm, welcoming end to the day, was a cheerless place. Clearly, the locals knew better than to patronise it, for we were the only people there as we drank the roughest of red wine and struggled through a greasy fry-up.

My spirits lifted slightly as we arrived at our first night's lodgings, at a nearby monastery, spacious and still, where silence is kept after 8.30. The guest-master, a charming Irish monk, showed us round. In a stage whisper, he explained the lighting system: 'It goes on automatically—rather spooky, but you'll get used to it.' Then he took us to our rooms, pointing out the whereabouts of soap, towels and hanging space and opening a drawer to reveal sheets for the next inhabitant. 'In the morning you will change the sheets—not the duvet cover—and you will drop them, disdainfully [suiting the expression to the word] on the floor.' He told us that the monks are the servants as well as the masters. Anyone who has used a washing machine will sympathise with his wish not to feed it with folded sheets. Continuing his merciless self-parody, he sought our patience if the local wildlife disturbed us during the night, adding, 'and if you walk in the garden in the morning, do not disturb the badgers, they're shy little people'. With instructions to meet him outside the dining room at two minutes to eight the next morning, he left us.

This warm welcome somehow gave us status as pilgrims. No medieval pilgrim seeking monastic hospitality would be refused: they would be met by a senior monk, the kiss of peace would be exchanged and food, drink and a place to sleep would be offered. In fact, the monasteries of the early Eastern Church were *required* to receive pilgrims and the tradition was incorporated into the Western Church, notably by the Benedictines, who laid aside money for hospitality to pilgrims; indeed, one of their abbots was renowned for personally washing the feet of every pilgrim. When, on busy pilgrimage routes, there were too many pilgrims for the monasteries to accommodate, guest halls and independent hospices run by the monks were specially built.

Admittedly, the practice did not always live up to the theory, for the monasteries did not provide great comfort. Jonathan Sumption, in his book *Pilgrimage*, says that life for the pilgrims was 'monotonous and comfortless…in many hospices no food was served at all…Where there were beds, they were usually dirty, and fleas were a common incident of life in a hospice.' Mostly, the pilgrims slept on straw-covered floors and rats and mice were frequent visitors.

We were luckier, but as I settled into the austere but comfortable room and unpacked before joining my companions for our evening meditation, I felt self-conscious. Was I a pilgrim, a tourist, a retreatant? I had little sense of identity.

'And the evening and the morning were the first day.' I could not keep the rather inappropriate phrase from my mind.

LIMPING TO PARADISE

ON TUESDAY MORNING, at two minutes to eight, we were waiting outside the refectory, as instructed by the guest-master. 'Orange juice to the right, cereals to your left,' he said. 'And when you've finished you will put your cutlery in the kitchen. Eat as much as you like now; you've a long way to go.'

Observing monastic silence, we helped ourselves to the cereal and the four pieces of toast in front of us, then went into the garden (careful not to disturb the badgers) to discuss the day ahead. My fellow walkers argued that we should skip the three miles from Ropley Dean to Four Marks, as Jane had very bad blisters and that in any case I had walked that stretch on a previous occasion.

I was split in two. On the one hand, the fact that I had covered the ground before did not seem relevant, nor did I like the thought of failing so early in my resolution to walk all the way. On the other, to force my friends to walk in discomfort was an option I was unwilling to take.

Perhaps I should have put pride on one side, but I could not do it. I suggested the obvious compromise, that I walk alone, but that was not accepted, so it was decided that just the two of us without blisters would walk the first stretch. With me feeling guilty at getting my own way, we got out of the car at Ropley Dean, where we had stopped the night before, shrugged on our rucksacks and made our way up the road to the village of Ropley itself.

In taking this route we were deviating from the straight road ahead, now the A31, but were in accord with two of the Pilgrims' Way's most scrupulous researchers. Mrs Adie, who wrote about the Way in the 19th century, agrees with the tradition that says the pilgrims would have passed through Ropley, and Belloc, writing a few years later, supports her, citing the discovery of Celtic collars, necklaces and bracelets as an indication of the road's even more ancient use. Though this way is slightly longer, we were glad to avoid the busy main road and to enjoy this quiet country lane, passing through fields, to the south was an old burial mound and a small copse.

LEFT *Carpets of bluebells are a spectacular sight in many of the woods of southern England. The flowers thrive in older, relatively undisturbed woodland.*

When Belloc walked this stretch it was an abandoned grassy path some twenty yards across, rutted by the passage of farm carts: 'It was treeless, wide, and the most of it neglected; never metalled during all the one hundred and fifty years which have transformed English highways. It was the most desolate, as it was the most convincing, fragment of the Old Road we had set out to find.'

Although now metalled, this lane still has a haunting authenticity and it was not hard to imagine the tramp of long-dead feet. But before fantasy could take over, we were engulfed by the bleak, sprawling bungalows of Four Marks. It has, however, a pleasant pub, where we met our companions for coffee and I recalled my previous visit. On that occasion, barely recovered from an operation, I had walked the eighteen-odd miles from Winchester in one day. I arrived exhausted, asking for a drink and boasting of my achievement. 'You must be mad!' said the barman. I had to agree with him.

Leaving Four Marks, we crossed the Watercress Line, lamenting the demise of all but a few of the country's steam trains. As the Pilgrims' Way almost certainly followed the route now taken by the railway line, we took a parallel path, through Chawton Park Wood to Alton. This was our first woodland walk and we rejoiced in it. It was that magic moment in spring when the beech leaves are almost translucent, trying to decide whether they are green or gold; when the bluebells

JANE AUSTEN'S HAMPSHIRE

JANE AUSTEN travelled to many parts of England during her short life, but it was in rural Hampshire that she was at her happiest, and at her most prolific as a writer. A love of the landscape, life and society in the country inspired this observant and witty novelist to produce her greatest works.

Jane was born in the Hampshire village of Steventon to a country rector and his wife in 1775. She grew up in a large, close-knit family, in a household in which there were plenty of books and lively discussions. The family made frequent excursions to local beauty spots, visited friends and relatives and attended dances, parties and other gatherings at country houses. It was these experiences that the young writer drew upon for her subtly perceived and often ironically depicted rendering of everyday life in middle-class provincial England, and by the age of 25 Jane Austen had completed early versions of three of her novels.

It was at this time, in 1801, that Jane's father retired, and the family moved to Bath. The years spent in Bath were unsettled, and Jane was never entirely

LEFT *This detail from the Jane Austen memorial window in Winchester Cathedral depicts King David with his harp. The window, by the well-known stained-glass artist C. E. Kempe, was erected by public subscription in 1900.*

RIGHT *A silhouette portrait of Jane Austen, said to have been 'done by herself in 1815', is housed in Winchester Cathedral Library.*

happy there, though the social life of this elegant city, so different from that of a country parsonage, provided endless opportunities for observation, and rich material for her work.

Jane returned to Hampshire in 1809, following her father's death and a period in Southampton, to live at Chawton with her mother and sister. Here began a prolific period of writing, a time often described as her most creative, in which she revised the earlier stories she had written, renaming them *Sense and Sensibility*, *Pride and Prejudice* and *Northanger Abbey*, and wrote *Mansfield Park*, *Emma* and *Persuasion*.

Jane suffered ill-health for the last two years of her life, and in May 1817 she moved to nearby Winchester, placing herself in the care of a Winchester doctor. But her health continued to deteriorate and she died on July 18, at the age of 41. She was buried at Winchester Cathedral, a building she had greatly admired, where her tomb has since become a place of pilgrimage for countless lovers of her work.

LEFT *Chawton Cottage, where Jane Austen lived with her mother and sister from 1809, is now a museum on the life of the great novelist.*

are still alert, upright and fully clothed in flower. Our delight was marred only by a solitary motorist, polluting the air with aggressive accelerations as he sped round the nearby motor-racing circuit. Yet even this failed to break my mood. I was touched by the circuit's use of battered old cars, in contrast to the huge budgets and publicity machines of the motor-racing world, and the noise served less as an irritant than as a way of highlighting the beauty that surrounded us.

In this wood, thoughts of Neolithic man and medieval pilgrims gave way to more recent associations. Jane Austen lived in the village of Chawton from 1809 till her move to Winchester just before her early death eight years later. Here she wrote *Mansfield Park*, *Persuasion* and *Emma*, and the surrounding countryside is believed to have provided the setting for some of the scenes in *Emma*. Jane Austen's house is now a museum honouring her memory.

At Selborne, only four miles distant, exhibitions in memory of two Englishmen, the naturalist and clergyman Gilbert White and Captain Lawrence Oates, a member of Captain Scott's ill-fated expedition to the South Pole, are housed in Gilbert White's House and the Oates Museum. Both led lives, that, in very different ways, reflect threads of thought that are woven into pilgrimage.

The story of Captain Oates is one of self-sacrifice in its purest form. Suffering from frostbite and gangrene, he could not keep up with his companions and he knew that he was delaying them and endangering their lives still further. On March 17, 1912, in the middle of the night, he walked out of the tent saying, 'I am

ABOVE *Selborne church, where Gilbert White was curate in the 18th century. He was born in the vicarage in 1720.*

RIGHT *The lovely village of Selborne seen from Selborne Common. Much of the area's hilly countryside is protected by the National Trust.*

just going outside and I may be some time.' His body was never found. Scott, Wilson and Bowers achieved only another fifteen miles before they died. Our trivial worries that we might delay each other with sore feet, tiredness and strained muscles were put firmly in perspective.

Gilbert White, by contrast, lived a quiet, unadventurous life, never moving far from the village of Selborne, with which he is always associated and where he was, for several periods, curate. But his meticulous observations of the natural world gave his life a rare richness, and I was curious to know what his diaries would reveal about this part of the country 200 years ago. His entries for the first week of May show that the weather was unkind: 'Dark, rain, rain', 'Great rain, wind, and thunder at night', 'Sad blowing, wintry weather'. The beech trees were set back by this unseasonable weather, for he writes that they were only just beginning to 'show leaves', yet in other ways the rhythm of nature seems to have been unaffected, for he reports sowing seed and cutting cucumbers grown on beds of hot dung, notes the vines beginning to shoot, and records seeing swallows, swifts, redstarts, house martins and 'a bird of the blackbird kind, with

THE NATURAL HISTORY OF SELBORNE

GILBERT WHITE'S BOOK, *The Natural History of Selborne*, is a meticulous record of his observations of the plants, birds and animals that inhabited the luxuriant wooded countryside of the Hampshire parish in which he lived. The book, combining objective fact and personal comment, and imbued with a genuine sense of scientific curiosity, makes engaging reading, and has almost never been out of print since it was first published in 1789.

White was born in Selborne in 1720 and spent most of his life at The Wakes, his family home, working as a curate. Here he pursued his interest in gardening, maintaining a journal in which he recorded plantings and flowerings and other events in the gardening year.

White's journal grew to encompass observations made beyond the garden at his home, and to reflect his growing interest in subjects such as the migration of birds and the hibernation of reptiles. He corresponded with the eminent

LEFT *Gilbert White's bedchamber is thought to be where he prepared his book* The Natural History of Selborne *for publication. The original manuscript may be seen today in his Selborne home, along with pieces of White's furniture, and family portraits.*

naturalists Thomas Pennant and Daines Barrington, and it was the latter who encouraged him to publish his observations. What emerged, nearly twenty years later, was *The Natural History of Selborne*, a collection of the letters White had written to the two naturalists, along with some he had composed specially for the book, using material from his journal.

The originality of *The Natural History of Selborne* lay in White's careful observation and first-hand recording of animals and plants in their natural environment, and it is for this reason that White is regarded by some as England's first ecologist. This, together with the vividness and passion with which he wrote, marks White's enduring classic as a major work of its kind.

white on the breast, that haunts my outlet, as if it had a nest there. Is this a ring ousel? If it is, it must be a great curiosity, because they have not been known to breed in these parts.'

As the ring ousel breeds in mountain and hilly areas, usually above 1,000 feet, it must indeed have been a rare sighting. Then there is a short, enigmatic entry about Timothy. Timothy, it turns out, was a thirty-year-old tortoise that White inherited from his Aunt Rebecca. Whoever named it was mistaken about its sex— it was in fact female. White knew his favourite pet's habits most intimately, noting its voracious summer appetite, the long periods for which it could go without food and that even when first awakened from hibernation, it ate nothing. Hence the triumphant entry, signalling the approach of summer, 'Timothy eats'.

We stopped for lunch at Alton, then, as the Pilgrims' Way was still usurped by the A31, walked round the edge of a school playing field to the village of Holybourne. Here we stopped to locate the site of the Roman town of Vindomis, discovered in 1969 during the building of Alton's bypass. It was hard to decide which of those carefully cultivated fields covered it, but we decided that the most likely place was a field that, like so much of the country at this time of year, was a glaring blaze of rape. We then walked (carefully) through a fruit and vegetable farm and (uncomfortably) across a ploughed field, to Upper Froyle. I felt quite indignant at again being forced off our route. Somehow when we were on, or at least very near, the original road, there was a sense of belonging, of purpose, of identification with those who had walked before. Picking our way round private land, even though we were entitled to do so, made me feel intrusive, a stranger in my own country.

THE VILLAGE OF SAINTS

As we three pilgrims came to the village of Upper Froyle, once more on the Pilgrims' Way, my perception of time was beginning to become more fluid, less firmly defined by the passing centuries, and the pagan origins of the village did not seem so very distant.

Roads and tracks crossing this area give clues to its ancient history. To the north is the Harroway, sometimes known as the Tin Track or the Drove, a highway that would have borne the feet of people and animals for at least 4,000 years; to the west, the Roman road once ran from Chichester to Silchester; and our route, the Pilgrims' Way, still passes through the village itself. Implements from the Stone Age and the Bronze Age have been found in the vicinity; Coldrey Farm, just to the south of the parish, is built on the remains of a Roman villa, and Norman pottery has been found on the very path we were taking.

The name 'Froyle' is believed to be derived from 'Froehyll' or 'Frija's Hill', the old name of the hill between Upper Froyle and Lower Froyle now known as Saintbury Hill. Frija was one of the wives of Odin, the principal god of the Teutonic peoples. In about the 5th century AD, when the Angles and the Saxons invaded Great Britain, it was Odin's name they invoked as they set out. Odin (or Woden) is still part of our daily lives, having given his name to the fourth

ABOVE *Small statues are found on many buildings in Upper Froyle. Some are in niches, or placed in a recess between windows* (top), *but most stand on platforms beneath a classical canopy, for example the saint and lamb* (middle) *or the saint and child* (bottom).

day of the week, Wednesday, as his wife Frija did to Friday. Her name originally meant 'well-beloved' or 'spouse', so she was well fitted to be the Norse goddess of love, protecting marriages and making them fruitful.

Upper Froyle is also known as 'The Village of Saints'. This refers, not to the holiness of the inhabitants, but to the statues of saints we saw in the doorways and recesses of the houses. The statues were brought from Italy in the late 19th century by Sir Hubert Miller, the last active lord of the manor, who lived until the beginning of the First World War.

Today, Froyle is dominated by the Lord Mayor Treloar School for physically disabled children, a fact curiously omitted from the 'Short History' on sale in the church. A hospital and a college were founded in Alton in 1908 as the result of a national appeal made by Sir William Treloar during his period of office as Lord Mayor of London. In 1948 the hospital was absorbed into the National Health Service and the college developed into the largest independent boarding school for severely physically handicapped children in the country. In fact, it became so large that it is now divided into two, the Lower School at Froyle, and the Upper School at Holybourne. Between them, they educate and care for some 300 boys and girls afflicted by disabilities such as spina bifida, cerebral palsy and muscular dystrophy, and handicaps resulting from traffic and sporting accidents. We saw many of them, mostly in wheelchairs.

We had intended to reach Bentley on this, our second day's walking, but Froyle had tempted us to linger and by the time we decided to continue on our way it was five o'clock and we were very tired. As we had only planned twelve miles for the following day and felt we could make up the distance then, we arranged with our driver, who was sketching the church, to meet us at the next village, a mile or so short of Bentley.

I was already so much in a walking mode that the speed of travelling by car came as quite a shock. The wayside flowers flickered past the window in a haze of texture and colour rather than brushing us gently as we passed, fields flashed by and the few minutes the journey took made a mockery of distance. The rapidly passing scene included a glimpse of Isington Mill, just south of the main road. Once a Saxon settlement on the banks of the River Wey, then a brick water mill with two oast-houses, it was derelict until after the war, when Field Marshal Lord Montgomery turned it into an attractive house, adding a shelter for his famous wartime caravan.

On my previous visit I had noticed a 'b. & b.' sign on the road near Isington and had booked us in for two nights. This was not done lightly, for the true pilgrim would go always forwards, sleeping where he found himself. But it was tempting occasionally to have time to settle in and have a chance to clean shoes, wash clothes and hair, and restful to have a morning free from packing up the car. We were to do this on four separate occasions, though I have to admit to a slight feeling of guilt each time.

On arrival at our lodgings I was shown into a room normally occupied by a teenage girl, at present away at boarding school. Here was a room sparkling with glorious adolescent vitality, throwing our previous night of monastic space and austerity into sharp relief. The walls were hardly visible beneath the photographs of serried ranks of schoolgirls, posters of lusty young men, pop stars and loving couples. The flat surfaces were so covered with the treasures and trinkets and toys accumulated during fifteen years of childhood that there was barely a square foot left for my possessions. In the chair sat a huge fat teddy bear.

We luxuriated in hot baths before a supper of homemade soup and spaghetti, and went gratefully to bed. Before sleep overtook me I thought of roads—from grassy paths to modern motorways. The next day we would reach Farnham, where the Pilgrims' Way at last finds a place on the Ordnance Survey maps. After a frustrating day when we had barely set foot on the Old Road, it was a satisfying thought.

THE WISDOM OF THE ROAD

There is no doubt that the route we were following, from Winchester to Canterbury, is an old road, hallowed by time and the footsteps of men, women and animals. It may not seem so now, bruised by building, scarred by highways and motorways, yet, as we were already discovering, there are long stretches where nature is still allowed to breathe freely and where the imagination can be transported back through the centuries to share the experience of those in whose steps we tread. Although much of it is very beautiful and surprisingly quiet, it is more than a pleasant country walk. The road does not reveal its secrets willingly, but I found that the more I learned about its history, the more I wanted to know.

A road does not just appear, but is the fruit of long years of trial and error. It is the supreme collective endeavour, a long experiment in which the individual can only be subsumed. And the road is wise. It takes us the easiest way, saves us from ravines, bogs and marshy land, prevents us from arriving at a river that cannot be crossed, or a mountain impossible to scale.

So whom would we be following? Who first trod this route, arching across the map and linking the two historic cities of Winchester and Canterbury, one a centre of temporal, the other of ecclesiastical, power? Though it is now called the Pilgrims' Way and associated with the Christian pilgrimages of the Middle Ages, it was not so called until the 18th century and did not appear on Ordnance Survey maps until the 1860s. In fact, the pilgrims were latecomers, using the route only for some 350 years between the end of the 12th century and the Dissolution of the Monasteries. There is plenty of archaeological evidence—pagan stone circles, heathen shrines, pit-dwellings, Druid stones, burial mounds and megalithic monuments—to suggest that it had already been used for thousands of years. The first tracks could have been made by Mesolithic people and their animals some 10,000 years ago, and it was certainly used by Neolithic man. Later, it was travelled by drovers, traders and merchants bringing ingots of tin from Cornwall. Its use by the Romans has been confirmed by villas, baths, pavements, coins, cinerary urns and pottery. It is probable that kings and courtiers, bishops and

ALONG THE NORTH DOWNS WAY

THE NORTH DOWNS WAY, stretching some 150 miles from Farnham to Dover, follows the ridge of the chalk downs of Surrey and Kent. First opened in 1978, it is one of 17 long-distance national trails established by the Countryside Agency in the British Isles, and traverses, almost all of the way, two designated Areas of Outstanding Natural Beauty—the Surrey Hills and the Kent Downs.

Areas of outstanding natural beauty they certainly are. Guided along the way by the familiar acorn symbol of the national trails, the walker, cyclist or horserider experiences each of the areas at its scenic best: the woodlands, with their seemingly endless stretches of beech, oak, ash, juniper and yew, carpeted in spring by wild flowers; rolling chalk grasslands, which also become a riot of colour in spring; panoramic views all the way to the sea, and the spectacular White Cliffs that drop steeply into the sea at Dover. Picturesque villages complete the image,

and make comfortable and convenient stopping-off points for weary travellers.

The areas surrounding the North Downs Way provide a variety of habitats for a wealth of animal and birdlife: the woodlands, in particular, accommodate such resident birds as tree creepers and goldcrests, and summer visitors like green woodpeckers, chiffchaffs and willow warblers; badgers, roe deer, foxes and hares are among the mammals that populate the countryside through which the trail makes its way, while butterflies like the Adonis Blue and the rare Chalkhill Blue and Marbled White flit across the summer meadowlands of grasses and flowers.

Although established relatively recently, the North Downs Way coincides in places with routes that have been used since ancient times, including the

LEFT *One of the signposts along the North Downs Way, displaying the acorn sign that designates the national trails.*

Pilgrims' Way, which runs just below the ridge of the Downs. Given the situation of the North Downs Way, high above the forests and their lurking dangers, and the inhospitable marshes of Kent, it seems likely that similar routes would have been followed by our ancestors. The full history of the trail will never be known with certainty, but its possible origins add a historical resonance, and a certain mystery, to the more obvious charms of the North Downs Way.

BELOW *A section of the clearly marked North Downs Way, viewed from the vantage point of the Hog's Back.*

clerics, would also have needed to travel between Winchester and Canterbury and would have had little alternative but to use the same road. It is even possible that Becket himself travelled this way.

Though we had decided to start at Winchester, for many that city would have been a stop on a journey starting from much further afield. In the Middle Ages, Christian pilgrims making their way to Canterbury came from all over England, and from France, Spain and Italy. Normans, Bretons and others arriving from the Continent, who disembarked at Southampton, would almost certainly have headed first for Winchester.

When the pilgrims neared Winchester, they would have passed the Iron Age fort of St Catherine's Hill (though the maze I walked would not yet have been made) on their way to honour the shrine of St Swithun, where they would have prayed for miraculous healing; they could have found refreshment at the Hospital of St Cross, though it was designed for 'the poor of Christ' rather than specifically for pilgrims, and might have claimed the free 'Wayfarer's Dole' at the porter's hatch at St Cross Hospital. (This tradition is still observed, and even now travellers can request a slice of bread and a horn of beer, drunk from the very cups used by the medieval pilgrims. I tried one weekend, only to find that, characteristic of true 20th-century bureaucracy, pilgrims are only expected to be hungry during working hours.) Perhaps, too, pilgrims would have bought provisions for the journey at Saint Giles's Fair, held for a few days during September on a hill east of the city from 1096.

ABOVE *Two visitors receive the traditional Wayfarer's Dole at the porter's hatch at St Cross Hospital in Winchester.*

Before leaving Winchester they would have been shriven and blessed, then, cleansed from the weight of their sins, would have followed, as we did, the river banks of the Itchen and the Wey to Farnham. There they would have been joined by travellers taking the Harrow or Hoar Way from Stonehenge, one of the most important temples in Europe. From Farnham the Pilgrims' Way broadly follows the North Downs Way, joining the route that Chaucer's pilgrims took from London at Harbledown, just two miles west of Canterbury.

The Christian pilgrims had set their feet on a well-used track shaped by centuries of tramping feet, breathing the elusive allure of ancient use. Long before we set out, my imagination had been stirred by the way Belloc entered into the minds of those travellers:

> The pilgrim set out from Winchester. 'You must pass by that well,' he heard, 'it is sacred.'…'You must, of ritual, climb that isolated hill which you see against the sky. The spirits haunted it and were banished by the faith, and they say that martyrs died there.'…'It is at the peril of the pilgrimage that you neglect this stone, whose virtue saved our fathers in the great battle.'…'The church you will next see upon your way is entered from the southern porch sunward by all truly devout men; such has been the custom here since custom began.'

This is the stuff of poetry, and pilgrimage is closer to poetry than to cartography. The same force that drew our ancestors to rocks and springs and holy mountains draws their successors in its wake. Belloc was sure that the Way, or Old Road, passed no fewer than thirteen churches. There must have been some significance in their position, for often Christian churches were built on sites once used for pagan worship; it is as if the magnet of holiness attracted worshippers to a particular place, even if the god was worshipped under a different form.

Apart from the practical advantages of following a track already beaten into the earth, a track that will lead to points where rivers can be crossed, where water might be found, it seems natural that medieval people should instinctively have followed their ancestors. Perhaps in doing so they performed a greater service than they knew, for Belloc argues that, with the decline of Winchester's importance and the decrease of traffic from west to east, the Road would have disappeared. It was, he claims, the murder of Thomas Becket and the pilgrimage to his shrine that saved it. Thus the road once used by pagans developed new sanctities of its own and, as Belloc said, 'Our remote ancestry was baptised again.'

How did Belloc plot the Road's course? First, he read all that he could find, talked to geologists and antiquarians, and studied maps. Then, on December 22, 1903, he and a companion set out to explore the route themselves, carrying 'no pack or burden' and timing their departure so that they would arrive in Canterbury on December 29, the very day on which Thomas Becket was murdered. They must have been strong walkers, for this gave them only eight short winter days—fifty-six hours of daylight.

Belloc considered geographical and geological conditions—wells, particularly those regarded as holy, confirm the presence of man and indicate use by travellers—and he made analogies with existing trails and suggested that place names hinted 'though only faintly' at the history of a village site. I, too, had been excited to hear of place names still in use, such as Pilgrim's Lodge, Pilgrim's Ferry, Palmer's Wood, Paternoster Lane and Pray Meadows, assuming that they supported the idea that the Road was used by Christians, but in fact these can only be used as corroboration of medieval use, not proof. Place names can claim a long lineage and indicate the history of a site, but many a modern street or house has ridden on the back of the associations of the area and adopted names associated with pilgrimage—I noticed roads in modern housing estates with names like Pilgrims' Lane.

Most of the arguments for plotting the course of the road travelled by prehistoric man have to be sought in the earth itself. The Road was not paved or embanked; its secret lies in the great masses of chalk hills between Winchester and Canterbury. While clay, sand, marshy land and rock retain no mark, chalk, firm yet not too hard, retains the trace of passage over the years, leaving the clear impressions that can be seen on chalk downs everywhere. It is also, as any walker will know, one of the kindest surfaces on which to travel. For early man the chalky uplands had a further advantage—they would have been safer than in the great, dark forest of Andredesweald which, until well into Anglo-Saxon times,

stretched across the southeast of England and where they would have had to brave wolves and boars, thieves, bandits and wild men.

So it was in the chalk itself that Belloc found several characteristics common to all the known, or at least probable, stretches of the Road, noting the habit the Road has of clinging to the southern slopes of hills and the northern bank of rivers, where it is warmer and drier, and that when the Road goes right up to the site of a church it would pass on its southern side. Finally, he found—reasonably enough—that the Road seeks dry ground where water has to be crossed and that a hill would always be ascended by the shortest route; it is the motor car that has led to modern roads zigzagging round a hill to reach the top. He collated these characteristics, and from them deduced the most likely way the missing stretches would have taken.

Belloc believed, and he may well have been right that, although many had written about the Road, no one since the days of the great pilgrimages to Canterbury had travelled it in its entirety. I completely shared his wish to tread, as nearly as possible, where my ancestors had trodden. But now, with motorways rubbing shoulders with the route, with the route itself sometimes a highway and land through which the Old Road once passed now taken into private use, the task is even harder.

My companions and I were agreed that we did not intend to be puristic to the point of masochism. Every traveller, every pilgrim, has some choice and who would want to walk along the A31? Where possible, we wanted to follow where Belloc believed the Old Road lay, but where it was prohibited by change of use, or made dangerous and disagreeable by highways, we would take quiet paths and tracks, without straying too far from the Old Road, with those who had been before us never far from our minds.

ABOVE *A pub sign for The Coach and Horses, one of the many old inns in Farnham.*

FARNHAM

On the third morning we set off at nine o'clock, rather later than we had intended, and Barbara drove us back to Lower Froyle, where we had given up the night before. There was a cool wind and the dry ground made for easy walking; but it was to be a sunless and rather grey morning and the route was as elusive as mercury, continually frustrating our attempts to follow it.

This set me wondering whether the medieval pilgrims ever lost their way. In those days, much of the land would have been covered by fields (where the view ahead would usually have been clear) or forest (much of which would have been impenetrable, dangerous and uninviting), and there would have been few buildings; thus the path etched by men and animals would have stretched ahead, presenting all kinds of dangers, but leaving little doubt about which way to turn. Pilgrims would have simply followed the road, uncluttered by motorways and towns, confident that it would guide them round natural hazards like marshy land or steep hills, and lead them to that point of a river where it could be crossed.

The chief dangers that menace the 20th-century pilgrim are busy motorways, highroads and urban sprawl. Despite the fact that one of us was carrying a guidebook and another an Ordnance Survey map (in the Pathfinder series, which has 2½ inches to the mile), there were quite a few occasions when, in our efforts to circumvent towns and the roads that have been laid over some stretches of the original Pilgrims' Way, we found that we had taken the wrong turning.

As we completed the mile from Lower Froyle to Bentley, three times we found ourselves with furrowed brows, studying map and guidebook and wondering which way to go. Each time we had to ask for directions and each time the locals treated us with the greatest kindness. On the first occasion we were rescued by a passing farmer who noticed our dilemma. 'You're on the Pilgrims' Way, my love?' 'Yes, we're going to Canterbury.' 'Then you're going the wrong way, my love.' So we took his advice and crossed a path scorched into a field of corn, allowing us to pass without trampling on the crops. No sooner had we been reassured by seeing the 'massive fallen oak' that our guidebook was confident would still lie where it had fallen, than we found ourselves in the middle of a nursery garden. The owner showed us through, generously refraining from pointing out the way we should have gone, and we rejoined the A31 at Bentley, one of the few places in which the Pilgrims' Way is identical with the main street. Again we were confused, and were put on our way by a man who told us we must see the church—it was very beautiful—of which he was churchwarden. 'Or rather,' he added, as honesty overtook pride, 'my wife is.'

Confident at last that we were on the right road, we followed a path by the railway line and the banks of the River Wey, past a huge sand quarry and on to Farnham. The walking was easy, but Jane was still struggling gallantly with blisters and sore toes, so on the outskirts of Farnham we left her to catch a bus to the pub at which we were meeting for lunch and the two of us took a quiet riverside path to the centre of the town.

LEFT *Farnham Castle, built by a bishop of Winchester during the 12th century and owned by his successors until the early years of the 20th century. The splendid, castellated brick entry tower was constructed by Bishop Wayneflete, and dates from the 15th century.*

ABOVE *A cobbled street in Farnham leads to the Church of St Andrew. One of the largest churches in Surrey, St Andrew's has Norman origins, but the present building dates mostly from the early 15th century, while extensive restoration was carried out in the 19th century.*

Farnham is one of the finest towns in southern England, and Castle Street, with its mainly Georgian façades, one of the broadest and most beautiful. Mesolithic pit-dwellings found nearby are believed to date from the 6th millennium BC, and, although the age of the town is unknown, indications as to its age are provided by the Iron Age fort known as Caesar's Camp, and in the town's name, which derives from the Saxon *Fernham*, a village among the ferns or brackens. Its long history is harmoniously reflected in a variety of architectural styles—the 12th-century castle, the medieval inns in which pilgrims and yeomen would have eaten, and the Old Vicarage in Church Lane, once a hostel in which they would have sheltered. There are imposing houses, such as the 18th-century Willmer House, now the town museum and, a few yards away, Vernon House, now the public library, whose Georgian façade conceals a 16th-century house.

Farnham is one of the few towns directly on the Old Road, which seldom passes through settlements. Travellers sought dry-going underfoot, but settlements, built after the roads were first etched across the countryside, needed water and tended to arise close to springs, usually found to the south of the Way. The lie of the hills round Farnham has given it an important position at the convergence of roads, and it is here that the Pilgrims' Way from Winchester joins the Harrow Way from Stonehenge. For thousands of years travellers reaching Farnham would have been able to determine the broad contours of the road ahead with confidence, for a ridge of chalk hills offers the traveller a route from which he would be unlikely to deviate. First the Hog's Back and then the rolling chalk ridge of the North Downs Way would lead him to Canterbury, and on, if he so chose, to Dover. But before we follow the road along the escarpment, we must do what many pilgrims before us would have done, and drop down to the River Wey for a mile to visit St Mary's Well and Waverley Abbey, another place where pilgrims could have found a free night's lodging.

Christian pilgrims would presumably have visited St Mary's Well for its water rather than for its associations, for the small cave where the stream joins the river was said to be the home of Mother Ludlum, reputedly a witch. It was once a hospitable place. Travellers could relax on seats beside the cave and drink from little iron cups fastened by chains beside the stream. These are long gone, but the great cauldron in which Mother Ludlum used to brew magic potions can still be seen in Frensham church. She was apparently a kindly lady, willing to lend her vessels for local weddings and festivities.

As we approached Waverley Abbey and walked round the carefully tended ruins, I wondered what the monks felt about their neighbour. The abbey was the first Cistercian house in England and was founded in 1128 by William Giffard, Bishop of Winchester, who brought a small group of monks over from France. Situated halfway between Winchester and London, it was a strategic siting and it grew fast: in just fifty years there were 70 monks and 120 lay brothers. It prospered for 400 years, though it had fallen on hard times by the time it was destroyed by Henry VIII's commissioners in 1536, and was valued at just £196.

The stone remains of the Cistercian abbey, glowing in the sunlight against the river bank, are beautiful in the way ruins so often are, and this first romantic impression was enhanced when I discovered the names of the meadows. Although the origins of the names are unknown, I like to believe that one, to the west of the abbey, is called the Saffron Beds because the monks grew the saffron crocus there, and another is known as the Parlour Field, because this is where the monks took their recreation. The Cistercians, or White Monks, tried to observe a stricter interpretation of the Benedictine rule and lived in puritanical simplicity, earning the praise of the contemporary historian William of Malmesbury. 'These monks', he wrote, 'have the surest road to Heaven.' It is easy to imagine that these stones must once have been the home of monks leading gentle pious lives in idyllic conditions.

On both counts, the reality, however, was rather different. Perhaps summer at Waverley would have been pleasant enough, but the winters must have been

piercingly cold and wet, for the abbey was built so near the river that it would not only have been damp, but would frequently have been flooded. It is hard, too, to reconcile the image of holiness perceived by William of Malmesbury with the reaction of the local people, who came to have an intense dislike for the monks and their 'greed for land'. The original sixty acres became over five hundred in less than the lifetime of a monk, and was used for sheep, for which English Cistercians were to become famous. At its prime the abbey owned thousands of sheep, who brought such rich returns that they were known as 'The Golden Hoof'. Not only was their wool exceptionally fine, but they provided meat, milk and manure.

There are many stories told about Waverley Abbey. There is, for instance, the tale of the shoemaker, accused of murder and a fugitive from justice, who sought sanctuary in the abbey. At the time this was his right—once a criminal had taken refuge in a church he could not, unless his crime was sacrilege or high treason, be removed from it. But the unfortunate shoemaker was tracked down by three ruthless men and, to the cries and protests of the helpless community, dragged away. For thus failing the fugitive the abbey lost its treasured right of sanctuary

TOP AND ABOVE *The romantic ruins of Waverley Abbey are said to have inspired Sir Walter Scott to name his novel* Waverley *after them. The interior of the storeroom is shown, top, and the exterior, above.*

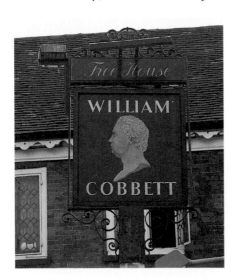

until it was restored by Henry III, who had the villains publicly flogged in Farnham churchyard and the shoemaker reinstated at the abbey.

I had read about an entry in the *Annales Waverleiae* that is of interest to the Canterbury pilgrim. There is a marked notice of the Martyrdom of St Thomas, outlined in wax with the words 'Saint Thomas' in red lettering. As the entry is dated 1171 and Becket was canonised in 1173, it may show that the martyr was considered a saint by the Waverley monks before formal canonisation by the Church.

EVENSONG

After lunch with Barbara and Jane and a happy woodland mile under beech, oak and rowan trees, Eileen and I crossed the River Wey and for a short while found ourselves on a tarmac road. Time spun a web around me as I became aware of links with three different centuries. In a field to our left some archers were taking aim at great green circles. Seen from afar they could have been knights from the Middle Ages or a band of Robin Hood's men. Ahead was Moor Park, with its associations with Sir William Temple, whose home it was in the late 17th century and where his secretary, the Irish satirist Jonathan Swift, wrote *A Tale of a Tub*. It is now a finishing school. Here, girls, many from Japan, learn English, flower arranging, musical appreciation and current affairs.

From here to Canterbury much of the Pilgrims' Way coincides with the North Downs Way, a national trail opened by the Archbishop of Canterbury in 1978. My spirits lifted at the prospect of spending several days on the flank of the hills, save where we would need to drop down to cross any rivers.

Soon we were walking in a cathedral of beech trees and I found a yearning for solitude creeping up on me. It was no reflection on my companion—perhaps she felt just the same as I did. Nor was it that I wanted the peace of that wood all to myself; it was more a need for solitude in which to absorb it.

All too soon we left the woods and were in the midst of expensive suburban houses

LEFT *The Church of St Lawrence, Seale, originally built in the Middle Ages, was extensively restored in the 19th century with a large central tower.*

and approaching a golf course. This was commuter land, the area known as 'stockbroker belt', the butt of ridicule since the days of William Cobbett. This robust and passionate commentator on the English countryside was born in Farnham—the house in which he was born is now a pub named after him—and rode round much of the south of England in the 1820s, describing it in *Rural Rides* with a mixture of loving evocation and indignant, sometimes choleric, outbursts as he lamented the death of rural England. He dipped his pen in venom before writing of stockbroking: 'this vile paper-money and funding system…born in hell'.

As the daughter of a stockbroker, I should perhaps have felt ambivalent about this, but I had to agree with him. The only redeeming feature about this section of the route was an old steam engine, parked on someone's front lawn. But even this spoke of nostalgia.

I must admit, though, to feeling envious of the weekday golfers, sauntering gently round the putting green, for by then the muscle spasm in my back was searing with pain and I wondered how I could reach the next village, still less Canterbury. We found a seat on the edge of the golf course and sat for a while, luxuriating in the bliss of stopping. Then somehow we reached Seale and tottered to the 12th-century church, undoubtedly one of the places at which early travellers would have sought both spiritual and material refreshment.

I went through the Norman porch and found two old men sitting in the choir stalls, one on each side. They invited me to join them for evensong, but I declined, saying that I was just passing through. As soon as they started I wished I had accepted, for there was something infinitely moving about these two men reciting

the age-old words together. After a few minutes I found I was drawn as if by a magnet to join them. I was still so deaf in my right ear that I could only hear the occasional phrase, but the atmosphere was calm and gentle as the words washed over me. Afterwards they told me that they say evensong together every night, just the two of them. This faithfulness shone like a little beacon of light.

My companions were waiting outside and we exchanged news of the day. Barbara and Jane had been to Guildford and Jane had bought some sandals; so her feet would have a chance to recover. But as she was not yet fit to continue walking she continued by car with Barbara and we arranged to meet at Puttenham, a couple of miles down the road. It was by then 5.30 and the rush hour was in full swing. The road was narrow and, for much of the way, without a verge.

Eileen and I set off carefully, passing, just outside Seale, Shoelands, a beautiful 17th-century house whose name is thought to derive from an old dialect word meaning 'to beg' and suggesting that

this was a place where weary pilgrims pleaded for alms. As the next house is called Monks Well, I wondered if they were sent on there for a drink and a wash.

The yearning for solitude overtook me again, and I asked Eileen if she would mind if I lagged behind and walked on my own. She looked doubtful, but agreed. So at last I was alone, not in a cathedral of beech trees but on a busy road—at least it was the Pilgrims' Way—at rush hour. I was engulfed in the fullness of evening that, especially in early summer, precedes the dying of the day. The noise of the traffic was somewhere at the periphery of my consciousness; almost in a dream I kept clear of the cars.

My solitary ecstasy did not last long. By the time I arrived at Puttenham I was again aching and tired, my cold had become slightly feverish, the spasm in my back a hard knot of pain, and I could hearing nothing with my right ear, unless a fierce hissing inside my head counts as hearing.

I thought of my garden, back in Oxford. I thought of the thalictrums and honeysuckle and my favourite *Allium bulgaricum* and *Papaver rupifragum*, all just coming into flower when I left. Why had I left the peace of my home for this? I began to sympathise with those people in the Middle Ages who felt the need to make a pilgrimage but, unable or unwilling to walk themselves, paid others to go for them, thus making 'pilgrimages by proxy'.

ABOVE *Shoelands dates from about 1618, but rises from the remains of moats, not visible in this picture, suggesting that there was a much earlier house on this site.*

OPPOSITE *This section of the North Downs Way near Seale crosses the high stretch of Downs known as the Hog's Back.*

CHAPTER THREE

GOLDEN DAYS

OUR FOURTH DAY was to be a short day: we had only about five miles
ahead of us. The driver took off, leaving us to have a look at Puttenham,
the village we had glimpsed only briefly the night before.

Puttenham is a pretty village, its cottages built either of 'clunch', a form of
hardened chalk, or mellow brick made from the local clay. Belloc is confident that
this would have been one of the villages on the Old Road, an argument supported
by the Neolithic and Bronze Age antiquities found at Puttenham Heath. There is
also evidence of the passing of pilgrims in the age of the church, dating from the
early 12th century. The church would have had a particular attraction for thirsty
and dusty pilgrims as there used to be a well close by the porch. Around 1750 it
was filled in, and for over 200 years there was no trace that it had ever been there.
Then, dramatically, on Palm Sunday in 1972, the contents suddenly subsided,
a yew tree was swallowed into the ground and the well was rediscovered.

For many years the winter fair was held in the churchyard. Many medieval fairs
seem to have been timed for the benefit of pilgrims, who would indeed have
brought good business: pilgrims would replenish their supplies—food, clothes,
utensils, weapons, candles and torches—and exchange gossip and information.
Puttenham held its fair in winter in order to coincide with the passing of travellers
aiming to reach Canterbury to celebrate the anniversary of Becket's murder in
December. So too, the fair at Shalford, a village we were to reach shortly, took
place on the Feast of the Assumption on August 15, to catch pilgrims returning
from the summer festival, when the translation of Becket's body from the
crypt to the Trinity Chapel was celebrated. For many years it was known as
'Becket's Fair'.

We tend to associate pilgrimages with penitence, guilt and piety, and indeed
they were often serious affairs, but they were also about going to fairs and having
fun: they were a break in the drab routine of life. The medieval pilgrims were a
noisy crowd who would have been chatting, singing and joking as they walked

LEFT *A path follows the edge of one of a series of ponds on Puttenham Common. This open area outside the village is a mixture of sandy heath and woodland.*

along. They would sometimes have been accompanied by travelling vendors, showmen and mummers, and when they rested by the wayside or stopped at an inn, they might have been entertained by Gypsy girls' sword dances, performing bears, or athletes turning endless somersaults. And everywhere droned the sound of the bagpipe, a popular instrument of the Middle Ages. But for some people it was all a bit much. A 15th-century writer living on the Pilgrims' Way complained to the Archbishop of Canterbury about the wanton songs and the bagpipes as the pilgrims passed:

> What with the noise of their singing, and with the sound of their piping, and with the jangling of their Canterbury bells, and with the barking of dogs after them, they make more noise than if the King came there away, with all his clarions and many other minstrels.

SIR EDWIN LUTYENS

Sir EDWIN LUTYENS is perhaps best known as the architect of the Whitehall Cenotaph, and for designing the city of New Delhi and its spectacular Viceroy's House, along with other great civil buildings like the British Embassy in Washington. But it was as an architect of English country houses that he first made his reputation.

Born in London in 1869, Lutyens spent much of his childhood in Thurley, Surrey. He explored the local countryside, developing a love of the vernacular barns and cottages, and teaching himself to draw. These experiences perhaps formed the basis of his lifelong appreciation of traditional country crafts,

ABOVE *Edwin Lutyens photographed in later life. Lutyens (1869–1944) used a number of architectural styles in his long and successful career.*

BELOW *Munstead Wood in early summer, with the iris and lupin border in full bloom.*

which was later to attract him to William Morris's Arts and Crafts Movement. He went on to study architecture and, at the age of 20, after a short apprenticeship, set up his own architectural practice. Soon afterwards he met garden designer Gertrude Jekyll, for whom he designed Munstead Wood, her home in Godalming, in 1896. The house, whose style reflected local building traditions, not only established Lutyens's reputation as an architect, but marked the beginning of a long and fruitful collaboration with Jekyll. During the following 30 years

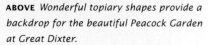

ABOVE *Wonderful topiary shapes provide a backdrop for the beautiful Peacock Garden at Great Dixter.*

they worked together, planning gardens for the houses Lutyens was designing, she bringing to his architectural genius a softness and simplicity that were products of her love of the natural garden. This collaboration had far-reaching effects, determining not only the direction that Lutyens's architecture would take, but also that of 20th-century English architecture and garden design in general.

Lutyens built about 200 houses in Surrey and the Home Counties. Some, such as Great Dixter in East Sussex, can be visited today. Now the home of renowned gardener and gardening writer Christopher Lloyd, Great Dixter was originally built in 1460. Between 1910 and 1912 the half-timbered building was restored by Lutyens, who added living quarters and a Yeoman's Hall from nearby Benenden, with such respect for the original style that his alterations are hardly discernible. Unusually, Lutyens designed the garden without the help of Gertrude Jekyll, and much of his original work, bearing testimony to the varied achievements of this great English architect, can still be seen today.

The Church, however, took a more lenient view than the laity and saw no reason why pilgrims should not enjoy themselves. Arundel, Archbishop of Canterbury at the time, was firmly on the side of the pilgrims and replied with a gentle reprimand:

> Thou seest not far enough in this matter, for thou considerest not the great travel of pilgrims, therefore thou blamest the thing that is praisable. I say to thee that it is right well done that pilgrims have with them both singers and also pipers, that when one of them that goeth barefoot, striketh his toe upon a stone and hurteth him sore, and maketh him to bleed: it is well done that he or his fellow begin then with a song, or else take out of his bosom a bagpipe for to drive away with such mirth the hurt of his fellow. For with such solace, the travel and weariness of pilgrims is lightly and merrily brought forth.

We 20th-century pilgrims were very boring by comparison, but at least we were quiet.

COMPTON TO ST CATHERINE'S

Belloc is convinced that the Pilgrims' Way passed to the south of Puttenham church, through land now occupied by Puttenham Priory, an impressive Palladian mansion, and thence to Compton. Unfortunately, a 19th-century owner of the house, more concerned with the traffic passing his windows than with pilgrimage, re-routed the road to the north; in any case, even if it were possible to go to the south of the church, it would now mean crossing the A3, so once again we were grateful to our guidebook, which took us off the road and into the North Downs Way. This led us along a quiet path to the north of Puttenham Heath and under two bridges crossing the A3, one a modern monstrosity, the other an old brick bridge designed by Sir Edwin Lutyens. On this bridge stand two huge wooden crosses, silently reminding motorists rushing down the modern road that they are crossing the Pilgrims' Way. It was a strangely moving sight.

Jane, now wearing sandals, was quite comfortable walking and it was not long before we were at the Watts Gallery, just outside the village of Compton. George Watts, the Victorian painter, was married to the actress Ellen Terry. When the marriage was dissolved he married Mary Fraser-Tytler, a wealthy young woman who not only devoted her life to him but, after he died in 1904, made a gallery they had built a shrine to his

BOTTOM *A bridge designed by Sir Edwin Lutyens takes traffic on the A3 over the Pilgrims' Way. Two wooden crosses on the bridge remind motorists that they are passing over this ancient route.*

BELOW *Signposts marked with the scallop-shell symbol guide travellers along the Pilgrims' Way.*

RIGHT *The Watts Chapel or mortuary was built from Surrey clay by local workers and the exterior surfaces are decorated with detailed terracotta friezes.*

FAR RIGHT *Natural light floods through the skylights in the Watts Gallery, illuminating some of the 300 or so works in the collection.*

RIGHT *In the basement of the gallery is the original large model that Watts used for his bronze statue of the poet Tennyson.*

work. Here, his pencil drawings, portraits, allegorical pictures and bronze figures can still be seen. She also designed a memorial chapel in the 'Arts and Crafts' style, planned as a Greek cross and rich in symbolic decoration—the labyrinth motif appears no less than five times. One, similar to the medieval Christian pattern, is on the altar, and outside the church are four angels holding circular shields, each shield incised with a unicursal labyrinth deriving from the pavement labyrinth at San Vitale, Ravenna.

I was struck by the ubiquity of the maze and by its persistence: it is found all over the world and can boast at least 4,000 years of history. On this walk alone there are associations with at least six mazes. There is the turf maze on the holy hill of St Catherine's, which I had walked before setting out; a pavement labyrinth is laid in brick beneath the altar of the church at Itchen Stoke, through which the Pilgrims' Way once passed; we were to pass quite near to a modern maze at Leeds Castle in Kent. Julian's Bower, the most celebrated turf maze in England, though far from our route, is connected with our journey in that it was thought to have been cut as a penance by one of the knights involved in the murder of Thomas Becket, and the mizmaze at Breamore Priory in Hampshire was constructed by monks who were supposed to crawl the maze on their knees as a substitute for a pilgrimage to Jerusalem. And now here were these strange angels, holding their shields in front of their bodies and reminding one irresistibly of the resemblance of the maze to human and animal entrails. In fact, it has been suggested that the labyrinthine pattern originated in the ritual disembowelling of animals and human beings for purposes of divination.

There would have been no maze-bearing angels when the medieval pilgrims passed this way, but they would undoubtedly have visited Compton church, dedicated to St Nicholas, only a short way further on. The modern pilgrim should follow their example, for it is one of the most interesting churches in England, the tiny crosses on the Norman window bearing witness to the presence of the pilgrims in whose footsteps we were following. It is very old, the tower and parts of the nave walls dating from before the Norman Conquest, and it has some unusual features. One is a tall, wide slit in the chancel wall near the pulpit, with a stone seat where the aged and infirm, unable to kneel on the bare stone floor, could sit, while still having a good view of the celebration of Mass at the altar. Hence the expression, 'the weakest going to the wall'. Another sign of the past life of the church is a small square window, once leading to the cell of an anchorite, who lived walled up in this tiny space, watching the altar day and night and surviving on the charity of the priest and congregation for food and drink. Excavations in 1906 revealed six skeletons, buried one on top of the other beneath this cell, suggesting a tradition of hermetic use, rather than the presence of just one eccentric anchorite.

Even more unusual, in fact unique in England and one of only two in Europe, is the upper sanctuary and its wooden balustrade, probably the oldest piece of ecclesiastical woodwork in the country. The purpose of this second sanctuary is unknown, though it could have housed a precious relic, and the doorway, now blocked up but once giving access from outside the church, suggests that it could have been used as a pilgrim chapel.

After this short diversion the route goes, for two miles or so, through the woods of the Loseley Park Estate, home of the famous dairy products that bear its name. The magnificent Elizabethan mansion faces in the opposite direction to our path and we only glimpsed it occasionally through the trees, but we did not feel deprived, for this stretch was quiet and beautiful. The sandy path, straight and clear, spared us endless consultations with the map; the ground rose slightly on each side of the path, wrapping us in a circle of brown earth and fallen leaves below, with arching green branches above.

BELOW *Flowers fill the walled garden at Loseley Park. Built between 1562 and 1568 by Sir William More, this Elizabethan manor house is still in the hands of his descendants, and is open to the public.*

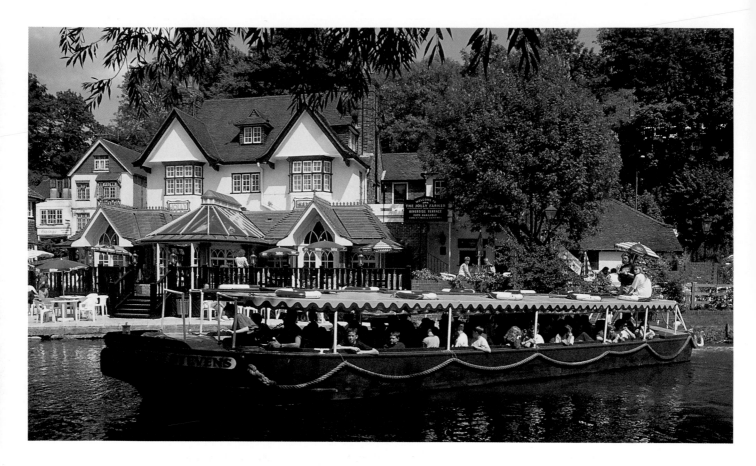

ABOVE *A canopied river boat cruises along a picturesque stretch of the River Wey near Guildford. Once part of a busy commercial waterway system linking the River Wey to the Thames, this area is now used chiefly for leisure activities.*

RIGHT *Today, Guildford is a busy commuter town, but the older buildings on the town's High Street speak of a historic past. Particularly distinctive is the 16th-century Tudor Guildhall with its overhanging clock.*

It was too good to last. 'Progress' interrupted us as all too soon we emerged on a tarmac road, a hill to the left covered with houses. 'Where are we?' I asked a pleasant-looking man, walking his dogs. 'Here,' he replied, enigmatically. 'Yes, I know. But where's here?' I persisted. It was Guildford. That lovely track of road was in the stockbroker belt, within yards of a big suburban city.

We had only to cross the road and go up a short sandy hill and we had reached our destination for the day—the recently cleaned ruins of St Catherine's Chapel, standing in dramatic silhouette on the top of the small hill. Opinions are divided as to whether this would have been on the medieval route. The notice at the foot of the hill assured us that it was not, but there are contrary arguments. As in Compton church, it is possible there was once a venerated relic on its upper floor, a belief based partly on the remains of no less than five doorways into a small chapel. Were they hewn out of the walls to give access to queues of pilgrims, seeking cures, offering their devotion? Then there is the existence, since 1308, of yet another fair, lasting for five days and surely an attraction to pilgrims. A spring at the foot of the hill, believed to have miraculous healing powers, would also have been irresistible to the medieval pilgrim. But the most

ABOVE *The stark ruins of St Catherine's Chapel are set on a hill above the River Wey. The building dates from the early 14th century.*

powerful argument in favour of St Catherine's being on the route is the chapel's geographical position. It is built on the highest vantage point in the area and has a commanding view of the winding course of the River Wey immediately below, the rough marshy ground on the other side and St Martha's Hill a couple of miles away. It would have been a natural place from which to survey the view up and down the valley and to consider where the river could be crossed.

We had lunch at an unassuming but excellent pub on the main road and then spent a contented hour sitting on the sandy beach by the side of the river watching boats, swans and ducks drifting past. Just to our left there was a fairly recent footbridge, which we would cross the next day and where Hilaire Belloc admitted to a piece of very curious behaviour. When he passed this way there was no bridge and he arrived after dark and too late for the ferry. This did not deter him. He and his companion clambered down the hill and stole a boat that lay moored on the bank. Using a walking stick as an oar, they reached the other side, to the accompaniment of outraged protests from the woman who owned the boat. They pleaded 'grave necessity', put some money in the boat and departed with all speed and, I imagine, little dignity.

We celebrated our 'short day' by going into Guildford. I was still very deaf, but it had been a good day's walk. Despite dipping into the 20th century to visit the hairdresser and taking a taxi to the Maryvale Pastoral Centre, where we were to spend the night, I was beginning to feel more like a pilgrim and less like a tourist, though still not entirely sure how I made the distinction. It had, I think, something to do with feeling completely remote from my ordinary life, of being immersed in what was happening moment by moment and of being aware of a sense of purpose, of going somewhere, having a destination, though it seemed a long way away.

ABOVE *The emblem of St Martha's can be seen inside the church.*

THE MAGIC OF ST MARTHA'S

The fifth day of the pilgrimage was to take us 570 feet above sea level to the church of St Martha on the Hill, on the hill we had seen from St Catherine's the day before. The two churches, the two hills, are only a short distance apart. Standing together yet separate, responding to each other geographically, they are also linked in legend. One tells of how the first buildings were begun in the valley below and how each day's work was carried up the hill by fairies. Another, on a more heroic scale, recalls how the stone for the twin churches was hewn by two giantesses, who had only one huge hammer between them. They would share it, hurling the great tool across the valley when the other had need of it.

We started from the foot of St Catherine's Hill, where we had rested the previous day, we crossed the bridge over the piece of river made famous by Belloc's theft and passed to the north of Shalford, where John Bunyan is thought to have once lived in a cottage called Horn Hatch. Slender though the evidence might be, this wisp of a possibility has led to suggestions that the Slough of Despond in Bunyan's great classic *The Pilgrim's Progress* was based on the marshy valleys around Shalford; that its famous August fair was the prototype for Vanity Fair; even that it was the Pilgrims' Way from Winchester to Canterbury that gave him the idea for his allegory.

Shafts of sunlight were streaming through the branches of the trees as we skirted Chantries Wood before reaching the car park at the foot of St Martha's Hill. From there it was less than half a mile up the sandy path through the woods before we were standing on a site that has been a place of worship for thousands of years.

The early history of St Martha's Hill is lost to us. A few prehistoric flints are the only clues to a belief that heathen

ABOVE *St Martha on the Hill, on the Pilgrims' Way, provides a high vantage point from which wonderful views of nearby counties can be enjoyed.*

rites were practised there; the great rings of earth to the south of the church—possibly druids' circles, more probably an Iron Age fort—have led some to put forward (and others to demolish) an argument that there was once an ancient labyrinth etched in the side of the hill. Later, and more confident, is the tradition of festivities that took place in an area known as Ben Piece or Bent Piece, an area of greensward at the foot of the hill. An eyewitness account in *The Times* newspaper of April 18, 1870, tells of the custom, whose origins are 'lost in the obscurity of time'. Every Good Friday would see a pilgrimage to St Martha's:

> Thither, from all over the countryside, youths and maidens, old folks and children betake themselves, and gathered together on one of the most beautiful spots in Surrey, in full sight of the old Norman church which crowns the green summit of the hill, beguile the time with music and dancing.

The paper does not mention that during the 15th and early 16th centuries, those who made the pilgrimage to St Martha's on the Hill earned themselves a 40-day 'indulgence' for their sins.

I was moved by the pilgrims' crosses, incised into the old nave doorway, some with a second beside them, proudly showing that the pilgrim had returned by the same route. They acted as a reminder that in visiting this site we, too, were making a small pilgrimage inside the longer walk—one whose rewards far outstripped the small effort of climbing the hill.

There has been a church here for over 1,000 years and, although nothing now remains of the original Saxon building, some 12th-century masonry was left when it was rebuilt in about 1848, leaving a heavy Norman-style church, only just worthy of its site. We wandered round, soaking in the atmosphere, trying to work out how many counties were spread before us—the pamphlet on sale at the church claims that the view takes in parts of eight. Certainly, the view extends over Surrey into Sussex (was that the sea at the edge of the horizon?), Middlesex to the north, back into Hampshire to the west and towards Kent to the east. To find three more seemed to be an exercise in imagination rather than geography.

St Martha's is still a living church, seating 110 people and holding services every Sunday, but the congregation must be reasonably fit, cars being allowed up to the church only for weddings and funerals. And what a place to be buried! The actress Yvonne Arnaud and General Bernard Freyberg, VC, who fought at Gallipoli, are among those who rest there.

The name borne by the hill and the church has no association with St Martha, though St Martha of Bethany, sister of Mary and Lazarus, is patron saint of the church and her day is kept on July 29. The name is in fact a corruption of Martyr's Hill, as it is thought that in about AD 600 Christians were martyred here.

St Martha's was the parish church of Chilworth, once the site of two industries— the gunpowder mills, the source of an explosion that caused the collapse of the old tower of the church in 1745, and a paper mill, whose product was used for banknotes. Both industries have long disappeared; both disfigured the landscape in Cobbett's day and were castigated by him:

> This valley, which seems to have been created by a bountiful providence, as one of the choicest retreats of man, has been, by ungrateful man, so perverted as to make it instrumental in carrying out two of the most damnable inventions that ever sprang from the minds of man under the influence of the devil!

ABOVE *This modest memorial stone marks the resting place of Yvonne Arnaud, the French-born actress who made her name on the English stage. Her career spanned 46 years and is commemorated in the Yvonne Arnaud Theatre, in Guildford, where she lived.*

namely, the making of *gunpowder* and of *banknotes!*…To think that these springs which God has commanded to flow from the side of these happy hills, for the comfort and the delight of man, should be perverted into means of spreading misery over a whole nation.

I often wondered what people like Cobbett and Belloc, who so deplored what man had done to the English countryside when they travelled it in the 19th and early 20th centuries, would think of what we have managed to achieve in despoliation since then. Here, however, was a rare place where the last case was, at least marginally, better than the first. From our high point on St Martha's Hill we could see no signs of industry besmirching the countryside surrounding us.

SPARKLING SHERE

We sat in the sun outside the church until we suddenly realised that we had lingered too long at this seductive site and needed to keep going if we were to reach Shere by lunchtime. So we continued down the other side of the hill, soon leaving the North Downs Way and walking through an oak plantation and across the top of Weston Wood. The path was straight, narrow and once again sandy: smooth underfoot, but with the roughness of a real country way. It seemed so authentic a pilgrim route that I ceased to bother if it really was the Pilgrims' Way or not, though at this point it is confidently believed to be so.

At the far edge of the wood the Pilgrims' Way crosses Albury Street, where a left turn leads to the Silent Pool. Intrigued by the name, I was disappointed to find that far from being a place for quiet meditation it is sombre and gloomy. There were not many people there at the time, but it had that unmistakable feel of a much-visited place. Whatever the reason, I found it hard to picture the scene set in the Silent Pool in a 19th-century novel by Martin Tupper, local writer who is buried at Albury. He writes of a beautiful maiden who was swimming there naked when she was surprised by King John, who called to her to come out. Too embarrassed to obey him, she waded deeper and deeper into the pool until, letting out a great cry, she drowned. They say that on a moonlit night you can still hear her cry echoing across the water. I doubt whether she would have been tempted into the murky water today.

Returning to the road, we saw an ornate Victorian Gothic building, an 'Irvingite' church built in 1840 for a sect called the Catholic Apostolic Church, but no longer used for services. Edward Irving, a close associate of the sect, was a Scottish minister who was excommunicated in 1830 for declaring Christ's human nature to be sinful. Neither the building nor the sect appealed to me, so I was not disappointed that the church was locked and I could hasten to satisfy my curiosity on something much nearer my heart, the famous yew hedge in Albury Park.

The gardens of Albury Park were laid out by the 17th-century diarist John Evelyn, who had planted many fine avenues of trees, most famously a yew hedge said to be a quarter of a mile long. Cobbett, also on his way to Shere, wished to see the gardens, as we did. Assuming that there must be a way through the park to

OPPOSITE *The dark reflections of trees in the waters of the Silent Pool add to the area's sombre atmosphere.*

ABOVE *A wooden bridge takes the pilgrim over the Tillingbourne ford and into Shere, often called Surrey's most beautiful village.*

Shere he simply rode up to the house and, 'pretty barefaced', asked permission to leave at the other end of the estate. His cheek was rewarded, for not only was his request granted, but he was allowed to ride all about the park and see the gardens, which he judged 'the prettiest…that I ever saw in England'. I wished I had Cobbett's temerity, as the Pilgrims' Way would almost certainly have gone directly through the park, but dutifully following the guidebook's instructions, we were not only deflected from our route, but never saw the famous yew hedge. I learned later that it is still there, now a row of noble trees rather than a hedge, but still a quarter of a mile long.

But fortune showered delights on us as we crossed the sparkling Tillingbourne stream by the Chantry Bridge and arrived at Shere. (The name derives from the Saxon *Schir* or *Essera*, 'the bright one'—perhaps referring to the clarity of its river.) We had arranged—as we usually did when in doubt—to meet Barbara at 'the pub nearest the church'; in this case, the White Horse Inn was the right one.

It is one of those enchanting 15th-century pubs that still abound in Great Britain, and we were once more thrown back into the past as we sat in the Pilgrims' Bar reading of previous visitors to the inn, like the diarist Samuel Pepys, the painter Augustus John and the writer J. M. Barrie. Looking round this pretty, rather overcivilised village, I found it hard to believe that this was once one of the wildest parts of Surrey and a centre for sheep stealers, brigands and smugglers. In fact, smuggled brandy dating from 1720 had been found in the cellars below the pub.

To a walker, the most touching thing in this delightful pub was the discovery, during recent alterations, of a pair of Elizabethan shoes in a wattle-and-daub wall; in those days building a pair of used shoes into the walls was thought to bring good luck to anyone living in the house. Shoes have been thought to denote liberty—presumably because they enabled one to walk on rough surfaces and thus to travel further. Certainly good shoes are the *sine qua non* of pilgrimage.

Like the church at Compton, St James's Church, which we could just see from the pub, can boast of its anchorite—a quatrefoil aperture and a squint once opened onto her cell—but some letters concerning her enclosure make one wonder if her incarceration was entirely voluntary. In 1329, wishing 'to vow herself solemnly to continence and perpetual chastity', she appears to have applied for perpetual enclosure and to have been given the consent she sought. Within two years she had returned to the world, only to beg to be enclosed again. The tone of the letter confirming her re-enclosure suggests that she was under considerable pressure to return to her tiny cell. Possibly, having a resident anchorite was good for the church's reputation. The unfortunate girl was to be 'thrust back' into enclosure; she must learn, 'how nefarious was her committed sin' in leaving a way of life that her judges had never tried for themselves; there was a suggestion that if she did not do as she was told she would be excommunicated.

St James's was completed in its present form in 1190: so the first pilgrims to Canterbury would have seen it rising from the ground. Many pilgrims scratched crosses and dials on the Norman stonework of the south door and one of those making the journey a few years later must have lost the top of his staff, a charming bronze Madonna and Child, for it was found in 1886 by a girl out walking with her dog in the woods above Shere and can now be seen in the church.

I was loath to leave Shere—it seemed a day when only curiosity about the next stage of the journey could nudge me away from the content of the immediate moment; present and future were in graceful harmony. So, indeed, were the three of us beginning to find a harmony in our walking. Or perhaps I should say that I, the tallest and thus the fastest walker, was learning to slow down a little. Pilgrimage means dovetailing with other people's speeds and inclinations; if one walker is compelled to stop and talk to every passing dog and another has to stop to change a film at what is, for the others, quite the wrong moment, so be it. I should admit that I, with my constant note-taking and occasional bursts of speed, probably provided more grounds for irritation than anyone else.

After just over a mile we were in Abinger Hammer, where the discovery of Mesolithic pit-dwellings, inhabited by hunters some 7,000 years ago, have led to this being called the oldest village in England. We had hoped to see the smith strike the hour on the famous clock, but had just missed two o'clock and did not

BELOW *The figure of a blacksmith chimes the hour on a bell beneath the Victorian clock in Abinger Hammer. The name 'hammer' refers to the nearby hammer ponds, which were used to supply water to the iron industry during the Tudor period.*

intend to wait for the next hour, so we turned into Hackhurst Lane and onto the heathland of Abinger Roughs. I was delighted to come across a flock of Soay sheep, one of the most primitive and rugged of all surviving breeds. A notice told us that the wool should be plucked by hand or allowed to fall to the ground. These tough nonconformists come from the island of St Kilda in the Outer Hebrides. It was curiously touching to see these independent little animals so far from their rocky, rigorous home.

The sun, the light wind and the charm of the day again tempted us to stop and stretch out on the heath for a while. We chose as our resting place the open grassy area marked by a noble granite cross, the Wilberforce Monument, where Bishop Samuel Wilberforce, the son of the Member of Parliament who devoted his life to the abolition of the slave trade, was killed when he fell from his horse. It says something for the luminosity of this day that, although my notes remind me yet again of the agony in my back, I have no recollection of aches and pains, just of sheer delight in my surroundings, and of amusement at seeing a couple emerging sheepishly from one of the farm buildings opposite us, brushing the straw off

VINEYARDS OF THE SOUTHEAST

ALTHOUGH ENGLISH WINE is more popular today than it has ever been, it may come as a surprise that there are over 400 vineyards in the country. These are situated mainly in the Southeast, where the region's characteristic lime soil and relatively mild climate provide suitable conditions for growth.

It is generally assumed that the grape was introduced to Britain by the Romans, but it is quite possible that vines were brought to these shores from mainland Europe at an earlier time. Nonetheless, wine-making flourished in Roman Britain, especially from the 3rd century, when the spread of Christianity created the need for wine for ritual use, and many monasteries produced wine from grapes grown in their own vineyards. Wine production continued under Saxon rule, and in 1080 there were 45 recorded vineyards. After the mid-14th century, however, production declined, due partly to a colder climate, and ceased almost completely in the 16th century after the Dissolution of the Monasteries.

Renewed interest in wine production since the early years of the 20th century has resulted in the emergence in some parts of the country of vineyards varying in size from a few acres to several hundred acres. Most of the wines produced are white, because red grapes generally require more sun, and many of the varieties grown originate from Germany, where climatic conditions are

ABOVE *Workers harvest grapes at Denbies Vineyard near Dorking. Some 265 acres of the estate's south-facing slopes were planted with vines between 1985 and 1991.*

similar. The largest vineyard in England is Denbies, near Dorking, which produces about 400,000 bottles of wine annually from vines grown on the slopes of the Surrey North Downs.

their clothes and trying to look as though they had been admiring its architecture.

Refreshed, we skirted Deerleap Wood and rejoined the North Downs Way. Frequently the choice of paths was confusing: there were those marked on the Ordnance Survey map—the Pilgrims' Way, one simply called 'Trackway' and the North Downs Way—there was the route preferred by Hilaire Belloc and there were the variations used by our guidebook. Sometimes the various routes coincided; sometimes they differed, most often because common land had fallen into private ownership or because of the interruption of modern roads, occasionally for no apparent reason. Now, from Deerleap Wood to just north of Dorking, Belloc's route, the Trackway, the Pilgrims' Way and the guidebook all sang with one voice, with only the North Downs Way wheeling off to the north.

So we were swept gently along the contour of the hills, passing Ranmore Common and continuing into Denbies Coach Road, once an approach to a now-demolished 19th-century house known as Denbies. Walking up this quiet, once baronial, drive is an experience of contrasts. The procession of yew trees casts a shadowy gloom along it, yet sometimes the leaf curtains are drawn and shafts of light illuminate the darkness. The sense of forgotten grandeur is enhanced by the vegetation along the road edges, an indiscriminate mixture of wild flowers jostling with shrubs—spiraeas, deutzias, buddleias—whose ancestors must have been planted in the long-demolished gardens.

ABOVE *There are some 300 types of plant to be found along the North Downs Way. One attractive species is the viper's bugloss, which produces blue, funnel-shaped flowers in June and July.*

The road continues into Dorking and out along the A24, so we left all recommended routes and wound our way round the country lanes. And we were right, for when we were forced to join the highroad it was, as we had anticipated, busy, noisy and smelly; we had made a good exchange. And we had the bonus of walking through Denbies, the largest privately owned vineyard in Europe. I later learned that the owner had made his money through what is now politely called 'water purification', but which most of us know as sewerage; he then bought the vast vineyard with the wealth he had acquired, no doubt influenced by the knowledge that the Romans had grown grapes there almost 2,000 years ago.

Almost hypnotised by the regularity of the stakes, weaving patterns across the fields, passing vines too young to have attained their mature gnarled knobbiness and wondering how they would possibly be ripe enough to harvest before our brief summer was ended, we walked in what we hoped was the right direction, by then very tired and looking forward to reaching our destination. Perhaps it was exhaustion, perhaps it was the serenity of the day, I don't know, but I found myself so lost in thought that I hardly realised how far we walked along the A24. We arrived at the Stepping Stones pub and a long, cool, bitter shandy brought an end to a wonderful day's walking.

WHERE CHALK IS KING

The Stepping Stones pub is named after one of the most charming ways of crossing water that can be imagined: a line of small, round concrete blocks, set a few inches above water level in a gentle curve across the River Mole, a walnut tree on one side, a chestnut tree on the other. It is not the sort of addition to the countryside one would normally associate with a Home Secretary, yet when the blocks were erected in 1946 it was Chuter Ede, who held that post, who footed the bill. They are thought to have replaced stones that had enabled travellers to cross the river at that point for many years.

Some have argued in favour of crossing the Mole a little to the north, at Burford Bridge, but it adds a mile and a half to the journey. The Georgian house that is now the Burford Bridge Hotel has its own claim to fame: it was once a small roadside inn, whose guests included Lord Nelson and John Keats, who wrote part of *Endymion* there. Nearby is Flint Cottage, once the home of the novelist and poet George Meredith and visited by his friends Max Beerbohm and J. M. Barrie.

It was the stepping stones we chose. There is always something magical about crossing water, so when we arrived quite early in the morning it was a little deflating to find several small boys exercising a dog and a radio-controlled boat, the one chasing the other round and round the river. I had a ridiculous desire for the crossing to be a quiet little ritual, so waited till the dog was exhausted (or the boat's battery spent) before setting foot on the first stone. I was aware of an apprehension similar to what I had felt when I walked St Catherine's maze. It was, however, entirely uneventful, and I was rather glad. Somehow I wanted the maze (any maze, not just St Catherine's) to retain its mysterious secrets, not to be found too readily elsewhere.

Now at the foot of Box Hill, we expected our path to lead us easily round the bottom of the hill. It could have done, perhaps it should have done, but we managed to miss the way and found ourselves set on a course that was to take us 600 feet up, to the very top. Thus I did not see the grave of an eccentric and very rich resident of Dorking, about which I had read. After his death in the 19th century, instructions were found that he should lie on Box Hill close to his fortune, which he hoped to enjoy in the next world. Apparently, he further insisted on being buried head downwards, so that when the trumpet sounds at the Last Day and the world (as he was sure it would) turned upside down, he would be the right way up and have a head start into heaven.

Taking the wrong turn was otherwise a happy mistake for, although it was a hard climb, the morning was bright and the views alone would have encouraged us to take that route. At one point we looked back on the rolling acres of Denbies Vineyard; at another we saw such a stretch of country to the south that the sizable town of Dorking was a mere blur of houses among the trees. At intervals we glimpsed the great expanse of the Weald, once covered by the forest of Andredesweald, and as we approached Reigate the Buckland Hills, Juniper Hill and Colley Hill stretched before us, one gracefully giving way to the other so it was hard to determine where one ended and the other began.

OPPOSITE *Light drifts of snow decorate a beautiful winter landscape extending to Box Hill. The woods and views from the hill have made this a popular beauty spot, and its rich natural history has earned it English Nature's designation as a Grade 1 Site of Special Scientific Interest.*

ORCHIDS OF THE NORTH DOWNS

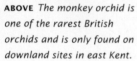

ABOVE *The monkey orchid is one of the rarest British orchids and is only found on downland sites in east Kent.*

THE NORTH DOWNS of Kent and Surrey, extending a little to the west into east Hampshire, are the richest area in all of England for wild orchids. The region is home to at least 31 members of this wild plant family, among them some of the rarest and most beautiful species.

The rich habitats to be found on the North Downs are largely chalk grassland. The areas that are particularly suitable for orchids are those where the turf is short and not overgrown with coarse grasses or scrub, as is now the case with so much of the country's chalk downland, partly as a result of the collapse of traditional grazing practices. The region's richest orchid-growing sites occur in Kent, the eastern part of the area, on the often steep slopes of the south-facing chalk scarp. This is a very warm habitat in summer, with the daytime temperatures often higher on the slopes than they are at ground level. For this reason, many species that are much more common in warmer parts of Europe, such as the beautiful lady orchid, the rare

monkey orchid and the late spider orchid, are able to flourish here, their seeds having been borne on the wind or by bird across the sea from regions including central and southern France, Spain and Italy.

ABOVE *Beautiful lady orchids, apparently so-called because their flowers resemble a crinoline, add a touch of colour to a shaded woodland setting.*

In Surrey, the western reaches of the North Downs are fairly rich in orchids, providing suitable habitats at such places as the famous Box Hill, where the man orchid, so-called because its shape resembles that of a human being, is typical. But far fewer species of orchid occur in Surrey than in Kent.

Throughout the North Downs, the woodland floors are home to several beautiful shade-tolerant species of orchid. Among them are the widespread common spotted orchid, the bird's-nest orchid, an unusual plant that is wholly yellow-brown in colour and contains no chlorophyll, and the handsome early purple orchid, whose delicate blooms grace woodland floors each spring.

LEFT *Another rare orchid found only in east Kent is the lovely late spider orchid with its distinctive shape.*

Another bonus was that this was a Saturday, a day when more people were free to enjoy the countryside. Though I am usually among those who delight in having a piece of countryside to myself, after several days of isolated stretches there was pleasure in what one might call The Companionship of the Way. We compared notes with experienced rucksacked walkers, who pointed out bugle orchids and told us of the terrain ahead; we commiserated with a young group who had set out ill-prepared and turned back saying sadly, 'We don't even have any water'; we asked the way from a man with an orange beard and a grasping face reminiscent of a character from Dickens; we congratulated others for the distance they had covered and boasted that we were walking all the way to Canterbury; often we just waved and smiled.

At about 12.30, we stopped at Betchworth Chalk Quarry, surrounded surprisingly by buddleias. We stretched out on the chalk downs high above the vast gleaming quarry, our view over the Weald partially obscured by an enormous ivy-clad tower, presumably once something to do with the work of quarrying. For a while we looked down on an army of brightly coloured skips and lorries, hidden from all but us, waiting to carry their white loads. We searched for—and eventually saw in the far distance—the sails of an 18th-century windmill on Reigate Heath.

Sean Jennett starts his book *The Pilgrims' Way* with the arresting phrase 'Chalk is king'. More and more I came to see what he meant as we passed chalk quarries such as Betchworth, where for centuries chalk has been dug and carried along the Old Road. We walked on chalk, caught its brightness shining across valleys and through woods, delighted in the gentle outlines, the steep escarpments, of the hills it forms. Chalk is soft, yet it conceals bands of flint, harder than steel, whose use for tools was discovered by primitive man. Later the Romans used it for the foundation of their roads, burning it to produce lime for cement. Chalk nourishes the yew tree, the beech and the holly, cakes our boots, gives a special clarity to the streams it carries and, at Dover, gladdens the heart of any homecoming patriot. I feel at home on chalk.

Climbing to the top of Box Hill meant that it was after 2.30 in the afternoon before we approached the pub at which we had agreed to have lunch. I knew it was on Reigate Hill, the A217, so for once we were happy to find ourselves on metalled roads. Thinking that the pub was some way down the road, I asked a friendly group of walkers the way to the A217. Imagine our delight when they said, 'Just there, by The Yew Tree pub.' It was the very pub we were looking for—and it was open and serving 'Bites and Pieces', the most delectable mixture of Lincolnshire baby sausages, Chicken Tikka and 'Wings of Fire'—spicy chicken wings.

FOLLOWING HENRY II

It was well after four o'clock before we were off again. We were passing north of Reigate, halfway along our route. Wonder at the countryside through which we were passing gave way to remembering again the goal of our pilgrimage,

ABOVE *The owners of Gatton Park erected this Doric-style temple in 1765, and it was from here that the foregone conclusion of the rotten borough's election result was read. The urn marks the loss of this practice following the 1832 Reform Act.*

temporarily forgotten in the moment-by-moment experience of the walk—the shrine of Thomas Becket.

Reigate remembers Becket. It would have given hospitality to pilgrims, who worshipped at a chapel in the main street named for him. Violated during the Reformation, it was later demolished and an 18th-century market house now stands on the site. But the significance of Reigate lies also in the speculation over its name. In the Domesday Book it was known as Cherchefell, then Crechesfeld; it was not until late in the 12th century, soon after Becket's murder, that it became Reigat or Regat, though the reason for the change is not known for certain. According to Jennett, 'The first syllable may come from Saxon *raege*, the female of the roe deer, and "gate" may be a gate as commonly understood, or be from the Icelandic, where it would mean a pass or path.' Hence it could be the place through which the roe deer pass.

There does not seem to be any strong reason to change the town's name to honour the activity of the local deer, so another argument, relevant to its position on the Pilgrims' Way, must be taken seriously, though it does not have scholarly approval. This suggestion has been made by Christopher Martin, an Anglican clergyman born and brought up in Reigate, who spent some time researching local documents for a paper he delivered to the Reigate Church Society and which was subsequently published in *The Times*. His argument is that Henry II went to Canterbury in 1172, and that the word derives from the Norman French, meaning 'the King passed through'. While scholars are united in affirming that the King did not make his penitential journey to Becket's shrine until 1174, Christopher Martin did find some documentary evidence to support his claim. Perhaps the King stayed in Reigate with his half-brother, to whom he had given a castle. The evidence may be slight, the claim controversial, but the conclusion is satisfying, lending substance to the belief that the pilgrims did indeed travel along this way, following in Henry's footsteps.

We soon reached Gatton Park, now home to the Royal Alexandra and Albert School Foundation for children, some of whom directed us most charmingly to the church. As we passed the lake, still and mysterious behind a curtain of trees, the sky darkened dramatically and, as if sensing that something untoward was happening in the cosmos, the cows streamed purposefully across the field towards what sanctuary I am not sure.

The village of Gatton, a manor house, a church and a few cottages, had, until the Reform Act of 1832, the ridiculous privilege of sending two Members to Parliament, by appointment rather than by election. Thus Gatton earned the scorn of the apoplectic Cobbett, who dubbed it 'a very rascally spot of earth', and considered it, together with Reigate, 'one rotten borough, one of the most rotten too, and with another still more rotten up upon the hill'. Ironically, the Reform Act, righting this political injustice, came into being just two years after these words were published. Had Cobbett been writing a few years later, he might have been better disposed towards the unfortunate object of his scorn.

We left Gatton to continue along the North Downs Way, passing Rupert Bowlby's nursery, where I had sometimes bought rare bulbs, walking through a strawberry field, once more touched that a path had been left clear for walkers, then past a gentle Saturday evening cricket match just outside Merstham.

Merstham was once a quarry village whose fine stone was used in the building of Henry VII's chapel in Westminster Abbey; it is also the place where pilgrims on their way from the Midlands to Canterbury may have joined the route. The church, whose chancel is believed to have been built with money from pilgrims, once had wall paintings of the death of Becket, and pilgrims are thought to have refreshed themselves at the wayside pool.

Now Merstham is a commuter town, scarred by the horrifying junction of the M23 and the M25. After a day free of motorways and modern monstrosities, this came as an unwelcome shock. We were to spend several days far too near the roar of the M25 for comfort.

We came into Merstham as the sun sank over the yardarm, looking forward to a drink. Again our luck was in—there was The Feathers, the pub at which we had arranged to meet, just across the road, and soon Barbara joined us. This time we drove a few miles ahead of ourselves, to Oxted, where we had arranged to spend two nights in one of the most delightful of our 'bed-and-breakfast' stops, one much frequented by pilgrims and walkers. Jenny and Tony Snell greeted us warmly, reminding us that the more prosperous medieval pilgrims could, and often did, find comfort in inns and taverns, although they were far from luxurious; no one would expect a bed to himself, meals were expensive and servants dishonest. But then, as now, standards varied. Chaucer's pilgrims were given a great welcome at 'that high-class hostelry known as The Tabard', where

> *… everyone*
> *Was given a place and supper was begun.*
> *He served the finest victuals you could think,*
> *The wine was strong and we were glad to drink.*

Sumptuous banquets were given to visiting royalty and prelates, but the ordinary pilgrim had to be content with humbler fare. Or worse. A contemporary chronicler writing of medieval innkeepers records:

> There was no crime that they did not commit. They displayed fine wines and served cheap ones. Their fish was bad and their meat putrid. Their candles did not burn. Their beds were filthy. They gave change in bad coin. Their inns were often brothels and always dens of drunkenness.

But at least they were cheap—a bed cost less than a penny a head.

CHAPTER FOUR

INTO KENT

AFTER TWO DAYS of pleasurable walking, this Sunday, the seventh day of our pilgrimage, started badly, with my obsessive desire to walk every inch of the way creating a problem. The complications of negotiating the motorway junction led to our being dropped off at a point about half a mile further than we had reached the night before; my companions must have been mildly irritated as I insisted on trudging back to the pub, simply in order to satisfy this obsession, but I soon caught up with them.

ABOVE Helix Pomatia, *an edible species of snail, has a shiny, banded shell.*

An unexpected surprise lay ahead. I had read about an unusual variety of snail, *Helix Pomatia*, said to be especially good for eating and thought to have been introduced by the French at the time of the first pilgrimages. There is even the possibility that it arrived much earlier, with the Romans. It is apparently now native to this area, but the only recorded finding I had come across had taken place over ninety years ago. I had no idea whether they were still found in the area, and had not really expected to see one, when suddenly there it was, a huge white snail, the size of a small onion, gliding along the Pilgrims' Way. My first find must have been the grandfather of them all, for we were to find ten others that morning, most of them a little smaller and a great deal more elegant, their shells a shiny chestnut-brown, circled with creamy-white bands. It was a living link with the pilgrims who had trodden before us. I need hardly say that we did not collect them for lunch, though we did sample some wild garlic, wondering whether it was related to the wild onions that we had seen earlier and which I knew the pilgrims had gathered to supplement the scant supplies they carried with them.

Finding these old inhabitants of the Pilgrims' Way made up in some measure for a double disappointment, first on passing The Harrow pub and finding it closed, then arriving at Arthur's Seat. I had earmarked Arthur's Seat early in our plans, convinced that it was an ancient hill-fort, a settlement, or at least a cairn. Indeed, Belloc thought there was a prehistoric camp on the southern side. So many legends surround the 6th-century king that his name is associated with sites all over Britain. But here, surely a likely spot, with the Pilgrims' Way, the Trackway and the North Downs Way all uniting in one road, we searched in vain for a romantic hilltop or ancient pile of stones. Arthur's Seat, it turned out, was simply a very beautiful house. I could find no Arthurian connections, no sign of a prehistoric camp. But the house has a quality of magic, and surely druids once danced round that circle laid out on the lawn. At this point we were only two miles from Chaldon church.

I had read that its wall painting of the 12th or 13th century gives a vivid insight into the mind of medieval man; in order to avoid making a detour on the long haul to Canterbury, I had made a separate trip to see it. It depicts the Ladder of Salvation and is divided into four parts, the ladder providing the vertical line, and a dense cloud separating Heaven and Hell horizontally. Peruse this painting and you enter the dark inner world of medieval man. In the bottom right-hand corner, the serpent, twined in the branches of the tree of the Garden of Eden, watches Adam's fall and the start of human sin; from this vantage point he can see men and women, balanced precariously on a thin, spiky bridge held over the fires of Hell, nervously picking their way across. In the next quarter, two devils stir a burning cauldron filled with doomed souls; a demonic wolf is gnawing the feet of another group of sinners; a woman's hand is being bitten by a hound of Hell.

Look at the top right-hand section and see those who have avoided the Devil's clutches; they have struggled up the ladder and are met by two angels, who lead them up the gentler slope that lies ahead. Now Satan lies bound and helpless,

ABOVE *The magnificent medieval wall painting in Chaldon church has probably been repainted many times.*

LEFT *The Church of St Peter and St Paul in Chaldon was built mainly in the late 12th and early 13th centuries; the stone tower dates from 1843.*

RIGHT *A delicate, finely crafted sign for the village of Chaldon shows a silhouette of the church.*

Christ has descended to his level and thrust a lance into his mouth. Finally, in the top left-hand quarter, the archangel Michael is weighing souls and a recording angel lists his findings. Satan is at work again, making a final desperate effort to reclaim souls about to disappear from his reach for ever. Some he has captured, but the virtuous fly upwards, with angelic assistance. The duality of Heaven and Hell, good and evil, could hardly be clearer.

The fear of Hell pervaded medieval life. Devils lurked round every corner. Man was helpless. In the face of these malign, uncontrollable forces, all that man could do was to supplicate, to placate, to perform rituals to expurgate sin and save himself from the powers of Hell, or of course he could make a pilgrimage.

STORMY WEATHER

By noon we had reached the top of Gravelly Hill, where we rested for a while in a meadow covered with buttercups and daisies, the staggering view marred only, as so often was the case, by the M25. The sky was darkening and, as we left, the rain began to fall. Soon it was pouring down. Worse, we knew of no pub for miles. Eventually I saw a parked car—the rain was too heavy even for comfortable motoring—and asked the driver where the nearest pub was. He told us there was one six miles ahead, another a mile and a half off our route. He must have seen our dismay, for he offered us a lift and I heard myself say pompously, 'It's very kind of you, but no thank you. We are puristic pilgrims.' So on we went, barely able to see, let alone appreciate, places whose names had evoked eager anticipation. Through the rain we glimpsed the Pilgrim Fort, just able to see that it was not an ancient stone building, but overgrown earthworks in the middle of a wood; we passed shapes that must have been the Devil's Hole, Winders Hill and Hanging Wood, though they were almost invisible behind a curtain of water. Eventually the birds, who always seem the first to know when rain has run its course, began to sing tentatively and I found myself humming the last movement of Beethoven's Pastoral Symphony—the one he calls 'Thanksgiving after the Storm'. And thankful we were, as the sun dried us off and I could examine my camera and notebook to see how they had survived. I was glad that we had experienced this downpour. So far, the weather had been too gentle, made too few demands on us. If we were to be real pilgrims, we had to face some discomfort from the elements.

Now the countryside was washed clean, the air clear, the colours of bluebells, yellow dead nettle, white cow parsley, pink campion refreshed and revitalised. I wish I could have said that I was refreshed and revitalised, but at least we were approaching Oxted, our goal for the day. Soon we were walking through Titsey Plantation, part of a 4,000-acre estate, where half a million trees were planted in the first half of the 19th century. I was not at all sure how we were going to cross Titsey Park, which lay beyond the plantation, as the path used by earlier pilgrims was closed to the public many years ago and there is no longer a right of way. We had tried to work out the various options with the help of maps and guidebooks, but were no wiser and had hoped that, once there, the route would be obvious. It was not, and I decided not to think about it until the next morning.

OPPOSITE *The summer flowering poppy is among the myriad wild flower species that grace the countryside near Oxted.*

As we circled Titsey Plantation, we heard unexpected sounds from behind the trees, though we could see nothing. A man's voice was saying prayers, a group of young voices singing hymns—in the middle of a wood…I was still too deaf to hear it well, but my companions assured me that it was a very pleasant sound. Later, we were to discover what was happening.

As we did not intend to negotiate Titsey Hill that evening, we deviated slightly from the route to return to the Snells in Oxted. This self-imposed detour made me appreciate the effort involved in the detours the early travellers would have made. I had often read of pilgrims 'dropping down' from the route: for instance at Waverley Abbey, where they left the route to find food and water or to stay the night, or at Compton, to worship at the church, or at Chaldon, to gaze fearfully at the mural depicting the soul's passage to Heaven or Hell. It seemed easy enough in theory, just a mile or so, but at the end of a long day's walking it is a different matter. I shall never forget that last stretch of road, stumbling along Bluehouse Lane into Oxted, exhausted. Never again would I underestimate the effort made by medieval pilgrims as they 'dropped down' from their route on the Pilgrims' Way to find food, water and accommodation, or to visit a nearby shrine.

ABOVE *The country house in Titsey Park was built in 1775, although the exterior dates from 1832.*

Though our day's walking was over, our day was not. We discovered that the local priest was disappointed that we were not staying with him—apparently pilgrims usually did—and that he had offered to give us Communion if we went along to the church immediately. I remembered going to Mass when I had come to 'recce' an earlier stretch of the route and how I had felt bound to those who had trodden the path before me with hoops of steel. So, although I did not know where I would find the energy, I knew I had to go, particularly as we had not been able to go to Mass in the morning.

The priest was very busy and could spare only a short time, so it was not a full celebration, just a few prayers and the giving of Communion. As we chatted to him afterwards, we discovered the answer to the mysterious singing we had overheard in Titsey Plantation. It was a healing service for animals and we learned that it was the priest's voice that we had heard saying prayers and that a group of schoolchildren were singing the hymn. His patients had included a sick pigeon, a lame dog and a goat with a mysterious skin disease.

In the course of this exchange the priest realised that I was having difficulty hearing and, to my surprise, said that he would anoint my ear and pray for healing. Then, asking us to pray with thanks, as though the healing had already happened, he touched my right ear with oil, which one of my companions was amused to notice was from the Body Shop. I had never received healing before and had not had time to form any preconceptions. My first reaction was to feel that this was a deep sharing with the pilgrims of the Middle Ages, seeking cures at holy shrines. I was very touched by his care and concern and wanted to be as open and receptive as I could.

Before we went out for dinner we shared a bottle of wine with the Snells and were regaled with stories of visiting pilgrims that put our slight sufferings firmly into place. One of their recent guests was a woman of eighty-two, walking the Pilgrims' Way on her own. Another woman, also alone, was doing a sponsored ride by bicycle, where the terrain permitted. She carried a legend on her back saying 'Jesus keeps me going', and each night she went into the pubs collecting money for her cause.

That night, in the comfort of my room, I wondered whether it was imagination or wishful thinking or miraculous cure, but wasn't my hearing just a little bit better?

TITSEY PARK

As soon as I woke I consulted my right ear. Yes, a slight improvement was noticeable, so I celebrated by turning on my radio. It was that time in the morning when the BBC's Radio 4 allows a space in the dramas and disasters of the daily news for reflection. On this particular day someone was talking about Moses, reverence and holy ground. My attention was immediately caught. To stand on holy ground was one of the objects of our pilgrimage. Some words of Elizabeth Barrett Browning floated over the airwaves:

> Earth's crammed with heaven,
> And every common bush afire with God;
> But only he who sees, takes off his shoes,
> The rest sit round it and pluck blackberries…

I was filled with a mixture of delight and shame. Delight at this beautiful expression of 'Finding God in all things'. Shame at how often I was one of those plucking blackberries; at all the occasions that could have been filled with joy and insights, instead of miserable self-pity.

But more practical considerations called us: could we cross Titsey Park without a long and very steep detour up the hill and down the busy main road? We decided to take a leaf out of William Cobbett's book and simply walk up to the house and ask if we could go through the grounds to the church at the other side. We reached some outbuildings, where four men were enjoying a coffee break and were happy to talk to us. We discovered that the last member of the Gresham Leveson Gower family, to whom the house had belonged for over 400 years, had recently died and most of the property was now run by a private charitable trust. Titsey Park was soon to be open to visitors and I got the impression that this would mean that the Pilgrims' Way would once again become a right of way, in addition to the four-mile walk already laid out through the plantation for use by the public.

One of the men was the head gardener and had worked on the Titsey Estate since 1947, when it was a typical Victorian garden, the borders surrounded by box hedges. He was going to supervise its return to Victorian splendour, then retire. I asked him about a spring that I had heard was known as St Thomas's Well, filling

BUTTERFLIES ALONG THE PILGRIMS' WAY

LEFT *The Holly Blue lays its eggs on holly in spring and on ivy in late summer or autumn, producing two generations a year.*

ABOVE *A Dark Green Fritillary feeds from a thistle, a favourite plant of this species.*

ABOVE *The Speckled Wood rests with its wings open, often on woodland plants.*

LEFT *The Holly Blue lays its eggs on holly in spring and on ivy in late summer or autumn, producing two generations a year.*

THE PILGRIMS' WAY, as it passes through Kent, follows for most of its route the southern flank of the North Downs. This ridge of chalk, which enjoys a mild climate and contains a variety of vegetation in its open grassland, woodland and farms, provides ideal habitats for many species of butterfly.

One of the first butterflies to appear in the spring after winter hibernation is the Brimstone, often seen feeding on the bluebells that carpet woodland floors. Late spring sees the emergence of such species as the black-and-white chequered Grizzled Skipper, which feeds on tiny wild strawberries and can be seen basking in the sun with its wings spread flat, while the brown and cream spotted Speckled Wood can be found in shady woodlands. This is also the time of the year that Britain's only true green butterfly, the Green Hairstreak, appears. It is in fact just the underside of the Green Hairstreak's wings that is green, the upper side being brown, but this provides the creature with effective camouflage when at rest with its wings closed. This species, particularly the male, is highly territorial, returning repeatedly to favourite perches. The bright blue Holly Blue, another territorial

species that appears in late spring, is the only British butterfly to change its two main sources of food, holly and ivy, seasonally.

As summer progresses, even more splendid species of butterfly appear on the North Downs. One of the most spectacular is the Dark Green Fritillary, whose wings are orange-brown marked with black on the upper side, and green with silver spots on the underside. These butterflies, which prefer open chalk grassland, fly so swiftly that they can often only be seen when they are at rest. Also present at this time of year is the attractive Chalkhill Blue, a species that is specific to chalk and limestone areas. As summer draws to a close and autumn approaches, migrant butterflies start arriving in Britain. The Red Admiral, with its dramatic black wings marked with red and white, the salmon-pink Painted Lady, and the rare Clouded Yellow, are among the species to grace the North Downs at this time of year.

BELOW *The pale green female Brimstone (left) and bright yellow male (right) at rest.*

me with hopes of a connection with Becket, but he had never heard of it, though he assured us that some remains of the Roman villa were still there.

They had no objection to our walking through the grounds, so we were soon back on the Pilgrims' Way, by the Church of St James. There is now no trace of the original Saxon church, though a 12th-century church known as the Pilgrims' Church occupied the site until 1775, when it was demolished. Memories of the heyday of pilgrimage are kept alive by the present church, which is dedicated to St James the Greater, brother of the Apostle St John and the patron saint of pilgrims, traditionally depicted with a scallop shell.

I was surprised to find that St James' scallop shell was sometimes drawn on the road signs saying 'Pilgrims' Way'—an imaginative touch, but surely the road to Canterbury should be indicated by a symbol special to St Thomas Becket? There are plenty to choose from: the saint on horseback, his mitred head between two erect swords, the ampulla, or miniature flask, containing drops of the martyr's blood (they had to be made of lead, as the sacred liquid was thought to possess such vitality that wooden flasks would have been split asunder); even the humble Canterbury bell, which was often stitched to the hats of pilgrims or tied to their horses' reins.

To decorate the signposts in this way would be true to the spirit of the Middle Ages, when every pilgrimage had its special signs and most pilgrims wore badges showing where they had been and proving that they had really undertaken the pilgrimage. So pilgrims to Jerusalem brought back a palm of Jericho, which was regarded as a symbol of regeneration, of the victory of faith over sin. Hence the word, and the surname, 'palmer', which was already part of the English language by the time Chaucer was writing *The Canterbury Tales*:

> Then people long to go on pilgrimages
> And palmers long to seek the stranger strands
> Of far-off saints, hallowed in sundry lands,

I have to admit that we did not have a single badge between us, nor did we see anyone wearing one. This might be a result of English reserve.

We left St James's Church and turned into a quiet country lane, the rolling North Downs to our left, great expanses of the Kentish Weald on our right. On each side of the road there was a symphony of green and white, the white dead nettles, which I learned to my delight are more poetically known as 'white archangels', greater stitchwort and endless shimmering heads, heavy with flower, of the ubiquitous cow parsley, which I shall for ever associate with this walk. Even the few butterflies were white, shining from the green verges.

We were now in Kent, though as the border had not been marked we were deprived of the childish pleasure of placing a foot in each county, saying, 'I am in two places at once'. Our period of walking in Surrey had shown me how much beauty remains in its quieter reaches and I promised myself that never again would I dismiss the county as mere commuter land. Nevertheless, I had looked forward to reaching the 'Garden of England', with its hops, its cherry and apple orchards, the county whose inhabitants distinguish between the descendants of the Saxon invaders—'Kentish Men'—and those of the Jutes—'Men of Kent'.

Kent occupies an area of nearly a million acres, once joined to the Continent and so close to France that the novelist and poet, Richard Church, writing only fifty years ago, reflected on 'a looming over of the geological past, so that the traffic, intercourse, modes of life that went on hundreds of thousands of years ago when there was no dividing sea *still goes on!*' Men of Kent, Kentish Men—and incomers, who are now affected by the Channel Tunnel and its consequent motorways—may not share this romantic approach, but they can still enjoy the chalk downs, the luxuriant fertility, the bittersweet smell of hops, the orchards, the oast-houses, now mostly converted into houses; they can rejoice in Kent's wild flowers and insects and remember a time when it could boast sixteen varieties of ant and more beetles than any other part of Britain. It was also famous for its immigrant butterflies—'they have so little way to fly'.

THE CHANNEL TUNNEL: A FEAT OF ENGINEERING

THE OPENING of the Channel Tunnel in 1994 brought to fruition an idea that had been in the making for nearly two centuries. Albert Mathieu drew up the first designs for a tunnel in 1802, and although these were apparently considered by Napoleon, the plan came to nothing. Several other designs, many fuelled by the advent of the steam train in the 1830s, would follow in its wake. A scheme of 1880 advanced so far that excavations were begun, but the project was abandoned because of a perceived threat of invasion from abroad.

The idea of a cross-Channel link continued to intrigue engineers in the

ensuing decades, but it was not until 1985, when the British and French governments invited developers to submit proposals for such a link, that it seemed set to become a reality. Several possibilities were considered, including a long suspension bridge, but designs

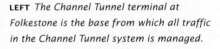

LEFT *The Channel Tunnel terminal at Folkestone is the base from which all traffic in the Channel Tunnel system is managed.*

for a twin-tunnel rail link, to be privately funded by a consortium of British and French corporations and banks, were eventually selected. Digging, on both sides of the Strait of Dover, began in 1987–8 and was completed in 1991. The Channel Tunnel was officially opened by Queen Elizabeth II on May 6, 1994.

The Channel Tunnel, which cost £4.65 billion to build, in fact comprises three tunnels, each about 31 miles long, two of which are for rail traffic carrying freight, passengers or vehicles. The central service tunnel provides access to the others, ensuring that this engineering masterpiece, lying some 130 feet beneath the seabed, meets the highest standards of safety and security.

LEFT *Eurotunnel operates two shuttle services—one for passengers and their vehicles, and the other for freight vehicles.*

TRAVELLING HOPEFULLY

For the first few miles into Kent the Pilgrims' Way is a metalled road, but it is so pleasant a walk that I did not miss the softer surfaces to which we had become accustomed. There were no stiles to scramble over, no hills to climb, no need to consult maps or wonder whether we were on the right path.

So as we walked that day, the remorseless tramp, tramp, tramp brought about a slightly hypnotic state, where thinking and dreaming came together, with the question so often in my mind: which is more important, the journey or the arrival? My instinct was still, as it had been before we set out, that it was the journey, that Robert Louis Stevenson was right when he said, 'To travel hopefully is a better thing than to arrive' (especially when I remembered that the next line is, 'And the true success is labour').

But such meditations were soon put to an end by an Act of Parliament. The Pilgrims' Way used to go across the Chevening Estate, past the handsome mansion built by Inigo Jones. It was for 200 years the home of the Stanhopes and in 1780 the 3rd Earl Stanhope, irritated by the continual passing of pilgrims, managed to pass an Act of Enclosure, which gave him the legal right to forbid anyone to walk through his property. So now walkers have little choice but to turn left up Sundridge Hill, which is very steep, and wend their way through woods and fields, keeping a discreet distance from the house and its attendant policeman, who is there because in 1959 the 7th Earl Stanhope gave it to the nation, and Chevening became the official home of the Foreign Secretary.

ABOVE *The burial plot of the Stanhope family, who lived on Chevening Estate, is situated in the graveyard of Chevening church. Monuments to members of the family are also to be found inside the church.*

We had heard that some people risk the police and simply walk across the estate, frequently getting away with it. But I suspected there could be guard dogs on patrol, so we resisted the temptation and set off up the hill.

The detour through the woods caused by the whim of the 3rd Earl Stanhope was so pleasant that we easily forgave him his lack of generosity. I also warmed to the thought of his daughter, an example of the eccentric English 'milady'. Lady Hester Stanhope had an argument with her father of such dimensions that she left home and went to London, where she acted as hostess for her uncle William Pitt. She must have exercised more control at Downing Street than she had at Chevening, for when Pitt died she was given a state pension large enough to enable her to take off again, this time to the Lebanon where, according to Richard Church, 'her craving for dominance, if not her social wit, could be exercised without restraint. She became a sort of Hippolyte among the natives, and maintained her hypnotic hold over them until her death in 1839.'

When we eventually saw her childhood home we thought we must have stumbled on an important international conference, for there were scores of cars and even more official figures than we were expecting. We later discovered that it was an antiques sale.

Our next stopping place was Chevening church, dedicated to St Botolph, a favourite saint of travellers and pilgrims. There was no pub nearby but Barbara

turned up with four bottles of beer. One of the patrons of the antiques sale saw our frustrated attempts to open the bottles on a stone wall and produced a bottle opener, so we sat on the grass verge, the graves of the Stanhopes in the churchyard behind us, drinking gratefully as we watched the expensive cars rolling out of the drive of Chevening House. It was after four o'clock before we set out on the road to Otford, apprehensively, for we knew it was a busy road and the rush hour was approaching.

It was worse than we had feared. We not only had to find our way across the M25, but had to walk for some way down an extremely busy, narrow road with neither verge nor pavement. Blinded and confused by traffic, we missed the diversion to the hamlet of Twitton that would have given us a little peace.

ABOVE *The leafless winter branches of trees in front of the pond at Otford allow a good view of the church behind.*

Once you are through the traffic and sprawling urbanisation of the outskirts of Otford, the centre of the village, with its old cottages, the church, the old pubs and the village green and willow-shaded pond, is delightful. But its ancient glory is long since departed. When the Domesday Book was compiled, Otford boasted a hundred small farms and six mills; by the Middle Ages an estate presented to the Church at Canterbury had become one of the largest properties owned by the archbishops. Kings travelling from Greenwich and heading for the coast passed through Otford, and in 1520 Henry VIII, with Queen Catherine of Aragon and a retinue of some 5,000, stayed here on their way to the Field of Cloth of Gold.

Otford also has many associations with Thomas Becket. Just off the green stands a ruined octagonal tower, part of the palace built by one of his successors and finished just in time to fall into King Henry's hands at the Dissolution of the Monasteries. This was the site of a previous palace much loved by Thomas Becket, where he often stayed. There is a spring to the east of the palace known as Becket's Well, as it is said that it was conjured forth by Becket striking the ground with his staff.

Another story about Becket is less flattering. It is told by the Elizabethan historian William Lambard, who refers to it as one of the saint's 'spiteful miracles':

> As Thomas à Becket walked on a time in the Olde Parke (busie at his prayers), that he was much hindered in devotion by the sweete note and melodie of a nightingale that sang in a bush beside him, and that therefore (in the might of his holynesse) he injoined that from henceforth no byrde of that kynde shoulde be so bolde as to sing thereabouts.

Perhaps one should be shocked by such churlish behaviour, but I have to admit that I warm to saints when I see their feet of clay; so I find this human irascibility

OPPOSITE *Built by Archbishop Warham in the early 16th century, Otford Palace, with a tower on each corner, originally measured about 440 feet by 220 feet. Today, one ruined tower and the walls of some adjoining buildings are all that remain of this once splendid palace.*

rather endearing, the more so as his command was not obeyed. As we crossed the bridge over the railway line I heard, I promise you, the song of a nightingale.

PRINCE OF THE CHURCH

In reaching Otford, only fifty miles now from our destination, we were coming under the indefinable aura of the See of Canterbury. The power of the State, once wielded from Winchester, was giving way to the power of the English Church, centred at Canterbury for nearly 1,400 years. If this feeling belongs largely to the realms of the imagination, it was embodied in the ruins of the great archiepiscopal palaces. We had already seen what is left of the palace at Otford and were approaching those at Wrotham and Charing. Canterbury's great Archbishop Becket had never been far from my mind but now his claims to my attention were becoming more insistent. It is time to take a break from our pilgrimage and remember something of the martyr's life.

The cult of Thomas Becket owes its existence to a quarrel and a murder. His cause, in essence his insistence that clerics should be tried by ecclesiastical, not royal, courts, does not sit easily in today's climate. Did he deserve the honours that were heaped upon him? Did his fame not lie as much in the violence of his death as in the quality of his life? Most poignantly of all, was his cause worth dying for?

Becket is not one of today's most popular saints. Father David Forrester of Oxford, one of his most loyal admirers, gave a rather unexpected answer to my question, 'What is it that you most love about him?' 'Because he is one of the last people you would expect to be canonised, so he gives people like me hope,' he said.

Becket was born in Cheapside in 1118, the son of Gilbert and Matilda Becket. Romance preceded his birth, indeed the strange, unsubstantiated tale became the subject of several popular ballads. The story is that Gilbert, when on pilgrimage to the Holy Land, was captured and reduced to slavery. In this sorry state he attracted the attention of the daughter of a Saracen chief, who fell in love with him, helped him to escape and followed him to England. Knowing only two words of English, 'London' and 'Becket', she used her first word to find a ship to take her to England, and the second to find her love; for, once in London, she ran round the city repeating 'Becket, Becket' until she had the good fortune to run into Gilbert's manservant. He took her to his master, who behaved honourably and married the faithful princess; it is romantically believed that Thomas was conceived the very next night.

Thomas received a good education with the canons of Merton Priory and at schools in London, then studied theology in Paris. There is no evidence that he intended to become a priest, though he took minor orders and some accounts say that he made a vow of chastity. When he was twenty-five, his father persuaded Theobald, Archbishop of Canterbury, to receive Thomas into his household. There, he found himself working at the hub of affairs during the turbulent war for the throne between Stephen and Matilda, nephew and daughter of Henry I. His intelligence and charm soon made him a favourite of the ageing archbishop, who, seeing his clerk's potential, sent him to study law abroad.

ABOVE *High above where St Thomas's shrine once stood in Canterbury Cathedral is the boss from which a pulley hung to lift the lid of his coffin. Some local stories attribute the crescent as a reference to the saint's Saracen ancestry, a trophy from the Crusades, or a sickle that was part of a picture of the Virgin Mary, now lost.*

Becket was the subject of at least ten biographies in the decade following his death, so we have a clear idea as to what he was like. He was intelligent, though no scholar, worldly yet ascetic, proud, obstinate, energetic. He soon found favour with Henry Plantagenet, Matilda's son, for in 1151 he was sent to Rome, where he succeeded in dissuading the Curia from sanctioning the coronation of King Stephen's son Eustace, thus leaving the way clear for Henry to succeed. So when Henry II was crowned in 1154, it was natural that the new king should show his gratitude by appointing Becket, then thirty-six, his chancellor.

At the heart of Becket's cause was the relationship between Church and State; the violent storms that beleaguered his life were caused by his conflicting and changing loyalties from one to the other. As a member of the archbishop's household Becket had stood firmly on the side of the Church and Theobald hoped that, as chancellor, he would continue to support the privileges that had been conferred on the Church by Stephen. But personal loyalty overtook loyalty to the Church and as soon as he was appointed chancellor he became the king's man. Now both courtier and churchman, he took the king's side, identifying with his military aspirations and taxing the Church heavily to pay for Henry's foreign wars.

So, too, did his lifestyle change. As chancellor he maintained a magnificent retinue, something noted—and questioned—both at home and abroad. If the chancellor travelled in such grandeur, how splendid must the king's retinue be? He became so wealthy that he was even able to give his master three fully equipped ships. But the contradictory impulses that threaded through his life led him to give alms lavishly, to indulge in secret penances such as wearing hair shirts and, in keeping with the medieval idea that there was a connection between mortification and sanctity, having himself flogged. And apparently he remained chaste.

Which was the true Becket, the ascetic priest or the worldly-wise careerist? It was universally agreed that his lavish lifestyle was to honour his master and that most of his huge expenditure was on the king's account. He was never accused of embezzlement or attempting to create a private fortune. One of Thomas's clerks argued that his behaviour was based on expedience. His job as chancellor was to reconcile Church and State and for this a little dissimulation was necessary. It is also possible that paradox was rooted deep in his nature; that he was genuinely torn between loyalty to Church and State, between God and man, between worldly grandeur and monastic simplicity.

Becket's tragedy, as with so many human tragedies, was brought about by a relationship, his friendship with the young King Henry II. It was in some ways a surprising liaison. Henry was coarse, restless, lecherous and blasphemous; he was also hardheaded, courageous and shrewd. But despite the difference in their temperaments, friends they were, both on and off duty, Becket flattered by the association with royalty, Henry respecting his chancellor's experience and intellect. Master and servant hunted, dined and gamed together, and for eight years were rarely apart. For all this period Becket put the king's wishes first, no longer favouring his previous master, Archbishop Theobald. Even so, and despite Becket's worldly life, Theobald, hoping that his former protégé would have

ABOVE *The personal seal of Thomas Becket was probably made from red carnelian stone and, it is thought, depicts a Roman god or hero. Seals made from gems were popular in 12th-century Europe.*

some chance of influencing the king, wanted Becket to succeed him as archbishop. When Theobald died, Henry, assuming that Becket would be as loyal as archbishop as he had been as chancellor, did indeed decide in his favour. It was said that the one person to doubt the wisdom of the appointment was Becket himself.

On June 2, 1162 Becket was ordained as priest, and the next day, in a splendid ceremony, he was enthroned as archbishop. It was a dramatic change in his life. He was not only a new archbishop, he was a new priest, new to the saying of Mass and all other priestly duties. It also brought about a change in his loyalties. To Henry's understandable disappointment, indeed outrage, his archbishop switched his loyalty from the king to the Church. To demonstrate this beyond any shadow of doubt, he gave up the office of chancellor.

He still entertained magnificently—his guests included scholars, knights and important people from every walk of life; boar, venison, pheasant and chicken were served at his table—but he himself now ate moderately and the dark hours of the night saw a new dimension to his asceticism. As he put it, he changed from being 'a patron of play-actors and a follower of hounds, to being a shepherd of

THE MEDIEVAL BANQUET

BY MODERN STANDARDS, the diet of most medieval people, consisting mainly of bread, weak ale and pottage, a stew made of cereals and pulses, was extremely dull. Everyday meals were equally humdrum affairs for wealthier citizens, although they ate meat and fish on a regular basis. But the feasts and banquets that punctuated the social calendars of the wealthy and powerful during medieval times were lavish affairs, sparing no expense and elevating eating to the level of theatre.

Great attention was paid to appearance: the best tableware was used, and the cook prided himself on presentation that dazzled the eye with colour and decoration. Dishes might include peacock, skinned and roasted, then bedecked with feathers, gilded beak and claws, or fantastic creatures created by combining two animals. Taste, too, was important, and cooks strove to use the rarest ingredients in unusual combinations, often with rich, exotically flavoured sauces, and

accompanied by fine wines. The use of expensive ingredients such as spices, indeed the sumptuousness of the entire banquet, were not only compliments to his guests but ways of demonstrating the host's wealth and maintaining his standing in the highly competitive and critical social circle in which he moved.

The medieval banquet might include many courses, though whether a guest would be served all of these often depended on his or her rank, as did the

ABOVE *A detail from the 13th-century Luttrell Psalter depicts guests partaking of a range of dishes at a banquet.*

size of the portions. They were leisurely affairs, punctuated with entertainments intended to surprise and delight guests. Paid performers, including fools, tumblers and minstrels, would wander between tables to entertain diners, while dogs lurked beneath the tables crunching on discarded bones.

souls'. Every night, around 2am, he secretly stripped to his stole and hair shirt and washed the feet of thirteen poor men, giving them 4p each. Every morning he studied the Scriptures with a tutor—he recognised that as a newly ordained priest he had much to learn—and then spent long hours in private devotion, continued to undergo scourgings and celebrated Mass frequently.

Becket had been archbishop for only a year when Henry asked the bishops to sanction the transfer of the trial of clerics accused of wrongdoing to the secular courts. When his approval was sought, Becket refused to sign.

This cause, for which Becket was to die, needs to be seen in its historical context. Today we are accustomed to one law applying, at least in theory, to all men; in the 12th century there were separate ecclesiastical and secular courts and Becket wanted it to stay that way. Henry, however, was anxious to re-establish earlier custom and to strengthen secular, as opposed to ecclesiastical, jurisdiction. There were arguments on both sides. In favour of Becket's argument that the Church should try its own offenders was the fact that clerics (and thus most educated men in the country, for they were nearly all in the Church's service) could be protected against the power of kings and barons, who were quite ready to forget the law when it suited them. Becket felt that he was defending the Church against the abuses of secular power. On the other hand, the Church itself abused its powers and there were many cases of criminal clerics sheltering under the Church's wing, where the punishments were lighter.

Church and State were now at war, and Henry, enraged and disappointed in his old friend, tried to humiliate his archbishop in any way he could. He even had him tried on a number of mostly baseless charges, unrelated to the central issue. Becket resolutely opposed the right of the king's court to try him. The trial ended in tumult and insult, the barons reviling him and shouts of 'perjurer' and 'traitor' following him as he left the hall. But outside, the crowds acclaimed him. To them Becket was a lonely figure championing the Church against oppression and cruelty.

Three weeks later Becket fled the country; he spent the next six years in exile in France. He zealously pursued his cause for all this period in exile. He wrote to Henry, he wrote to the Pope, and as every literate person joined in this copious and often acrimonious correspondence, the original issue was drowned in a sea of words. Each side brought out their heavy artillery. Henry confiscated Becket's possessions, took over his residence at Saltwood Castle, ordered the seizure of all the churches and revenues of Becket's clerks, and exiled all his relations and members of his household, together with their families. Thomas issued excommunications and threatened ecclesiastical censures.

This is as much a human as a political story, both men wanted a reconciliation— at the very least it was in their own interests—and they arranged to meet in a field in France. By now, the bitterness had been replaced by a weary sadness. 'Oh, why will you not do my wishes?' lamented Henry. 'All things would be put in your hands.' Becket could only reply, 'My Lord, my soul tells me you will never see me again in this life.' They parted without exchanging the kiss of peace. Becket, though well aware of the risks, decided to go home. He had four weeks to live.

ABOVE *A detail from a stained-glass window in Trinity Chapel, Canterbury, depicts Thomas Becket and Henry II in what is thought to be their attempted reconciliation.*

CINQUE PORTS

BEFORE THE ESTABLISHMENT of a permanent navy by Henry VIII in the 16th century, England's vulnerable southeastern coast was defended by the so-called Cinque Ports, a confederation of ports on the English Channel that supplied manned ships for the use of the Crown in times of need. They were granted special privileges, including freedom from certain taxes, in exchange for this service. Originally comprising the five, or *cinque*, 'head ports' of Hastings, New Romney, Hythe, Dover and Sandwich, the confederation grew to include the 'Ancient Towns' of Winchelsea and Rye, and some 30 lesser members, or 'limbs'.

The association between these ports probably originated during the reign of Edward the Confessor, in the 11th century, and their importance grew after the Norman Conquest. During the 13th and 14th centuries their powers increased almost to the level of self-government, with the Cinque Ports holding complete control of a vital section of the English Channel. This led to fierce rivalry between the Portsmen and fishermen in other towns, and repeated outbreaks of violence. The Portsmen also had a reputation for

piracy and when, for example, they were granted leave to raid the French coast, did so with ruthless ferocity, often robbing and killing indiscriminately. Eventually, an attempt was made to bring the Portsmen under control, and the office of Lord Warden of the Cinque Ports was created. The Lord Wardenship, now merely an honorary office, has survived to the present day, and recent bearers of the title have included Winston Churchill and Queen Elizabeth, the Queen Mother, who was made Lord Warden in 1979.

By the end of the 14th century, the role played by the Cinque Ports in the country's defence had begun to decline, owing to the increased use of royal ships, which eventually led to the establishment of a permanent navy. In addition, many of the harbours were gradually lost as a result of silting up

ABOVE *Although the sea has receded, leaving little more than a creek, Rye has retained much of its charm, standing on a hill above the surrounding marshes.*

or erosion and, like the one at Sandwich, have now vanished. Today, the thriving port of Dover provides the only hint of the enormous power and importance once held by the Cinque Ports.

LEFT *The present Constable of Dover Castle, Lord Warden and Admiral of the Cinque Ports is HM Queen Elizabeth, the Queen Mother, shown here at her installation.*

ABOVE *The coat-of-arms of Sandwich shows a device common to all the Cinque Ports, the foreparts of three lions joined to the sterns of three ships.*

egales 7 brokentel

MURDER IN THE CATHEDRAL

Becket's arrival at Sandwich must have warmed his heart, for he was not, as he had expected, greeted by armed men, but by a welcoming crowd running into the water shouting, 'Blessed is he that cometh in the name of the Lord.' When he reached Canterbury he was greeted by music and bells and a procession of chanting monks. Becket dismounted, took off his boots and arrived at the cathedral on foot, prostrating himself and greeting each monk with the kiss of peace. On Christmas Day the contradictory elements in his nature were dramatically shown when he first preached on the text 'On earth peace to men of good will' and told the congregation that they would soon have another martyr. He then pronounced excommunication on all who had violated the rights of the Church, including specifically Ranulf de Broc, who had been responsible for implementing the king's orders in appropriating the revenues of Church property and who still held Saltwood Castle. 'May they all be damned by Jesus Christ,' he is believed to have said, hurling flaming candles to the ground.

Meanwhile, in France, several prelates joined Henry at Bayeux, complaining about Becket, fearful that he was going to arouse the country against the Church. They incited the king perhaps more than they intended and eventually he uttered those fateful and famous (though variously phrased) words: 'What miserable drones and traitors have I nourished and promoted in my household, who let their lord be treated with such shameful contempt by a low-born clerk!' Four knights were present: Reginald Fitzurse, William de Tracy, Hugh de Merville and Richard

ABOVE *An illustration from a medieval manuscript depicts Thomas Becket's return to England from exile. The king's agents await him on the shore as his boat approaches the port of Sandwich.*

le Breton. They interpreted his words in their own way and left immediately with murder in their hearts. They travelled to England, where they were welcomed by de Broc and spent the night of December 28 with him at Saltwood. The next morning they rode the remaining fifteen miles to Canterbury, mustering support as they went. They arrived at the archbishop's palace at three in the afternoon, demanding, in the king's name, to see the archbishop.

The knights found Becket still at table, talking to members of his household. The knights had concocted a message from the king, demanding that Becket give way on everything for which he had stood for so many years. They must have known that Becket could never agree to their demands and indeed he did not.

At this the knights shouted and gesticulated, thrusting their heads into his face. Becket joined in the verbal abuse and the knights left, yelling, 'It is you who threaten.' As they left, Becket followed them, shouting that he had not returned to Canterbury to run away. 'You will find me here. And in the Lord's battle I will fight, hand to hand, toe to toe.'

Becket had known what was coming. He had spent much of the day in prayer, calling on the saints to come to his aid; he had made his confession, assisted at Mass and three times had asked to be flogged. It is said that he had considered flight, but had decided that 'God's will be done'. Clearly his monks understood what might happen, for they urged him to seek refuge in the cathedral. When he scorned their timidity they dragged him away, through the cloisters, into the north transept of the cathedral, where vespers had begun. Darkness was falling and it would have been easy for Becket to hide in the vast cathedral, lit only by candles, but he insisted that the door be left open and turned to await the knights. The uproar had so frightened the monks that many abandoned their prayers and hid in the aisles; terrified servants scattered through a door Becket had ordered to be left open to allow them to escape. The archbishop was left with just three of his companions.

Soon the knights stormed into the cathedral, shouting, 'Where is Becket, a traitor to the king and kingdom?' 'Here I am,' replied Becket, 'not a traitor to the king, but a priest of God. What do you want of me?' The knights tried to drag him out of the cathedral so that no sacrilege should be committed, but Becket struggled and somehow stood his ground. By now all had deserted him save Edward Grim, a visiting cleric from Cambridge. Becket stood with his back to a pillar and said, 'Into thy hands, O Lord, I commend my spirit.'

When the attack began Becket managed to fell William de Tracy, hurling him on the stone floor with torrents of abuse; Fitzurse closed in, shouting 'Strike! Strike!', but only succeeded in removing the archbishop's cap. De Tracy leapt up and struck hard, but the blow fell on the faithful Edward Grim, whose arm was cut to the bone, merely grazing the archbishop. De Tracy struck again, this time stunning Becket, who fell to the ground. Grim writes that as he fell he murmured, 'For the name of Jesus and the protection of the Church I am ready to embrace death.' The *coup de grâce* came from Richard le Breton, who struck with such violence that his sword sliced off the top of Becket's skull and shattered in two pieces on the hard floor.

LEFT *In a 12th-century depiction of Becket's martyrdom, Reginald Fitzurse, identified by the device on his shield, attempts to kill Becket but succeeds only in knocking off his cap.*

Still they were not done. Shouting 'The king's men! The king's men!' they ransacked the palace for evidence of treason, beat the servants, and made off on stolen horses, saddlebags crammed with their spoils. They spent the night at Saltwood, at one time the residence of the man they had murdered.

Once the knights had left, the monks and clerics found the courage to attend to the body of the murdered archbishop. Blood and brains were collected and the body carried to the high altar, with bowls placed under the bier so that every drop

THE MIRACLE WINDOWS

ONE OF THE GLORIES of Canterbury Cathedral is its medieval stained glass, much of which survived the destruction of images in the Reformation period. Particularly fascinating are the windows of the Trinity Chapel, which depict miraculous cures attributed to St Thomas Becket—stories of the saint's ability to heal began to circulate only a few days after his martyrdom in 1170. With their rich radiant colours the 12 windows—only eight of them remain— would have impressed the thousands of pilgrims who sought cures at the saint's shrine, which stood in the chapel before the Reformation.

The miracles shown by the windows were based on stories recorded by two Canterbury monks who were contemporaries of Becket. One set of images, for example, in the chapel's north arcade, depicts what happened when the plague visited the house of a certain Sir Jordan Fitz-eisulf (*see below*), a moral tale reminding people to keep any pledges made to St Thomas.

The north arcade windows also display the healing of two crippled sisters after they had seen a vision of St Thomas during their pilgrimage to Canterbury, as well as the story of Robert of Rochester. This young lad was throwing stones at frogs with his school friends by the River Medway when he fell in and nearly

drowned (*see above*): he was revived by sipping water of St Thomas, that is water sanctified by drops of the martyr's blood.

In the south arcade can be seen the healing of Brother Elias, a monk who suffered from leprosy, and the cure of Adam the Forester, who was wounded by a poacher's arrow. There is also the story of William of Gloucester, accidentally buried under a mound of earth while

ABOVE *Robert, surrounded by his school friends, falls into the River Medway. The frogs they were hitting are on the left.*

laying water pipes on the Archbishop of York's estate. In a vision St Thomas told a woman that William was still alive— even though his friends had given up hope—and this led to his rescue from the ground.

LEFT AND FAR LEFT *When Sir Jordan's son nearly dies, he recovers by drinking St Thomas's water and, in gratitude, his father vows to offer money at Becket's tomb—but fails to do so. St Thomas appears to a beggar and orders him to prompt Sir Jordan to fulfil his vow. But the warning goes unheeded until the plague strikes down Sir Jordan's elder son (far left) and Sir Jordan finally makes the offering (left).*

of blood should be saved. Few of them knew about Becket's ascetic practices and they were amazed to discover the monk's habit and a hair shirt, seething with lice and worms, under the ecclesiastical robes. The monks were deeply impressed and burst into cries of, 'Look, he's a true monk!' and 'Saint Thomas'. The eagerness to save every drop of blood became more intense. Already Becket was being seen as a martyr and the townspeople crowding into the cathedral dipped their fingers into the blood and made the sign of the cross on their foreheads. Fearing that someone should try to steal his body, the monks clothed it in his consecration clothes, together with the insignia of his office, and buried it in the crypt.

Immediately the miracles began. On the very night of the murder a paralysed woman of Canterbury was cured with some of Becket's blood that her husband had wiped up on a cloth. Within days, news had spread and miraculous cures were reported in Sussex, Gloucestershire and Berkshire. By Easter at least twenty miracles had been claimed, and in June public acclaim had defeated official hostility and pilgrims were openly wearing ampoules of 'the water of Thomas'— a few drops of his blood diluted with gallons of water. A few months later news began to arrive of miracles in Germany, France, Italy and Holland. By then some of the Canterbury monks had travelled to Rome to give the Pope their version of the story and within a year legates were sent to investigate the miracles. Becket was canonised in 1173, his feast day being commemorated on the day of his murder, December 29. Becket's cause not only received popular support, but had the official backing of the Church.

From that momentous day in 1170 until Henry VIII ravaged the shrine in 1538, pilgrims flocked to Canterbury from all over England and the Continent and Becket's shrine became the most popular in the whole of England. An official register was kept of the miracles wrought by the relics of the saint (there were as many as 700 recorded miracles in the fifteen years after his death) and plenary indulgences were given to those who visited the shrine. On July 7, 1220 the saint's body was translated from the crypt to the new Trinity Chapel behind the high altar, and the shrine was magnificently adorned with gold, silver and jewels offered by the pious. Now the saint had a second festival, in summer, a time that was rather kinder for pilgrimage. The number of pilgrims increased and the coffers of Canterbury became correspondingly richer.

ABOVE *An enamelled reliquary depicting Becket's martyrdom. Many such caskets were made in Limoges in the 12th and 13th centuries.*

The arguments for Becket's canonisation rested on three planks: the issues for which he had fought, the manner of his death and the miracles. Even if the issue over which he fought is no longer deemed worthy of canonisation, it is impossible not to admire the courage with which he fought for it and the dignity with which he died. And there is no question that he died a martyr's death.

CHAPTER FIVE

PAGAN BONES

WE SPENT THE NIGHT in Otford, a couple of miles from the ruins of Becket's favourite palace and quite close to the bridge where I had heard the nightingale. The next morning I allowed myself to be talked into a deviation, which led us to lose our way.

Our landlady knew that the direct route from Otford to Wrotham was, like the road into Otford, which we had negotiated the day before, narrow, busy and without verges. She advised us to avoid the road by taking the North Downs Way. Although it sounded a lovely walk, I did not want to stray so far from the Pilgrims' Way, which at this point coincided with the road; also, I knew that our guidebook suggested walking along a small path running beside the road, which would have been tolerably quiet. However, in the face of advice from an Otford local, I thought perhaps I had misunderstood the guidebook and that the road might indeed frighten one of my companions, who, I had by then discovered, was really scared by heavy traffic.

We set off, climbing high up to the north of the Pilgrims' Way, and were at first glad that we had done so, for the day was fine and the views spectacular. As we were no longer on the route suggested by the guidebook, we relied on our map and the acorn markers indicating the North Downs Way. After about two hours we came to a main road and when we asked to be directed to Wrotham were told to go up the hill and we would soon be there. It did not feel right, but we did as we were told and walked another couple of miles, eventually reaching a small village, a signpost marking a variety of places, all unfamiliar to us except Brands Hatch, and we knew we did not want to be there.

We had been walking for over three hours and it was already twelve o'clock, the time we had arranged to meet Barbara in Wrotham. What should we do? There were some pretty cottages in the village and we rang a doorbell to ask if we could use the telephone. A charming elderly lady, looking like someone from *Cider with Rosie*, greeted us warmly. She told us we were at West Kingsdown and that

Wrotham was almost six miles in the other direction, but that she was going there to do some shopping and would give us a lift.

We did not hesitate to accept but I was distraught by the interruption of the continuous line from Winchester to Canterbury. It was like a physical wound; in fact it was worse, because it could not be healed. We had not only lost our way but we had missed several miles of the journey and, short of starting all over again, there was no recovering it. Our pilgrimage was scarred and mutilated.

I wondered if I should ask to be taken back to Otford and retrieve the walk along the Pilgrims' Way to Wrotham, but dismissed this idea, as my companions would have had to wait and we would not reach our destination for the day by

ABOVE *Fields of ripening crops sway in the wind in this arable landscape sweeping from the area near Wrotham towards the Medway Valley.*

ABOVE *The rural charm of Trottiscliffe village attracted the artist Graham Sutherland (1903–80) who lived in an attractive house there.*

evening. I even thought of returning after we had completed the pilgrimage and walking the missing miles. But it was too late to mend the situation; we had made a mistake and I was going to have to live with it.

Once in Wrotham, after our circuitous deviation, we were back on the Pilgrims' Way—indeed, The Bull Inn is a 14th-century coaching inn, once a stopping place for pilgrims. We wandered round the delightful old village, trying to imagine how the archbishop's palace must once have looked, then visited the church. Here, as at the churches of St James at Shere and St Martha on the Hill, Chilworth, there are a number of little crosses incised into a piece of sandstone, often thought to indicate the passing of pilgrims, though the writer of the pamphlet on sale at the church thinks that it is more likely that the crosses were to ward off evil spirits.

Before we continued on our way we took advantage of being in a quiet village during working hours to do some shopping. Jane bought a bottle of wine for the evening and told us of the following exchange. 'Haven't seen you before. Where do you come from?' 'From Winchester,' she said, 'and we're going to Canterbury.' 'Ooh!' he said, clearly impressed. 'Thomas Becket?' 'Yes, that's right. I'll say a prayer for you.' 'Lovely. Nobody's ever done that for me before.'

We left Wrotham, crossed the M20 and followed the Downs in a northeasterly sweep along another of those long stretches where the North Downs Way, the Pilgrims' Way and the Trackway are harmoniously one and the same.

There were woods on the hills above us, exuberant arable fields to our right, chalk underfoot and, as always, cow parsley embroidering the verges. We passed Platt Hill Wood, Hognore Wood and a house appropriately named Pilgrim House, from where we could see Trottiscliffe church, which by then we knew was pronounced 'Trosley'. Then we walked along the south side of Great Wood until we reached the turning to the Coldrum Stones, which lie just half a mile off the Pilgrims' Way.

The Coldrum Stones are a Neolithic long barrow. In 1910 excavators found the bones of twenty-two people—men, women and children—some of which were taken to Trottiscliffe church. The bones revealed that these people were short and strong in stature, with long heads and broad feet. The presence of the bones of ox, cat, deer, rabbit and fox suggest that they were meat-eaters. Their teeth were healthy, but the elderly apparently suffered from rheumatism and all the shin-bones had been flattened by the squatting posture they favoured. They were members of the Neolithic farming community who were the first to settle in this part of Kent and these twenty-two people were among the most prestigious of the community, possibly even members of the royal family.

ABOVE *The Coldrum Stones once formed a circle of about 160 feet in circumference over a long barrow, or burial chamber. Only part of the circle has survived, and some stones lie as great slabs flat on the ground.*

Careful study of the barrow and the bones during the excavation suggested that the bodies of the dead were laid in a separate wooden structure until the flesh had rotted, and then, when the bones fell apart, they were gathered up, separated and placed in the tombs with great care. Although the religious beliefs of Neolithic farming communities are not known, experts believe that the planning and thought given to these long barrows speak of well-organised communities with a belief in some sort of life after death. It is interesting that the larger end of long barrows, containing the main sepulchre, frequently point, as do the altars of

LEFT *The Pilgrims' Hall, Aylesford Priory, reflected in the River Medway. Probably built in the 13th century, it served as a hospice for pilgrims on the road to Canterbury Cathedral.*

Christian churches, in an easterly direction. The distinguished archaeologist Jacquetta Hawkes suggests that these monuments must have served as religious meeting places and that the cult associated with the tombs was concerned with ideas of rebirth:

> I do not think it is allowing the imagination too great liberty to say that the faith, for it is very truly a faith, which made the New Stone Age communities labour to drag, raise, pile thousands of tons of stone and earth, was in resurrection, the resurrection of their corn and beasts, of themselves. They laid their dead in the dark, earth-enclosed chamber with something of the same conviction with which they cast the seed corn into the soil.

As we neared the site, there they were, the massive stones, four standing upright in the centre, many more fallen to the ground in a stone circle. The light was bright, the wind blustering round as it had blustered for 4,000 years, the grass mown close and clean, the simple fence surrounding the burial chamber discreet and solid. I was tempted to scramble over the fence to touch the stones, to get closer to those far-off ancestors; it was respect that prevented me. This was holy ground.

Too moved for discussion, we stayed silently for some time. I was standing at the back of the circle of stones, looking east, when suddenly I saw, in the far distance and exactly above the central stone, the spire of a church. It was a wonderful moment of completion; the burial chamber, built by pagans seeking resurrection in their way, the Christian church, proclaiming the resurrection of Christ.

ABOVE *A friar chopping wood at Aylesford Priory. Each friar has a specific area of work at the priory and many work outside in the community at large, too.*

THE FRIARS OF AYLESFORD

It was fitting to our mood that, for the next two nights, we should be staying at The Friars, the Aylesford home of a community of Carmelite friars. It was founded in 1242, when the first Carmelites arrived from the Holy Land. Five years later,

OPPOSITE *Aylesford's Gatehouse, seen here from across a pond, was built by Sir John Banks, one of the owners of the property. He bought The Friars and turned it into a fine mansion in the 1670s.*

St Simon Stock, who was believed to have been born in Kent (a late tradition even suggests Aylesford itself), was elected prior general of the order. During his time, the Carmelites became an international order, with foundations in Oxford, Cambridge, Paris and Bologna.

There is a tradition that St Simon experienced a vision of the Mother of God, who touched his scapular and promised her protection to anyone who wore one. Although the vision lacks contemporary documentation it has always been a tradition in the Order, and is honoured with a carved plaque in one of the chapels and a medieval wooden statue, normally in the Relic Chapel but carried in procession during the pilgrimages. The Relic Chapel is so called because in it is a tall reliquary covered with ceramic tiles, which houses the saint's skull. It was brought back from Bordeaux, where he had died nearly 700 years before, in 1951.

After the Dissolution of the Monasteries the house became a private dwelling and it was not until 1949 that it returned to the friars, Carmelites from all over the world contributing to the recovery of their ancient home. Almost immediately coachloads of people began coming to Aylesford to pray, and The Friars became,

THE CARMELITES AND ST SIMON STOCK

KNOWN AS THE WHITE FRIARS from the colour of their mantles, the Carmelites grew in size and prestige during the Middle Ages to become an important order of mendicant friars, next to the Franciscans and Dominicans. The origins of the order are obscure, but it seems to have arisen out of Christian hermits living on Mount Carmel in northern Palestine during the 12th century. In about 1210 the hermits began to follow a strict religious rule of solitude, poverty and abstinence, which they maintained until about 1238, when hostility from Muslims forced many Carmelites to flee to Europe. One of these refugees was probably St Simon Stock, who was elected prior general of the order at Aylesford in Kent in 1247.

Little is known of St Simon. He was never formally canonised as a saint; and the surname 'Stock' was first attributed to him a century after he died in 1265. Under his leadership the Carmelites reorganised their rule along the less severe model of the Dominicans: the friars were allowed

to eat together, the hours of silence were reduced and insistence on abstinence was tempered. Also, friaries were founded in towns, which led to greater expansion of the order across Europe. Although there was a reaction to these reforms by die-hard Carmelites, the order grew: by the end of the 13th century there were 150 Carmelite houses in Europe, with 30 of them in England.

ABOVE *Aylesford's Reliquary Chapel with the reliquary holding the skull of St Simon.*

Today, the Carmelites of Aylesford continue the work of their forebears, adapting their traditions to the modern world. In addition to their life of prayer and worship they organise pilgrimages and retreats and serve the community at large by visiting prisons and schools.

by popular acclaim, a Marian shrine and a place of pilgrimage. A great deal of work, not to mention money, has been devoted to restoring the old buildings and now The Friars is not only the home of a small community, but a well-established conference and retreat centre with five chapels and a guesthouse accommodating up to 100 people. Its main purpose is to be a centre for prayer and pilgrimage and the friars estimate that around 200,000 people come every year, gathering when the weather permits in a huge outdoor area known as the Piazza or Shrine Area.

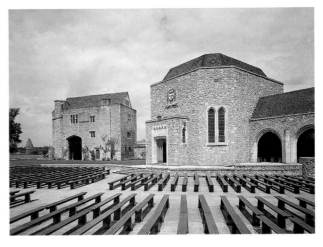

The old buildings, lovingly renovated, were glowing in golden evening light when we arrived. We collected our keys from the reception desk and settled into our rooms on one side of the huge old courtyard. We were delighted to find them not only spacious, but with timbered walls and ceilings, some of the beams dating from the 12th century, some added in the same style during the 20th-century reconstruction and so well done it was hard to tell the difference. We were delighted, too, to find that there were hot pipes running round the rooms, enabling us to wash and dry our clothes. We opened Jane's bottle of wine and spent an hour or so chatting before going over to the Pilgrims' Hall for our evening meal.

ABOVE *A view across the Piazza where pilgrims from across the world gather to worship at Aylesford Priory.*

In this beautiful hall I was aware, with a sense of poignancy, of the pilgrims who had been before us. They would have known these stone walls, these satisfying proportions; they would have sat at wooden tables very like the one at which we were sitting. They would even have looked up at the same oak beams in the roof, for when the hall was restored the original beams were in such good condition that they did not need to be replaced, and were simply cleaned off and put back where they had been for hundreds of years. In fact, when they were sent for carbon dating they were found to date from 1170, the very year of Becket's martyrdom. So the assumption must be that the hall was built in time for the first pilgrims who travelled to the saint's shrine at Canterbury.

After a good helping of cauliflower cheese I explored the two galleries above the dining hall. One is now a library and the small top gallery is at the moment unused, but for the early pilgrims they were the sleeping quarters. There would have been a big log fire in the middle of the hall and a hole in the roof to allow the smoke to escape. Above this hole there would probably have been a square wooden structure for keeping out the rain, or at least the worst of it. The softwood balustrades round the galleries are now open railings, though they would originally have been panelled, in order to keep the draughts away from the sleeping pilgrims.

The day ended with night prayer in the small Cloister Chapel. This was how the friars ended their day, every day. While we were with them, this was how we would end ours.

JEWELS IN SHADOWLAND

The next day, as we drove back on our tracks from Aylesford to the place where we had stopped the night before, I no longer felt uneasy. Whatever the minor irritations and frustrations, despite upsurges of violent emotion and pain, I was, at a deep level, content. Perhaps pilgrimage was purging my guilt.

The two miles from the Coldrum Stones to Paddlesworth church were in keeping with my peaceful mood. The track continued its gentle sweep round the foot of the Downs, the day was slightly misty and sultry, but quiet and warm. There was a long stretch when we walked through trees, enclosed in a tunnel of branches meeting over our heads.

In Belloc's time the little chapel at Paddlesworth was a ruin, and we are indebted to the Redundant Churches Fund, an independent charity who took it over in 1976, for its restoration. It is a tiny, yet beautifully proportioned Norman building, standing alone and vulnerable on the edge of a field, opposite a farm. It would have been known to the medieval pilgrims and can just lay claim to being a living church once more, for it is open at weekends, and services are held there twice a year.

The village of Snodland (apparently it can blame a Saxon landowner called Snodd for its name) spills over almost into Paddlesworth and on its outskirts stands Woodlands Farm, a half-timbered house with a long and eventful history. I had heard about it in the bar of The Bull Inn at Wrotham. 'You must go and see my parents,' said the girl from whom I bought a drink. 'They live in a house that used to be a pilgrim hospice.'

Mr and Mrs Meyers greeted me warmly and showed me round the house. It was built in 1450, but the foundations could have been built much earlier. Neolithic axes found nearby indicate the presence of prehistoric peoples and there are signs that there was once a Saxon barn on the site. Its use by pilgrims was indicated by an outside staircase, no longer there, which led to an upstairs room. Apparently the pilgrims would have gone straight up to sleep, without disturbing the owners, who trusted them to settle up in the morning before they went on their way.

The Meyers also told me something of the local history and legends about the Pilgrims' Way in that part of Kent. William Caxton married a girl from the nearby village of Halling and set up a printing press there. A 17th-century owner of Woodlands Farm started the first scheme for apprentices, which still helps the young people of Snodland. In more macabre vein, I heard how people thought to be witches were tried in the ecclesiastical court in Snodland and how those found guilty were condemned to death by drowning. The Medway at this point is a deep and dangerous river and the women were put in a damaged old boat, the oldest pushed to the front where they would perish soonest. A point of the river where the tide was fast was chosen, and the boat was then pushed mercilessly out into the turbulent waters.

There is a legend that says that Jesus travelled here with Joseph of Arimathea. It is said that He came up the river, passed the front door of the Roman villa, the remains of which have been found near its banks, and walked part of the Pilgrims' Way.

There was once a ferry across the Medway at Snodland, used by Belloc, who claims also to have seen a hard-bottomed ford. It would then have been only a short walk, passing Burham and Little Culand, to the megalithic monument known as Kit's Coty House. Now there is neither ferry nor ford and plans for a bridge have not yet materialised, so the nearest points to cross the river are to the north, over the Medway bridge near Rochester, or to the south, at Aylesford. The North Downs Way leaves the Pilgrims' Way just before Paddlesworth and makes a huge loop to Rochester and down again to Kit's Coty. The Aylesford route takes a shorter detour to the south, meeting the other two routes at the White Horse Stone near Kit's Coty House.

Over a cup of coffee we discussed the options and considered ways in which we could reach Burham, tantalisingly close across the river. We had been told that it was sometimes possible to hire a boat, but we should have made arrangements beforehand, as none of the locals seemed sure who to approach. In the end we opted for the shortest route, which would take us right past The Friars, where we were staying.

It was a dreadful walk. I would sooner have trebled the distance than walk those few miles. I wondered how Cobbett would have fumed over the monstrosities bequeathed to us by the 20th century, for not only were we deprived of the river crossing, but we saw our industrial heritage revealed in its worst and drabbest colours as we made our way down the river's side. Now I knew why someone has called the Medway 'the dustbin of Kent'.

We started through a maze of modern buildings, crossing a car park and passing under a railway bridge. The Blue Circle Lake had sounded attractive,

ABOVE *Chalk quarrying for the cement works on the River Medway. The area surrounding the Medway is a centre of industry in Kent.*

ABOVE *The early morning light shimmers across the River Medway as it flows past the pretty old village of Aylesford. The medieval bridge is said to be one of the finest in the area.*

and it was at least a redeeming feature, but soon we were funnelled between wire fences close to the railway line, processed through a trading estate and across the track by New Hythe station. Then, squeezed between more wire fences, which were now even higher and stretched over concrete posts, we came into a bleak industrial area bought up by a Swedish packaging business. Our senses, spoilt by so much countryside, were assaulted on all sides: downland now replaced by charmless factories, hedgerows by these forbidding fences, the fresh wind by a heavy sulphurous smell. I discovered later that the most likely explanation for the smell was the coal-fired boiler house that produces steam for drying the paper.

Once through the factory buildings we were walking on the towpath and assumed that the worst was over. But before we had time to breathe a sigh of relief I saw that not only was the Medway at this point sluggish and dirty, but, even worse, that one vile smell was giving way to another. The reason was not far to seek. As we rounded a bend in the river, there was the sign: SEWER. We were now passing the local sewerage works.

My reaction to these scenes of desolation surprised me: I was glad, just as I had been glad that the previous Sunday had given us a taste of walking in really dreadful weather. Apart from frequent confrontations with motorways and traffic, we had spent most of the last ten days in quiet, sometimes idyllic, countryside. If pilgrimage is an image of life, then it too must have its shadow side. This was brought poignantly home as across the river, nestling in this ugly industrial wasteland, we saw the sparkling old houses of the village of Aylesford. Jewels can exist in shadowland.

We had lunch in one of Aylesford's oldest pubs, only half a mile from The Friars, and continued along our enforced detour, modernity still oppressing us as we passed Safeway's massive storage depot. Once we had left that eyesore behind, the route took us past a cherry orchard and into fields, but the constant throb of traffic, probably from the M20, was still with us. On these occasions I was quite grateful for my continuing (though slightly improving) deafness.

My spirits rose at the thought of the three prehistoric monuments we were approaching: the Countless Stones, Kit's Coty House and the White Horse Stone. We saw first the Countless Stones, which from a distance appeared to Jacquetta Hawkes as a 'small shoal of stranded whales'. We must have seen them from even further away, for they could have been mistaken for sleeping sheep. They have fallen in such a way that it is not always easy to tell where one stone ends and another begins. Some say that they are called 'countless' simply because there are so many and because they lie so confusingly; others say that a magic spell cast over them prevents them from ever being correctly counted. The only certainty is that they once formed a burial chamber, a thought that became very real when I learned that holes in the hillside may once have been the rudimentary homes of the folk who worshipped there.

PAPER-MAKING IN THE SOUTHEAST

THE SOUTHEAST, whose rivers provide a plentiful supply of water, has a long association with the manufacture of paper. Some of the region's paper mills date back as far as the 18th century and are still active today.

The process by which paper is manufactured has, over time, become highly mechanised, but the basic technique remains unchanged. The fibres, usually of wood, though sometimes of other materials including rags and straw, are separated and made wet, and a pulp is produced. The pulp is then flowed onto a wire-mesh belt, and a sheet of fibre is formed. This is pressed and compacted, which squeezes out most of the water, and evaporation removes any remaining water. Heated rollers further compress and dry the paper which, depending on its intended use, may then be coated with some other substances.

LEFT *An example of traditional paper-making. Small quantities of handmade paper are still produced in the Southeast.*

Several different types of paper are made in the Southeast, including handmade paper, tracing paper and tissue paper. Recent years have also seen a revival of large-scale newsprint here, and a new approach aimed at conserving resources: instead of using wood pulp to produce the paper, millions of used newspapers and magazines are collected from special bins and recycled. This involves mixing the existing paper with water and pulping it, and releasing the ink from the fibre using soap and chemicals. The process is then completed in the traditional way, yielding a range of papers on which many of the nation's newspapers and magazines are printed.

RIGHT *Protected by railings, Kit's Coty House stands on high ground. Probably once part of an ancient burial chamber measuring 180 feet long, the stones would have been covered by an earth mound, now completely eroded.*

Kit's Coty House is a megalithic tomb, one of the best-known prehistoric monuments in the whole country. It stands in a cornfield called Blue Bell Hill just over a mile northeast of Aylesford, three massive upright stones supporting a fourth. It, too, was almost certainly a burial chamber, and an 18th-century drawing shows that there was a long barrow running westwards from it. Even in the 17th century it was sufficiently well known for the diarist Samuel Pepys to break his journey to visit it. He wrote that the stones were 'of great bigness, although not so big as those on Salisbury Plain. But certainly a thing of great antiquity, and I am mightily glad to see it.'

So was I, but I have to admit to being disappointed. The imagination is stirred by the theory that it marked the burial place of Catigern, a British chief killed nearby in the battle against the Jutes, Hengist and Horsa; even more by the thought that the site was probably known to cave-dwellers who worshipped the sun. But I had no sense of a living link with ancestors, of the place still being inhabited by the spirits of the dead, as I had had at the Coldrum Stones.

The last of these old stones was the White Horse Stone, a large sarsen stone standing unceremoniously by the side of the lane, now once again the Pilgrims' Way. We walked round, peering at it from many different angles, until at last, like seeing a face in the clouds, we could trace the form of a horse's head, its eye a deep hole in the stone. There were the remains of a fire beside it. Had modern druids or witches been sacrificing there?

MIRACLES AND MAZES

A sign to Boxley forced me to leave prehistoric times and leap forward some 3,500 years to the Middle Ages, which in contrast now seemed quite close to the 20th century. It has been suggested that Boxley received special attention at the Dissolution of the Monasteries, as it was here that the adjudicator decided against Henry's divorce; certainly, there is little left of the 12th-century Cistercian abbey, now a private house and far too close to the M20 for the comfort of the owners. However, Boxley Abbey is still remembered for the two miraculous images that were shown to pilgrims, neither of which can be seen today: the celebrated crucifix, the Rood of Grace, and the image of Rumbold, the child saint.

Tradition has it that the miraculous crucifix arrived at the monastery on the back of a stray packhorse, which refused to leave until the monks had given the sacred object a home. The crucifix turned out to have extraordinary powers, the hands sometimes raised in blessing, the head able to bow in sorrow and the face assuming different expressions as the eyes rolled or wept and the mouth moved. These gifts were not put to pious use, for whether the image expressed pleasure (by its heavenly smile) or sadness (by a disappointed frown) was dependent not on the state of the pilgrim's soul, but on the size of his offering.

But worse was to come. After the Dissolution the man employed to pull down the buildings made a disconcerting discovery. He wrote to Thomas Cromwell about what he had found in the Rood of Grace:

> Certain engines and old wire, with rotten old sticks in the back, which caused
> the eyes to move and stir in the head thereof, like unto a living thing, and also
> the nether lip likewise to move as though it should speak.

The image of St Rumbold also involved deception. He must have been quite the youngest saint, for he died when he was just three days old, having already recited the Lord's Prayer and the Apostles' Creed—hence his canonisation. This small statue had the power to change its weight at will. Sometimes it could be moved by a child, on other occasions it resisted the greatest strength; it all depended (or so it was believed) on the state of the soul of the pilgrim. Women who had lost their chastity stood to risk public exposure, for to them St Rumbold would be as immovable as the walls of the abbey itself. An offering to the priest could spare their blushes—he would operate some hidden device behind a nearby pillar and the statue moved freely. The iconoclasts loved this, though some bishops had been aware of the fraud and had chosen to look the other way.

As we stood at the turning to Boxley, we were propelled into the 20th century by roadworks, for at this point their presence had diverted all the local traffic onto the Pilgrims' Way. The lane was so narrow that a small van brushed the cow parsley on both sides at once, there were no verges and it was rush hour. This time I could not help hoping that naive pilgrims, cheered by a 'heavenly smile', did not discover that they had been cheated (perhaps I was learning to cope with scruples). I had no qualms and flagged down the first car going in our direction.

LEEDS CASTLE: THE JEWEL OF KENT

WITH ITS CASTELLATED WALLS, fine towers and romantic island setting in a lake surrounded by beautiful parkland, Leeds Castle is an impressive sight. It began life as a Norman fortress in the 12th century, later becoming a royal palace and residence of a succession of kings and queens, including Henry VIII, who enlarged and improved the castle. It subsequently passed into private hands in 1522, and after a succession of owners was bought in 1926 by an American heiress. Lady Baillie, as she became, lived at Leeds Castle for nearly 50 years, restoring it in great style and creating large parts of the beautiful landscaped grounds seen today.

When Lady Baillie died in 1974 she bequeathed Leeds Castle to the nation. Her wish that the castle be preserved as a 'living castle' is reflected in the lively calendar of events the castle now hosts, including the Festival of English Food

LEFT Leeds Castle, called 'the loveliest castle in the world' by historian Lord Conway, rises majestically out of a snowy winter landscape.

and Wine, historical storytelling for children and the Festival of Floral Art. Especially popular are the open-air classical concerts, where picnicking visitors are entertained by some of the country's foremost conductors, orchestras and soloists, and the Great Balloon and Vintage Car Weekend, when brightly coloured hot-air balloons drifting serenely above the castle provide a dramatic sight.

The castle's more permanent attractions also have something to offer everyone: grand rooms lavishly decorated with art, antiques and *objets d'art*; a fine collection of dogs' collars,

some of which date from the 16th century; the maze, planted with 2,400 yew trees, and the grotto, which provides an alternative route out of the maze via a series of mysterious underground tunnels. For nature-lovers there is the Wood Garden, carpeted in daffodils and wood anemones in early spring, and the Pavilion Garden, which blazes with colourful rhododendrons and azaleas a few months later. Exotic touches are provided by the Aviary, which houses over 100 species of rare bird, and the subtropical plants that flourish in the Lady Baillie Garden, opened in 1999 in honour of the woman by whose inspiration Leeds Castle, with its ancient heritage, has been preserved for the nation.

BELOW *Fireworks arch high over the castle as a grand finale to a night of music, at one of the summer open-air concerts.*

BELOW *Gently floating hot-air balloons take part in the Great Balloon and Vintage Car Weekend, a popular event at Leeds Castle.*

It was a large white Mercedes driven by a charming Indian businessman, so we travelled the remaining mile into Detling in the utmost comfort. I recalled 'the chariot in weariness' we prayed for when Canon Teare read the *Itinerarium* and wondered if 'a protection in danger' might not also fit the case. But this time my conscience was clear—or do I protest too much?

After a drink at The Cock Horse (so named because it kept a horse to hitch to coaches and help them up hills), I left my companions in the pub and carried on a little further. This was partly inclination, and partly because we had made a small mistake in our calculations and realised that we would not reach Canterbury by midday on Saturday unless we did a little extra. The two and a half miles to Broad Street was an ecstatic walk, the Downs rising gently to my left and the fields bathed in a rosy evening light. I was quite sorry when I saw the car and my three companions coming to pick me up to return for a second night of monastic hospitality at The Friars.

ABOVE *The maze at Leeds Castle was designed by the architect Vernon Gibberd and planted in 1988. It will in time grow into a topiary castle, with towers and bastions formed by castellated hedges.*

Before continuing to Canterbury, however, let me take you on a short detour to Leeds Castle. It is not on the Pilgrims' Way and I had no reason to believe it was visited by early pilgrims, but I could not resist the chance to walk another maze. Having walked the unicursal maze on St Catherine's Hill and seen how that was a microcosm of pilgrimage, I wanted to have the experience of walking a multicursal maze. As it was at least two miles off the route—and meant crossing the M20 at that—I had visited it some weeks before.

All the world was there, enjoying the first spring flowers, admiring the famous moated castle, an island fortress whose stones span about 1,000 years, from the 9th century, when it was the site of a manor of the Saxon royal family, to the 1930s, when the elegant drawing room was created. We milled around, eating ice creams, drank cups of undrinkable tea, then wandered round the lake. I could hardly take in the beautiful gardens, so impatient was I to reach the maze. Knowing I would be faced with choice, I was apprehensive. 'Children love getting lost in the maze and it's fun for grown-ups too,' says the leaflet cheerily, but I was not so sure.

My premonitions were right. Seconds after I set foot between the trees, still only some three or four feet high, the first choice was presented to me. Did I turn left? Or right? Or go straight on? There was nothing indicating which I should choose, and I was filled with panic. The panic increased as choice followed choice among the small, winding paths between the young trees. Eventually I began to take one or the other path in an arbitrary way; in no time, I was within a stone's throw of the centre. What had I been worrying about? It was quite easy after all. Fool's gold! I was not there at all, the centre smiled triumphantly at me, unattainable beyond a line of trees I had thought I could penetrate but could not.

What should I do? Perhaps head for the outside and thus succeed. I took the path that seemed to lead away from the centre. It was, as I half suspected, too self-conscious a move and once again I was choosing one path after the other and going nowhere. The initial feeling of panic was changing into irritation. How silly it all was, this endless trudging, these interminable paths and futile choices. So, now in a daze of confusion, I walked interminably, no longer caring much which path I took. 'Nearly there!' said a voice somewhere on my right. And I was.

No sense of achievement. No reason for any turn, any choice. Once at the centre I had no wish to stay, it held no magic. I was not sorry when the keeper told us that it was time to close.

I was 'amazed' (yes, the words are philologically connected) at the difference between walking a unicursal and a multicursal maze. The unicursal maze gave me a sense of trust—I knew that I had just to keep going and I would reach the centre. On the other hand, the multicursal, infuriating though it was with its bewildering and apparently pointless choices, seemed a more accurate mirror of life, so I was surprised to discover that for the first 3,000 years of its history, until the Middle Ages, the maze was unicursal. Perhaps art was reflecting life. When life was simpler it was just a question of survival, of keeping going along one's given path; when life became more complex, as choices multiplied, the maze became multicursal. Pilgrimage, I now knew from experience, included both. There were those delightful occasions when there was no doubt as to the route, and walking was, if not easy, at least uncomplicated; and there were the moments of confusion, doubt and choice. The spiritual pilgrimage also includes both, though I suspect most people find—I certainly do—that they spend more time on ways of confusion than on ways of simplicity.

IN PRAISE OF PUBS

We had stopped at Broad Street the night before, so it was to Broad Street that we returned that morning, the eleventh day of our pilgrimage. This was to be a day when the path was clear and uninterrupted, and we were soon at Hollingbourne.

Hollingbourne is a beautiful village. A red-brick Elizabethan manor house, once home of the Culpeper family, crowns a street of houses so perfect that Richard Church, writing in 1948, was lulled into fantasies of a life already becoming history, when he wrote:

ABOVE *Hollingbourne village sign shows the Culpeper family crest, top; a watermill, top left; oast-houses, bottom left; and the church tower, right. The Pilgrims' Way crosses the middle of the stream that runs through the village.*

I cannot think of a more suitable village than Hollingbourne in which to spend one's latter years. To settle there, in one of its period houses (I should choose a William and Mary piece higher up the village), with a devoted gardener, a good cellar of claret, and rooms in the Albany so that comfortable reading should be done in London when in the mood, seems to me the height of civilised living.

We were tempted to linger in Hollingbourne, but it was too early in the day for leisurely stops: the day was fine and the countryside beckoned. For the rest of the morning, from Hollingbourne to Lenham, the Way was so straight that it could have been a Roman road. The path took us over rough dirt tracks and soft grassy paths, over gravel, chalk, hard flinty clay and occasionally a metalled surface. For some miles we walked along the edges of arable fields, the Downs rising on our left, providing a constant reassurance and sense of direction. I felt deeply content, even glad, when at one point we took a wrong turn, for we found ourselves under an avenue of beech trees arching so gracefully over our heads that we welcomed the mistake.

The day was marred only by rape—I mean oilseed rape. All around us, for mile after mile, stretched endless acres of that glaring, shallow yellow that has become such a faceless feature of spring in northern Europe. No doubt it brings millions of pounds to the farmers, but it adds nothing to the countryside and is harmful to brassicas and humans alike.

A short diversion across a field brought us to Lenham in time for lunch. This is another delightful village, boasting a magnificent tithe barn, a 16th-century forge house and the 'Saxon Warrior's Chemist', so named because a Saxon grave was discovered under the half-timbered building. In the heart of the square is a 17th-century pub called The Dog and Bear, and there we settled down.

ABOVE *A log pile is stacked outside the tithe barn in the pretty village of Lenham, with the church in the distance.*

ABOVE *A painted village sign for Lenham features a chalk cross carved into the hillside in remembrance of those who died in the two world wars.*

I would like to sing a paean of praise for the pubs along the Pilgrims' Way. The pub became for us a symbol of comfort, hospitality and welcome. We would arrive hot and tired, strew our rucksacks and jackets along benches, shed our shoes under the table, drink shandies and relax as if in our own sitting rooms. Sometimes, for the price of a drink and a sandwich, perhaps later a cup of coffee, we would spend over an hour talking, resting, using the telephone, seeking advice from whoever was at the bar. Nobody bothered us, hurried us on, or even seemed to notice us particularly—we were simply allowed to be. Pubs were our second homes and publicans the salt of the earth. 'There is nothing which has yet been contrived by man,' wrote Samuel Johnson, 'by which so much happiness is produced as by a good tavern or inn.' I had to agree with him.

We were not in a hurry to leave the comfort of The Dog and Bear, but eventually we made our way back to the Pilgrims' Way across a field, slightly alarmed by popping sounds, as if we were being shot at (it was, we learned later, a device intended to scare the birds, not us), and rejoined the North Downs Way on a greensward path by a huge chalk war memorial. We were well on schedule to complete the day's walk and that reassurance, coupled with the charm of the day and the hospitality of The Dog and Bear, had left us very relaxed, so when the glare of the remorseless rape gave way to soft green cornfields and sheep, we celebrated by lying down and having a dram—from the hip flask I had been given for the pilgrimage.

Then we dropped off the route again to visit Charing, where the archbishops had a manor house, which Becket would undoubtedly have visited as he went about his diocesan business and where Henry VIII is believed to have stayed. The remains of the palace are now a farm and can only just be glimpsed beyond a notice saying 'Private', but the main street, with its Georgian house frontages is so charming that I could not see how the village could have earned its unkind slogan:

Dirty Charing lies in a hole
Has but one bell and that she stole.

It was the church, built on a site given by King Ethelbert of Kent, that most interested me, for in the Middle Ages the pilgrims would have visited it to see Charing's famous relic—the block on which the head of John the Baptist is said to have been struck off. It was believed to have been brought from the Holy Land by Richard Coeur de Lion, but even if it escaped the attention of King Henry VIII's commissioners it would certainly have been destroyed in 1590, when a fire, started by a Spaniard shooting into the dry shingles of the roof, caused serious damage to the church. I had little heart for so gruesome a trophy, but the cult of relics was at the heart of pilgrimage, so, walking as I was in medieval footsteps, I was curious to understand something of their power, to know how they would have been a source of forgiveness, guidance and healing.

Orthodox and Roman Catholic Christians believe that the grace of God present in saints' bodies during life remains active in their relics when they have died, and

LEFT *The Dog and Bear Hotel, Lenham, was built in 1602. One of its bedrooms is said to be haunted by a friendly ghost, who rearranges the furniture.*

that God uses these relics as a channel of divine power and an instrument of healing. So precious relics in magnificent reliquaries drew medieval pilgrims in their thousands. There was also the seductive spin-off of the pilgrims' offerings, which filled the coffers of the churches and monasteries that owned the relics.

However, very important relics were often so carefully housed and guarded that they could not be seen, so pilgrims would seek healing from the humblest objects that had been in contact with the saint's body—dust, stones, scraps of paper. Becket's followers claimed cures from 'the water of Thomas', but as the demand so greatly exceeded the supply, the dilution became weaker and weaker until the cure was effected by a liquid innocent of the slightest trace of the saint's blood. Examples of miraculous healings are so numerous that even sceptics must wonder if there is not something in it, if only that believing a cure is possible itself leads to cure.

Once we had seen Charing church we were not tempted to linger—tearooms, pub and restaurant presenting us with firmly locked doors—but we had made good time and, as it was too early to return to Lenham, where we had arranged to meet, we decided to go on to the village of Westwell. Although it was a pleasant evening walk, we had been overoptimistic. A wrong turning added a mile or two to our journey and by the time we reached Westwell we had walked nearly seventeen miles since morning. Utterly exhausted, we rang for a taxi to take us back to our meeting place in Lenham. It was like a home from home, being able to spread ourselves gratefully over the hospitable benches of The Dog and Bear.

ABOVE *The coat of arms of Queen Anne is displayed over the entrance to The Dog and Bear Hotel, in honour of her visit in 1704.*

CHAPTER SIX

ARRIVAL

O N FRIDAY, MAY 14, the twelfth day of our pilgrimage, we were less than twenty miles from the spot where St Thomas Becket was martyred, our journey's end and a place for hundreds of years regarded as holy ground. I did not realise that within a few miles we would be standing on ground that was not, as far as I know, made famous by visions or martyrdom, but which, to me at least, was a place of overwhelming holiness.

St Mary's Church, Eastwell, is not on the Pilgrims' Way, but on this occasion I felt nothing but gratitude to the owners of Eastwell Park, whose notice 'Private Grounds. Keep Out' forces walkers onto a parallel path and thus past the church. It is a ruin now, shattered by the guns that were sited nearby during the Second World War; in 1951 it was again assaulted, this time by an unusually tempestuous wind. Now only the tower remains, with a few walls and the vestiges of once-graceful windows.

The ruins stand alone, no other buildings are visible. There are trees close to the tower, some overshadowing it, others clustering round protectively. Rough grass borders a large, still lake to the south. I had rarely experienced so deep a sense of peace. I read the notice on the church tower: 'This ancient house of God is being repaired by the Friends of Friendless Churches…It remains a consecrated building and the churchyard is sacred ground. Please respect them accordingly.'

I was touched by this appeal, reminded yet again of that question at the heart of pilgrimage: what is sacred ground, what makes a holy place? The awareness of a holy place is elusive, unavailable to us when we most long for it, striking us with the force of revelation when we least expect it. I have never forgotten my first visit to the Holy Land and my conviction of the presence of Jesus on the Sea of Galilee and in the quiet of the Judaean hills. Then the shock of going to the Holy Sepulchre in Jerusalem and seeing priests from various denominations each lifting a cloth covering the tomb, saying, 'This is our piece.' For me, holiness fled from the place at that instant.

Yet I know that holy places can and do survive such treatment, that it is possible to see beyond the greed and possessiveness that can tarnish holy places. Holiness cannot easily be banished. At the end of *Murder in the Cathedral*, T. S. Eliot writes:

ABOVE *A section of the west wall and the Perpendicular tower are all that remain of the 15th-century St Mary's Church in Eastwell.*

Wherever a saint has dwelt, wherever a martyr has given his blood for Christ,
There is holy ground, and the sanctity shall not depart from it
Though armies trample over it, though sightseers come with guidebooks looking
over it.

The sanctity may not have departed, but it can become harder to perceive.

Certainly, I was in no doubt as to where, so far on this pilgrimage, I had felt awe, timelessness, peace, and yes—love. The first time was in the maze on St Catherine's Hill, the centre emanating its own extraordinary power. Then at the Coldrum Stones, where our ancestors lie timeless on the Downs, and here, among the ruins of St Mary's Church, Eastwell. Whether this was partly due to the quiet and the loving care with which these sites are tended (who could fail to be moved by 'The Friends of Friendless Churches'?), or whether by some more mysterious, elusive presence, I do not know. But I do know that in these places I found spiritual nourishment and a sense that God is, in some very special way, there. I was in no doubt that they are sacred places and that I was standing on holy ground. I wondered whether we would feel the next day, when we reached Becket's shrine, that we were standing on holy ground.

ABOVE *Undulating green fields outside Boughton Aluph. Near here, the North Downs Way divides into two routes, one going to Canterbury and the other to Dover.*

TIME SUSPENDED

When we could bring ourselves to leave, we passed near Plantagenet's Well, so called because an unmarked tomb is believed to mark the resting place of Richard Plantagenet, bastard son of Richard III, who lived there as a humble bricklayer. In less than half a mile we rejoined the Pilgrims' Way at Boughton Lees. Here, the Way changes its southeasterly direction and follows the contours of the Downs to the northeast—a natural turning that lends support to the belief that we were indeed on the Old Road. Our next stopping place was the church at Boughton Aluph, where, I had read, the medieval pilgrims would have rested before facing the dangers of the robber-infested King's Wood. It would have been a good place to rest, for the south porch contained an unusual comfort, a fireplace; the brick chimney, thought to be unique, still survives. The church is now less hospitable, open only at weekends and on bank holidays, the explanation no doubt contained in the notice: 'Please close door to keep out sheep.'

ABOVE *Set in rolling farmland outside Chilham, restored oast-houses such as this one are typical features of the Kent landscape.*

Time was passing not only in hours and days, but in visible change. When we left Winchester (was it twelve days ago or a year and twelve days?) the bluebells were fresh and upright; here, they were drooping and coming to the end of their short lives. In Hampshire the elderflower trees were innocent of flowers; now we had reached Kent they were tentatively dressed in white, wafting reminders of homemade wine. The lambs were noticeably larger, clinging less urgently to their mothers. The innocent yellow-green of very early spring was darkening to the bluer green of the middle of May.

So too was time thrown into the melting pot as we walked in medieval footsteps, surrounded by reminders of man from Neolithic times to the 20th century. By now I was tired for much of the time and at one level longed to reach Canterbury, for the pilgrimage to be over and to be able to take my aching back to the comfort of my own home and to see my neglected garden in its spring freshness. Yet I also knew I would be heartbroken if anything were to prevent me from finishing the journey, from meeting the challenge.

From the church at Boughton Aluph it was a five-mile walk to Chilham. The semi-hypnotic state that had come over me at intervals was now almost continuous and my memory for the detail of the next two hours of walking is shaky. I remember a beautiful stretch of rolling Kentish countryside, then passing Soakham Farm, derelict and silent apart from a few chickens, apparently left to fend for themselves. We resisted the temptation to rest in a barn full of soft, comfortable hay and continued past Soakham Downs, walking for the next hour or so in a daze of content along the edge of King's Wood, imagining the bandits of medieval times, admiring the beautiful way it was now managed by the Forestry Commission. We were now on the summit of the Downs, some 500 feet above sea level; the air was bracing, the day one of those fresh, light May days that Britons dream of when they are abroad in spring. We saw no one for miles.

My tiredness—and perhaps my state of mind—was beginning to affect my walking and I was constantly falling over; on one occasion, I came a real purler and was amused by one of my companions, who could finally put to use the antiseptic wipes and plasters that she had been gallantly carrying for over 100 miles. I remember, after the application of first aid, things like stones underfoot suddenly giving way to soft wood chippings; a grass snake, still as a Buddha; hearing birdsong with my right ear for the first time since we left Winchester; miles of bluebells and the feeling of walking in a tunnel of young, sweet chestnut trees, occasionally glimpsing the wooded acres of Godmersham Park stretching out to our left between the trees.

The sight of Godmersham Park lifted me temporarily from my trance. This massive Palladian mansion was often visited by Jane Austen, whose brother Edward inherited it in the 1790s. No doubt she would have visited the local church and seen an early representation of Thomas Becket, a carved bas-relief that shows him seated, dressed in vestments and mitre.

Jane Austen frequently mentions Godmersham in her letters, and scenes from *Mansfield Park* and *Pride and Prejudice* were influenced by her visits here, charmingly remembered by one of her nieces:

> I remember when Aunt Jane came to us at Godmersham she used to bring the
> MS of whatever novel she was writing with her, and would shut herself up with
> my elder sisters in one of the bedrooms to read them aloud. I and the younger
> ones used to hear peals of laughter through the door, and thought it very hard
> that we should be shut out from what was so delightful.

PICTURESQUE PERFECTION

The Pilgrims' Way would originally have continued straight through Chilham Park, but, as at Albury, Gatton, Titsey, Chevening and most recently Eastwell, there is no longer right of access, so we followed a lower route, staying on the North Downs Way for the last mile to Chilham. Chilham is probably one of the most beautiful villages in England. It was our last stop before Canterbury, and the last of the thirteen places where, according to Belloc, the Old Road passes right up to a ruined or existing church. It was after two o'clock and we did not intend to walk any further that day, so we made ourselves at home at The White Horse and had an excellent lunch.

The guidebook claims that Chilham is 'a microcosm of the history of England' and the facts support the claim. Julliberrie's Barrow, nearby, dates from the same period as Stonehenge, suggesting that Chilham could be the earliest known settlement in this part of Kent. The castle has Roman foundations; when the Romans left, Chilham remained an Anglo-Saxon stronghold for several hundred years. Its list of distinguished residents includes Withraed, the 8th-century King of Kent and legendary figures such as Lucius the Briton, Vortigern the Dane and Hengist the Jute. The village is also associated with King Canute, William the Conqueror, King John and the Peasants' Rebellion of 1450.

It is a picturesque village, winning awards for 'Best Kept Village' and much frequented by film crews and tourists. It has the antique shops, tea shops and gift shops typical of the sort of British village that is eager to attract tourists. Every year

MORRIS DANCING: A MODERN REVIVAL

MORRIS DANCERS, often dressed in white, with bells fastened to their legs and sporting ribbons and flower-bedecked hats, are a familiar sight to country-dwellers and city folk alike. They can be seen performing in town squares and village greens in many parts of England, especially in summer and on festive occasions.

There are two main forms of this ritual ceremonial dance. The most familiar is the Cotswold morris dance, which involves six dancers who perform 'set' dances, accompanied by a musician and often a brightly dressed 'fool'. Each dance has a central theme, which may involve stick-clashing, hand-clapping or leaping. In the processional morris dance, larger groups of performers proceed through the streets in two lines, carrying brightly coloured ribboned sticks, stopping occasionally to perform a set dance, before moving on with the procession.

The origins of morris dancing are obscure. One theory links the custom

to pre-Christian pagan religions, although this has largely been discredited. Another theory explains it as a Moorish invention—hence the name 'morris'—which spread through the courts of the nobility and was taken up by the common people. Certainly, dancing of this kind has been associated with holiday celebrations since Tudor times, although it has not always been as

RIGHT *Members of a team of morris dancers display their talents in an energetic stick-clashing dance.*

popular as it is today. The tradition owes its current popularity to a revival of interest in folk dancing early in the 20th century, and again in the 1970s, which has seen the number of morris-dancing teams grow from a few dozen in 1911 to over 400.

there is a May fair, morris dancing, a 'Young Men and Maidens' race round the village, and a garden safari. Its weekly market dates back to 1260 and the heronry to 1280.

For all that, it is still a living village, clearly much loved by its residents, and its history has been absorbed into its bricks and stones. Its oldest symbol, an ancient yew tree, is reputed to have been planted in about AD 690, within ninety years of St Augustine's arrival in Canterbury and centuries before Becket was its archbishop. In fact, Chilham was at one time the home of the bones of the great St Augustine, which were brought here in 1535, in anticipation of the plundering of the monasteries by Henry VIII. The bones are lost, but the ancient sarcophagus remains.

My wanderings round this beautiful village were cut short by the pain in my back. It was so bad that, as it was midafternoon and the pub was empty (though still open), I asked the friendly landlord of The White Horse if I could make use of the hospitality of his floor for a few minutes. He said that of course I could, so for a blissful half-hour I stretched out in a corner, once again grateful to 20th-century hospitality to aching pilgrims.

This generosity to virtual strangers, dirty and tired strangers at that, made me think of the hospitality of the desert, of the days when hospitality was a sacred duty, of the instinctive kindness of man to man now so often drowned out by the pressure of modern life, perhaps even more by fear.

Just as we were so indebted to the kindness of publicans, so I must pay tribute to our overnight lodgings, our modern hospices. The cleanliness and kindness, the size of the breakfasts and the warmth of the welcome impressed us all along the route, but never more so than at Mannamead, a bed and breakfast on the Pilgrims' Way near Harrietsham, where we returned when we had seen all we had the energy to see of Chilham.

ABOVE *The White Horse pub, with the tower of the Church of St Mary behind it, stands in a corner of Chilham's main square. The brick façade was added to the Tudor building about 200 years ago.*

ABOVE LEFT *Chilham Castle seen through an avenue of trees. Inigo Jones designed the Jacobean mansion for Sir Dudley Digges, and it was built between 1603 and 1616.*

As it was our last evening together we wanted to celebrate the near-completion of our walk, so we asked Mrs Atkins, the proprietor, if there was somewhere special nearby, and she suggested we try The Ringlestone Inn, just up the road.

The Ringlestone Inn was built in 1533, originally as a hospice for monks, but around 1615 it became one of the early 'ale houses'. It still has its original brick and flint walls and floors, oak beams, inglenooks and old English oak furniture. When the dining room was added, the tables were specially made from the timbers of an 18th-century Thames barge.

ABOVE *Desserts are served to customers eating al fresco on a summer's day at the Ringlestone Inn.*

TOP *A roaring fire welcomes visitors to the snug bar in the Ringlestone Inn.*

But what appealed to me even more was its recent history. Apparently, for twenty years after the Second World War, it was run by two eccentric women, a mother and her daughter, whose cross-eyes held a powerful attraction for the local gallants. (Apparently it is good luck to sleep with a cross-eyed woman.) They ran the pub like a private house, with wine in crystal glasses and spit-roast game served mainly to their friends, who preferably came from the forces, though it was considered better still if they were officers. The rest of the world had to knock to gain admission and the women would admit only people of whom they approved. Even more curiously, they would only serve whatever drink they felt disposed to offer. Assuming that you were allowed in, you might ask for a half of bitter and find yourself holding a double whisky, or the other way round, depending on their whim.

All this came to the ears of a national newspaper, who sent a reporter down to do a story. As he came into the bar, he found himself facing neither a pint of bitter nor a double whisky, but a twelve-bore shotgun, held by one of the women. And she used it, the shot glancing across the top of his head and only just missing him. The women seem to have escaped lightly, simply being persuaded by the police that it was time they retired.

The fame of the pub reached some Americans, who wanted to transport it, stone by stone, to the States. I am glad they didn't, for with its medieval atmosphere, the excellent food and the best elderflower wine I have ever drunk, it was the perfect way to celebrate our last evening meal together.

THE LAST LAP

It was a bright day and very quiet as we packed up to set out on our last day's walk; even the gentle thrum of the Marley Tiles factory down the valley seemed to be only my own nervousness made audible.

I was as apprehensive as on that first day nearly a fortnight ago. We were nearly there, we had almost reached our goal. What would it be like? Would arriving at Canterbury be an anticlimax, or would it bring a feeling of great achievement? Most of all, I wondered whether I would find the martyred Becket's shrine a holy place or merely a tourist site.

Barbara left us at Chilham, the residents quiet behind closed doors, the shops not yet open, and we set off, going almost directly north to Old Wives Lees, under an avenue of poplars, planted as shelter for the nearby orchards. The apple blossom had fallen and the fruits were just beginning to form, though they had a

ABOVE *A tree-lined road near Old Wives Lees stretches into the distance over the undulating Downs.*

THE GARDEN OF ENGLAND

KENT, LONG KNOWN as the 'Garden of England', is blessed with fertile clay and limestone soil that is ideal for fruit-growing. Since the 16th century, when Henry VIII's fruiterer established a large collection of fruit trees and bushes at Teynham, Kent has been a major supplier of fruits such as apples, pears, cherries and blackcurrants.

These fruits, and many more, can be found today at Brogdale Horticultural Trust's centre, which in itself merits the title 'Garden of England'. The centre is located near Faversham in Kent, close to Henry VIII's orchards. It is home to the National Fruit Collections, which together constitute the world's largest collection of fruit trees and plants. Apples, of which there are a staggering 2,300 varieties, and pears, with some 550 varieties, are just two of the fruits grown in the centre's 150 acres of

LEFT *Gathering in the apple harvest at a Kent orchard. Imports are a problem for the industry, but apple varieties are now protected.*

orchards. Brogdale is a testament to the work of those enthusiasts who in the mid-20th century searched out varieties of fruit that had been mentioned in historical periods, but had been 'lost'. Eventually it also took on the responsibility of awarding Plant Variety Rights to those who produced new types of apples. The collections also include a fascinating range of lesser-known fruits, like quinces and medlars.

Brogdale is a fruit-lover's paradise, with something to offer throughout the year, particularly in spring, when the orchards burst into blossom, and in late summer and autumn, when the ripening fruits are a blaze of colour. Here, the visitor can see and buy fruit enjoyed by peoples of times past, such as the 'Decio' apple variety, which was eaten by the ancient Romans, or fruit raised in other countries, such as the American Mother, an apple produced in Massachusetts. The Trust also runs courses about every aspect of fruit cultivation and holds many events, including the Summer Fruit Festival and the Apple Celebration, as well as guided tours of the orchards.

long way to go before they would be picked and put in the huge boxes stacked expectantly in a corner of the field. As we continued through hop fields, we passed what is now an unusual sight, an unconverted oast-house.

There were no problems with the route; we had no fellow walkers; we did not even see any farm workers. The mind was free for fantasy, to imagine medieval voices pleading, 'St Thomas, heal me', to wonder what I hoped for.

We were walking through this charmed land of orchards when the skies darkened and the rain began to fall. In moments it had become a hailstorm, windy, cold and very wet. The day had started so auspiciously that we were not dressed for such a downpour, but hardly had we begun to wonder what to do, than we found ourselves approaching a private house and a collection of farm buildings. We gratefully took cover in a huge Dutch barn, hoping that the owners would not mind, and wondered how long we would have to wait. In ten minutes it was over. Once again, the birds announced the return of fair weather and the sun shone.

What made this so extraordinary was that these were the only buildings we were to pass that morning and this ten-minute storm was the only break

OAST–HOUSES: SYMBOLS OF A BYGONE AGE

OAST-HOUSES, with their unusual conical or pyramid-shaped roofs, were originally built to dry hops for use in brewing beer. Although they were built in many hop-growing areas, oast-houses are a particular feature of the Kent landscape. Most oast-houses date from the latter part of the 18th century and the 19th century, when hop-growing was at its peak.

Oast-houses comprised two main areas: the square or circular kiln, or kilns, also known as oasts, and the stowage, or processing areas, usually next to the kilns. The ground floor of the kiln housed the heat sources, above which the drying-floors were suspended. The hops were spread over the drying-floors and allowed to dry at carefully regulated temperatures, a process that might take up to 16 hours.

LEFT *Kent's largest complex of oasts, with 20 kilns, is at the Hop Farm Country Park, Beltring, Paddock Wood. It is open to the public.*

The cowl, attached to the top of the kiln, was an inverted cone-shaped structure with an open vent and a wind vane. The cowl played an important role in the drying process: able to rotate freely, it would swing round against the wind and create a draught, which helped to draw up the hot, moisture-laden air, thus increasing ventilation and the speed of drying.

Once dry, the hops were transferred to the stowage, and allowed to cool. They were then pressed into pockets hanging from a frame that was fitted to a trap door in the first floor of the stowage. The filled sacks, or pockets, were then sewn closed and stored on the ground floor, ready to be taken away.

Today, hop-drying is a mechanised process, and few oasts are used for their original purpose. Many have been converted into domestic dwellings, however, giving them a new lease of life and ensuring that their distinctive shapes will remain a presence along Kentish skylines for some years to come.

in the weather during the whole day—and only the second time it had rained since we left Winchester.

Soon we crossed the site of Bigbury Camp, an Iron Age settlement which, when excavated 100 years ago, yielded iron cart-tyres, horseshoes, bits, plough coulters, sickles and adzes. Little remains to be seen, but in any case my mind was not on the Iron Age. It was on the immediate future, for we were approaching the point where we would get our first view of Canterbury Cathedral. The Pilgrims' Way became a 'No Through Road', passing some expensive houses. To our right, the Great Stour River wandered in a leisurely way through fields and woods, and straight ahead, framed by large trees, was the cathedral.

It was an amazing moment. I thought of our predecessors along this route, who might have stopped at just this point. I thought of *The Revelation*: 'And I saw the holy city, new Jerusalem, coming down from God out of heaven, prepared as a bride adorned for her husband.'

Yet just to see the object of our journey was clearly not enough; we had to be there. At considerable risk we negotiated the A2. It amazed me that crossing a dual carriageway and scrambling over the barrier in the middle of the very busy road was not only allowed, but seemed to be the only way. We climbed Golden Hill and at last met the road taken by Chaucer's pilgrims from Southwark at Harbledown, the town Chaucer called 'Bob-up-and-down'. And there were the almshouses, built in the 1840s on the site of the leper hospital, whose floor sloped down to allow it to be washed after lepers had passed through.

In the almshouses there is still a part of one of Becket's shoes, encased in brass and crystal. The Dutch humanist and scholar Erasmus and John Colet, Dean of St Paul's, visiting Canterbury in about 1514, were apparently invited to kiss this relic. For the dean, having already declined to accept a piece of a linen handkerchief used by Becket, this was too much. 'What, do these asses imagine we must kiss every good man's shoe?' he exclaimed. 'Why, by the same rule, they might offer his spittle or his dung to be kissed.' Erasmus, although at the forefront of those who denounced pilgrimages, referring to them quite explicitly as merely tourist excursions, felt impelled to make the peace by giving a rather larger donation than he might otherwise have offered. An even more significant visitor to Harbledown was Henry II, and it was of him that I was thinking when we went into the pub opposite the almshouses for lunch.

There is no doubt that it was Henry's remark that had triggered Becket's violent death, but there is no reason to believe that he had murder in his heart. How then did he react to the news of the murder of his friend turned enemy? That he had no thought of violence is indicated by the fact that, as the knights were travelling to England with murderous intent, he was summoning a council to decide what to do about the troublesome archbishop. It was decided merely that he should be arrested. All reports agree that when he heard the news of Becket's death, Henry was distraught. He could not unsay his rash words, but he could, and did, admit that they had been the cause, if unwittingly, of the archbishop's murder.

ABOVE *Lines of trees like those in the distance beyond these hopfields near Old Wives Lees were once used to shelter the hops from strong winds. Today, netting or screens are more often used for this purpose.*

ABOVE RIGHT *A 16th-century house, now The Dickens Inn at The House of Agnes, on St Dunstan's Street in Canterbury, is said to have featured in Charles Dickens's* David Copperfield *as the home of Agnes Wickfield.*

ABOVE *St Dunstan's Street, with the 15th-century Falstaff Hotel on the left, leads to the West Gate, beyond which lies the city centre.*

Whether his distress was out of fear for his reputation, especially in the face of Becket's popularity with the people, guilt at his involvement, or sadness at losing a once-close friend, is hard to determine, but that it was genuine is not in question. He clothed himself in sackcloth and ashes, shut himself up for three days, eating little but milk and almonds and protesting his innocence. The Bishop of Lisieux wrote to the Pope, saying that the king was so tormented that they had begun to fear for his life and beseeching him to indicate the king's innocence by punishing the perpetrators of the crime. But, ironically, one of the causes for which Becket stood—that laymen who murdered priests should be tried only by clerical courts—meant that his murderers could not be punished with more than excommunication. It is believed that they were simply sent on pilgrimage to the Holy Land and may have died there.

It is generally thought that Henry did not make his penance until 1174, but he was not one to do things by halves: his remorse might have been slow in being publicly admitted, but it was at least whole-hearted. An additional spur to penitence could have been that the king needed the martyr's support, for his kingdom was in serious trouble: his sons were rebelling against him and he was facing an invasion from Scotland. He set off from Normandy and arrived at Southampton in July 1174. Living on bread and water, he travelled, probably along the Pilgrims' Way, as we had done, to Canterbury.

When he reached Harbledown, he stopped at the leper-house and ordered that they be given 20 marks a year from the royal purse (still today the sum of £13.33 is paid annually by the Crown). As the cathedral came into view, he dismounted and walked to the outskirts of the city. Here he took off his boots and, his bare feet bleeding as he walked over the cobbled roads, made his way to the cathedral. In tears, he kissed the ground where Becket had fallen and went to the crypt, where he prostrated himself before the coffin. He then removed his cloak, put his head and shoulders through one of the openings in the tomb and asked for the prayers of those present and for punishment. He received five strokes of the rod from every bishop present and three from every monk. As there were eighty monks present, they must have stayed their hands, otherwise he could hardly have survived such a flagellation. Weak and bleeding, he offered £24 and a silk pall at the shrine, assigned land to the convent and promised to build a monastery in honour of Becket and to restore the rights for which the martyr had died.

Even this was not enough for the king to feel purged of his sin. He spent the whole night lying on the ground in full view of the visiting pilgrims, who he had insisted should be allowed to enter to witness their monarch's shame. The next morning he attended Mass and left, a phial of water mixed with the blood of the martyr hanging round his neck. Soon he heard that the invasion from Scotland had been quelled and that his sons were no longer able to sustain the rebellion against their father. His former friend and archbishop must have looked kindly on him, for the tide of his fortunes had turned.

JOURNEY'S END

Perhaps we should all have travelled the last two miles to the cathedral together, but my wish to walk alone was strong; also, I wanted to leave plenty of time to wander round the cathedral before evensong at 3.30. So I asked my companions if they would mind and set off on my own, across a roundabout, onto the London Road, past the old pilgrim hospices, now hotels, along St Dunstan's Street and in through the West Gate, the last surviving city gate.

All the way I was in a state of such excitement and apprehension that I hardly took in my surroundings. I suppose it was fear of my arrival being an anticlimax that was at the root of my nervousness, but my fears took more concrete form as I became convinced that now, at the eleventh hour, something was going to prevent me from reaching the shrine—a turned ankle, a traffic accident, perhaps. Fantasy went into overdrive as every bus seemed about to dispatch me to the next world. Once at the West Gate I calmed down a little, the milling tourists becoming modern pilgrims as I sought the calm of the Eastbridge Hospital, founded by 1180 as a lodging place for poor pilgrims. Eight hundred years later and its doors were still open; I could enter freely, and spent a few moments seeing where the medieval pilgrims would have slept and worshipped.

Then through the Christ Church Gate, and I was standing before the cathedral. I half closed my eyes and imagined the scene so vividly depicted by Jonathan Sumption:

BELOW *The entrance to Eastbridge Hospital, which was originally founded to meet the needs of pilgrims visiting Canterbury but now accommodates elderly people and is open to the public.*

ABOVE *The eastern arm of Canterbury Cathedral was gutted by fire in 1174, and most of the magnificent features seen today are the result of restoration work carried out between 1175 and 1184 by the Frenchman William of Sens and his successor William the Englishman.*

The pilgrim was greeted at his destination by a scene of raucous tumult. On the feast day of the patron saint a noisy crowd gathered in front of the church. Pilgrims mingled with jugglers and conjurers, souvenir sellers and pickpockets. Hawkers shouted their wares and rickety food stalls were surrounded by mobs of hungry travellers. Pilgrims hobbling on crutches or carried on stretchers tried to force their way through the crush at the steps of the church. Cries of panic were drowned by bursts of hysterical laughter from nearby taverns, while beggars played on horns, zithers and tambourines.

On this 20th-century day in the middle of May I was disappointed that it was building and repair work that was causing the noise and confusion; the cathedral's great west door was covered with scaffolding and firmly closed. My first view of the cathedral would not be the magnificent nave. I followed signs directing visitors (and pilgrims) round the cloisters, and suddenly a new excitement gripped me.

The silver lining round the cloud of frustration caused by the building work was, surely, that I would enter as Becket had on the fateful day of his martyrdom, by the northwest transept.

Becket was walking with me as I followed the directions this way and that, passing an old man being helped down the steps by a St John's Ambulance man. Through the cloisters and I was there, not quite, as I had hoped, by St Thomas's shrine, but in the Jesus Chapel. I was about to sit quietly for a while, when I realised they were beginning to clear the cathedral for evensong and I had only a short time to spend at the places in the cathedral that are particularly associated with Becket.

First I went to the site of his martyrdom, the Altar of the Sword's Point, so named after the tip of the knight's sword, which broke off in the fatal struggle. It is impressively simple: replicas of three swords outlined starkly against the white wall, a plain table and the word 'Thomas' inscribed on the floor. Then to the eastern crypt, where the body originally lay, now marked only by a stone slab, and up the flight of stone steps leading to the Trinity Chapel. Many of the pilgrims would have climbed these steps on their knees, and the undulations made by their constant passing are a vivid reminder of the devotion the saint inspired. From 1220 until Henry VIII had it demolished in 1538, they would pray before a magnificent shrine; now it is a bare space, an expanse of stone flags with a candle in the middle.

This austere space is very moving, leaving more to the imagination than an ornate reliquary. But how impressive the huge golden tomb must have been, once one of the richest shrines in the Christian world. It stood in the centre of the chapel, a gold-covered chest encrusted with jewels, supported on pink marble columns standing on a stepped plinth. A Venetian diplomat who saw it in the 16th century described it thus:

> Notwithstanding its great size it is entirely covered with plates of pure gold. But the gold is scarcely visible beneath a profusion of gems, including sapphires, diamonds, rubies and emeralds. Everywhere that the eye turns something even more beautiful appears. The beauty of the materials is enhanced by the astonishing skill of human hands. Exquisite designs have been carved all over it and immense gems worked delicately into the patterns. Finest of all is a ruby, no larger than a man's thumbnail, which is set into the altar at the right hand side, and which…I believe, was the gift of the King of France.

King Louis, the first king of France to visit England, also left a gold cup; indeed, so many gifts were left by the pilgrims that it took eight men to lift the chest of

ABOVE *Inlaid marble roundels set into the floor of Trinity Chapel, Canterbury Cathedral. The floor was once in front of St Thomas's medieval shrine.*

TOP *Restored in 1986, the Altar of the Sword's Point marks the spot where Becket died. Prior to its destruction in 1538, the shrine here displayed the tip of a sword, broken off in the fury of the attack on Becket.*

treasures when Henry ordered their removal. A small light in the 'miracle windows' depicting the miracles of healing attributed to St Thomas, gives some idea of how it would have looked.

I could have spent a long time looking at these glowing windows, some of the oldest and finest stained glass in the cathedral, but it was time for evensong, so I joined my companions, who by this stage had arrived, and relaxed as the choir sang all seventy-two verses of Psalm 78.

We had done it, we had walked 150 miles and we were there, in Thomas's cathedral, where he worshipped and celebrated Mass, very near the place where he was murdered and the site of the shrine at which so many had come to pray for his intervention in their lives. I felt closer to him, warmer towards him. (It seemed significant that at last, like a true Becket-lover, I could refer to him as 'Thomas'.) Somehow I saw him as a brave and stubborn man, standing up for his beliefs, and I could admire him, even love him, for his courage and doggedness. But could I revere him as a saint? At that moment it did not seem important. I felt a deep peace, not to mention considerable physical relief that the long days of walking were over, and a small sense of achievement. But my mind had slipped into neutral, overwhelmed by the ancient beauty of the cathedral. The timeless chanting of the psalm took me beyond thought. I could identify now with Richard Church, visiting the cathedral in the 1940s.

> My immediate desire, when I first saw the massive but featherweight pillars receding in perspective up the aisle, with their fellows along the nave crowding together through the angle from which I saw them, was to lift my arms likewise, and to seek a high place to add to my endeavour. I wanted to shout with the voice of an army of men entering somewhere in triumph. But of course I stood there, doltlike and dumb...I can see myself standing there, hat in hand, with an agonised attention flickering away from the superb spectacle before and above me, flickering away to read the tickets on the collection-boxes and the booklets inside the door, then coming hopelessly back to that grandeur again, and once more failing.

I, too, sat 'doltlike and dumb', until the psalm at last ended and Canon Christopher Lewis introduced the lesson by saying that 'Moses is telling the people of Israel that when they arrive in the Promised Land, they must not forget to be grateful to God and generous to others'.

We each had to find our own way. I was very conscious that there were many aspects of pilgrimage—saints, relics, shrines, for instance—that I had not been able to relate to as fully as the medieval pilgrims would have done, and as some Christians still do. Aware, too, that the places I had found most holy were not the traditionally sacred centres of Christendom. Yet I knew I had been changed by this pilgrimage, and that it had not ended on my arrival at my destination, any more than life ends with death. It did not matter then that I had no great thoughts. For the moment, gratitude was enough.

OPPOSITE *The choir of Canterbury Cathedral with Trinity Chapel beyond. The chapel was built in the 13th century and housed St Thomas's shrine from 1220 until it was destroyed in 1538, during the Reformation.*

HIGHLIGHTS

The best that southern England has to offer

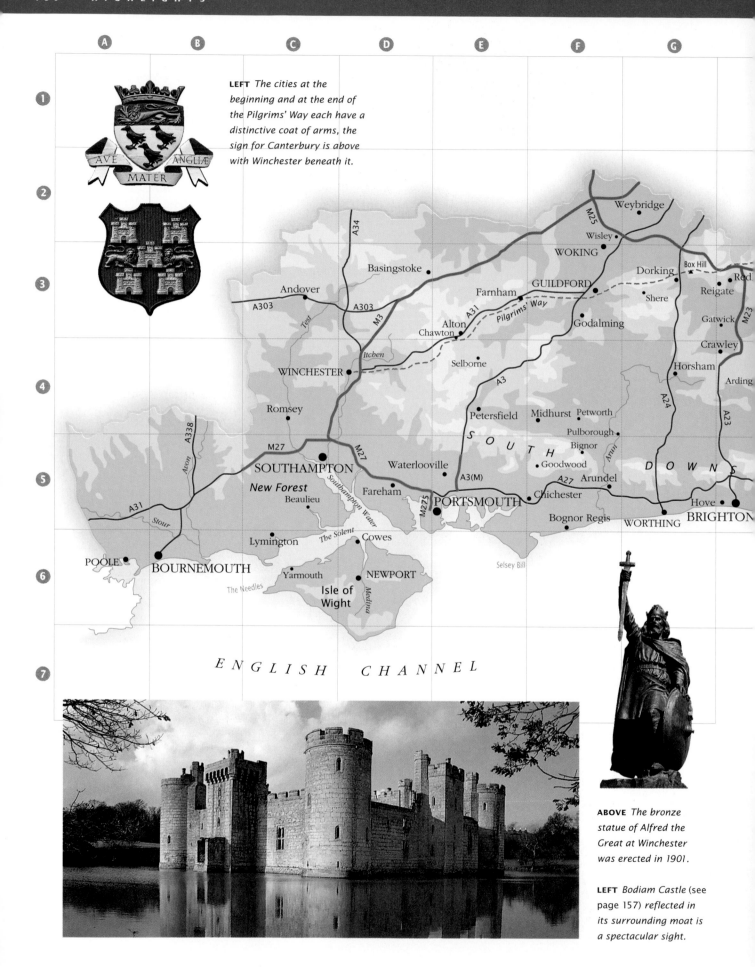

LEFT *The cities at the beginning and at the end of the Pilgrims' Way each have a distinctive coat of arms, the sign for Canterbury is above with Winchester beneath it.*

A34

M25

Weybridge

Wisley

WOKING

Basingstoke

Dorking

Box Hill

Red

Andover

Farnham

GUILDFORD

A303

Reigate

Shere

A303

Pilgrims' Way

Godalming

Gatwick

M3

Alton

A31

Chawton

Crawley

Test

Itchen

Selborne

Horsham

A23

WINCHESTER

A3

Arding

Romsey

Petersfield

Midhurst

Petworth

A24

Avon

A338

Pulborough

Bignor

S O U T H

M27

M27

Waterlooville

Goodwood

D O W N S

SOUTHAMPTON

Fareham

A3(M)

Arundel

A27

A27

New Forest

Beaulieu

Southampton Water

M275

PORTSMOUTH

Chichester

Hove

Lymington

The Solent

Cowes

Bognor Regis

WORTHING

BRIGHTON

Stour

Selsey Bill

POOLE

BOURNEMOUTH

Yarmouth

NEWPORT

The Needles

Isle of Wight

Medina

E N G L I S H   C H A N N E L

ABOVE *The bronze statue of Alfred the Great at Winchester was erected in 1901.*

LEFT *Bodiam Castle (see page 157) reflected in its surrounding moat is a spectacular sight.*

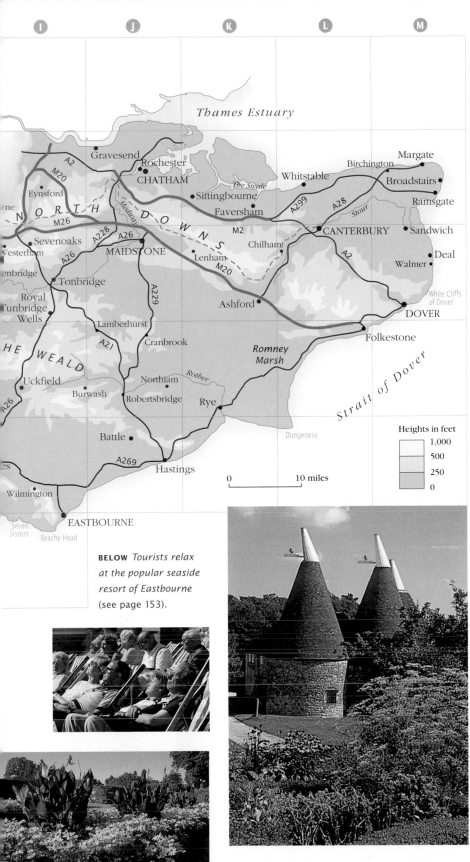

Thames Estuary

Gravesend
Rochester
CHATHAM
Eynsford
NORTH DOWNS
Medway
The Swale
Sittingbourne
Faversham
Whitstable
Birchington
Margate
Broadstairs
Ramsgate
M20
M26
A2
A299
A28
Stour
M2
Sevenoaks
Westerham
MAIDSTONE
A228
A26
A26
A229
Lenham
Chilham
CANTERBURY
Sandwich
A2
Deal
Walmer
enbridge
Tonbridge
Royal
Tunbridge
Wells
Ashford
M20
White Cliffs
of Dover
DOVER
Lamberhurst
THE WEALD
Cranbrook
A21
Romney
Marsh
Folkestone
Uckfield
Burwash
Northiam
Rother
Robertsbridge
Rye
A26
Strait of Dover
Dungeness
Battle
A269
Hastings
Wilmington
EASTBOURNE
Seven
Sisters
Beachy Head

Heights in feet
1,000
500
250
0

0   10 miles

BELOW *Tourists relax at the popular seaside resort of Eastbourne (see page 153).*

LEFT *Summer flowers at The Royal Horticultural Society Gardens, Wisley (see page 160).*

ABOVE *An oast-house set in lovely grounds at the Museum of Kent Life (see page 163).*

CONTENTS

ABOUT THIS SECTION

THE PILGRIMS' WAY from Winchester to Canterbury covers much of the varied landscape and features of southern England. In the pages that follow, the whole area, encompassing east Dorset, Hampshire and the Isle of Wight, Sussex, Surrey and Kent, is covered, revealing even more attractions of the region. From the spectacular jagged cliffs, seaside resorts and yachting centres of the coast, to the attractive villages and towns set in the rural idyll of the Weald and Downs, all parts of the region have many places of interest. Beautiful stately homes, gardens and archaeological sites include some of the most famous in the country. Museums reflect local history, especially the role played by the area in the defence of the realm and agricultural life. The 'Fame of Southern England' on pages 166–7, includes a few of the region's many famous residents.

Information about opening times, entry fees and so on should be sought from local tourist offices. Details of a selection of offices in the region are supplied on page 169.

Where appropriate, the entries that follow contain grid references for the map opposite.

CITIES, TOWNS AND VILLAGES

Arundel F5

This West Sussex town is dominated by its impressive castle which, although much restored in the 18th and 19th centuries, dates from the 11th century and retains its Norman keep and 13th-century barbican. Arundel's other two great landmarks are the majestic Roman Catholic cathedral, on a hilltop setting to the west of the castle, and the parish church of St Nicholas, which was built in the late 14th century. Other attractions include the Arundel Museum and Heritage Centre, with displays about the town's past, antique shops, leafy riverside walks, and the Wildfowl and Wetlands Trust, with its award-winning visitor centre.

Bognor Regis F5

This south-coast town began life as a fishing hamlet and was converted into a health resort by Sir Richard Hotham in the 1790s, acquiring the title 'Regis' after George V convalesced there in 1929. Now a popular destination for family holidays, it boasts several fine Regency buildings, along with sandy beaches, funfairs, bandstands, a pier with amusement arcades, cafés, nightclubs and several parks.

Bournemouth B6

Set between two pine-clad hills at the mouth of the River Bourne, Bournemouth first became a resort in the mid-19th century, after the advent of the railways made it accessible from London. Today the public gardens, two piers, pavilion, elegant arcades and Victorian parades of shops serve as reminders of this period in the town's history and, along with its seven-mile stretch of sandy beach, seaside amusements and myriad hotels, continue to draw holidaymakers and day-trippers alike.

Brighton and Hove H5

Originally a fishing and farming village called Brighthelmstone, Brighton first became widely known after the publication in 1750 of a book by Dr Richard Russell, who extolled the benefits of sea-bathing. Visits by the Prince of Wales and his circle in the 1780s guaranteed its ongoing popularity, and much of its architecture dates from this time in the town's history. The Royal Pavilion, built in the style of an Indian mogul's palace, is one of Brighton's most visited attractions (*see pages 17–19 and 159*). Others include the Lanes, the town's oldest quarter, with its antique and jewellery shops, the Palace Pier and its amusements, the Brighton Museum and Art Gallery, the Booth Museum of Natural History, and the beachfront area, with its restaurants, bars, pebble beach and other attractions. Hove, Brighton's smaller, more refined neighbour, also boasts a pebble beach and elegant Regency terraces and squares, as well as a floral clock in Palmeira Square and the Hove Museum and Art Gallery.

Broadstairs M2

Broadstairs has strong associations with Charles Dickens, who spent many summer holidays in the Kent seaside resort, and in 1849–50 wrote *David Copperfield* there. The mansion overlooking Viking Bay in which he stayed, since renamed Bleak House, is now a maritime museum. The Dickens House Museum, on the seafront, was once the home of Miss Mary Strong, on whom Dickens modelled the character Betsey Trotwood. The town's Dickens connections are celebrated each June, in the week-long Dickens Festival.

Canterbury L3

Canterbury first became a settlement under the Romans, and later the capital of a Saxon kingdom. It is famous as the birthplace of English Christianity, as it was here that St Augustine established an abbey in AD 598—the ruins of which can be seen outside the medieval city walls—and, with his followers, began the conversion of the Anglo-Saxons in the 7th century. The magnificent cathedral, begun in 1070, became a place of pilgrimage after 1170, when Archbishop Thomas Becket was murdered there, and its stained-glass windows portray scenes from the saint's life.

Other reminders of the city's medieval history include the West Gate, the only one of eight city gates still standing, the 12th-century Eastbridge Hospital, established for poor pilgrims, and the Falstaff Hotel (*see page 168*) and House of Agnes, for pilgrims arriving at night, after the city gates were closed. The Roman Museum, built on the site of a Roman town house, has original mosaic floors. The city's wealth of literary associations include Charles Dickens's *David Copperfield*, Geoffrey Chaucer's *Canterbury Tales* and T. S. Eliot's *Murder in the Cathedral*. (*See also page 22.*)

Chichester F5

Founded by the Romans in about AD 70, the city still displays elements of the typical Roman town-plan, in that its four main streets, partly surrounded by a circular wall, converge at right angles at its centre, where an ornate market cross dating from 1501 now stands. The cathedral, nearby, with its 277-foot spire, was built between 1091 and the early 15th century. Chichester also boasts some fine Georgian merchants' houses, including Pallant House, now a gallery of paintings, furniture, textiles and modern British art. Walks can be taken along the medieval city walls, affording impressive views of the town and surrounding countryside.

Cowes D6

Cowes is Britain's yachting capital and the setting of the world's most famous regatta, Cowes Week (*see below and page 169*).

ABOVE *Crowds gather in front of the Royal Yacht Squadron, housed in Cowes Castle on the Isle of Wight, to watch the start of one of the many yacht races to which the island plays host.*

Cowes has two parts, situated on either side of the Medina River and linked by a chain ferry. The long promenade of East Cowes offers excellent views of yacht-racing outside the harbour. West Cowes, on the left bank, is home to the headquarters of the Royal Yacht Squadron, the world's most exclusive yacht club, which is housed in Cowes Castle. A mile to the southeast is Osborne House (*see page 159*), seaside home of Queen Victoria, where she died in 1901.

Deal and Walmer M3

Deal was once a 'limb' of the Cinque Ports (*see feature on page 106*), and is now a quiet fishing town, with Georgian houses and a steep shingle beach. On the seafront is Deal Castle (*pictured right*), built in 1539–40 by Henry VIII. The Time Ball Tower, near the pier, was built in 1854 and used by sailors anchored in The Downs, the stretch of water between Deal and the Goodwin Sands, to check their chronometers. Deal Museum and a naval communications museum document the town's maritime history. A mile to the south is Walmer Castle, similar to Deal Castle, and also built by Henry VIII, which is now the official residence of the Lord Warden of the Cinque Ports.

Dover M3

Dover, at the English Channel's narrowest point, has been a port since Roman times, and was one of the original medieval Cinque Ports (*see feature on page 106*). Its White Cliffs (*see page 165*), which are crowned by the magnificent Dover Castle (*see pages 157–8*), dominate the cross-Channel visitor's first view of land and have become a famous symbol of England itself. In the castle grounds stands a huge octagonal stone *pharos*, or lighthouse. The Roman Painted House, in New Street, dating from the 2nd century AD, has impressive frescoes, the oldest paintings to have been discovered in Britain, and a complete underfloor heating system. Scenes from different periods in Dover's history are brought to life at the White Cliffs Experience, and at the town's museum. Today, Dover is a vast, busy passenger port.

Eastbourne I6

Its 3½-mile-long esplanade lined with majestic hotels and fine houses, Eastbourne retains the dignified charm that has attracted visitors since the 18th century. The Wish Tower, in the middle of the esplanade, was one of the Martello towers built as protection against Napoleonic invasion, and now houses a

ABOVE *An aerial photograph shows the rounded gun emplacements of Deal Castle, built by Henry VIII to deflect possible invasion by French and Spanish forces.*

puppet museum on the period. The Towner Art Gallery has works by British artists of the 19th- and 20th-century, including Henry Moore. Among the town's many splendid parks and gardens are the Carpet Gardens (*pictured below*), Hampden Park and Motcomb Gardens. In the summer months, traditional band concerts are held at the Grand Parade Bandstand.

ABOVE *A formal planting in Eastbourne's Carpet Gardens makes a fine summer display. The elegant hotels in the background, typical of this seaside resort, complete the picture.*

Farnham E3

The centre of Farnham is believed to have been laid out by the Bishop of Winchester in the 12th century. Its castle, dating from the same period and until 1927 the palace of the bishops of Winchester, overlooks the town from the top of Castle Street, which has fine Georgian houses. Built in 1619, the gabled Windsor almshouses, in the same street, reveal how Farnham might have looked before the Georgian rebuilding. At Willmer House, the Museum of Farnham, with its Georgian façade and fine carving and panelling, has displays including archaeological finds and items produced by local inventors and artists. William Cobbett (*see page 166*) was born in a house on Bridge Square in 1763, which is now the William Cobbett pub.

Faversham K2

Situated at the head of an inlet of the Swale Estuary, Faversham was a prominent manufacturing centre and busy port as early as the 12th century. It later became a centre for the gunpowder industry, documented at the restored Chart Gunpowder Mills, and is home to one of Kent's major breweries, Shepherd Neame. Displaying a harmonious mixture of architectural styles dating from the 15th century onwards, the town has a number of notable buildings, including the Guildhall, which dominates the Market Place, and the parish church of St Mary, with its distinctive spire. The Fleur-de-Lis Heritage Centre documents Faversham's history.

CITIES, TOWNS AND VILLAGES (CONTINUED)

Lewes H5

Lewes, the county town of East Sussex, stands on a spur of the Downs beside the River Ouse, dominated by its Norman castle. Anne of Cleves's House, dating from about 1500, was given by Henry VIII to his fourth wife on their divorce, and is now a folk museum. Southover Grange, nearby, was the childhood home of the 17th-century diarist John Evelyn, and Bull House, in the High Street, was the home of the 18th-century revolutionary writer Thomas Paine. Other interesting buildings include the remains of the Cluniac Priory, the Elizabethan Shelley's Hotel, and a number of tile-hung houses, typical of this part of Sussex.

Lymington C6

Situated on the tidal estuary of the Lymington River, Lymington is one of the busiest sailing resorts on the south coast, and the terminal of a ferry service to Yarmouth on the Isle of Wight. An ancient market town, it still hosts a weekly market in its Georgian high street (*pictured right*), and was for centuries a centre for salt refining. Lymington is well situated for walks along the Solent Way, one of the region's major footpaths.

Maidstone J3

The county town of Kent, lying on both banks of the River Medway, Maidstone has since the Middle Ages been a centre through which fruit and vegetables grown in the surrounding countryside have been transported to London. Weaving, hop-growing and paper-making have also played their roles in the town's history. All Saints' Church, The Archbishop's Palace, which was once a country house of the archbishops of Canterbury, and Chillington Manor House, now the town museum and art gallery (*see page 162*), are among Maidstone's fine buildings. The Museum of Kent Life, which has a hop garden, oast-house and orchard, is at Cobtree, just outside Maidstone.

Margate M2

Margate, where the first covered bathing machine was invented by local glovemaker Benjamin Beale in 1753, has many Regency and Victorian buildings dating from its early days as a seaside resort. It is still a popular destination, especially among day-trippers from London. The town's attractions include a long stretch of sandy beach, a promenade, and the Dreamland theme park, which boasts the oldest scenic railway in Britain, along with the Shell Grotto and Margate Caves.

ABOVE *Lymington's genteel high street today reveals nothing of the era when the town was the haunt of smugglers who, it is said, moved contraband between houses via underground passages.*

Newport D6

Situated at the centre of the Isle of Wight, and at the head of the River Medina, Newport has been the island's marketplace for centuries, and its capital since Saxon times. Its history dates back even further, as shown by the Cypress Road Roman Villa, where Roman hot and cold plunge baths can be seen. Other attractions include 17th-century houses, and a guildhall and square designed by John Nash. On the town's outskirts, near the village of Carisbrooke, is Carisbrooke Castle (*see page 157*), which apparently once belonged to Alfred the Great, although much of the present building was constructed later.

Poole A6

Poole, which has Europe's largest natural harbour, was well established as a port by the 12th or 13th century. Today it is largely a business centre and holiday resort, popular for its 3-mile stretch of beach. The town has some fine buildings dating from different periods, including the 15th-century Town

ABOVE *Poole's Guildhall, one of many Georgian buildings that line the town's quayside, houses a display of the town's history.*

DICKENS'S ROCHESTER

CHARLES DICKENS once said of his beloved Rochester, which he had often visited from his childhood home in nearby Chatham, 'I peeped about its old corners with interest and wonder when I was a very little child'. He retained his ties with Kent throughout his life, ending his days in 1870 at Gad's Hill Place, in Higham-by-Rochester, a house he had admired as a child and which he purchased in 1856.

Rochester provided the backdrop to many of Dickens's novels. It appeared under its own name in *David Copperfield*, *Great Expectations* and *The Pickwick Papers*, as Dullborough Town in *The Uncommercial Traveller*, and as

Cloisterham in *The Mystery of Edwin Drood*. The Royal Victoria and Bull Hotel, on the High Street, was The Bull Hotel in *The Pickwick Papers*, and The Blue Boar in *Great Expectations*. At the Guildhall, young Pip was formally apprenticed to Joe Gargery. Jasper's Gatehouse and Tope's House, now a restaurant of the same name, appeared in *Edwin Drood*, while Eastgate House featured as Westgate House, a school for young ladies, in *The Pickwick Papers*. It is now the Charles Dickens Centre, with displays from Dickens's life, tableaux from his novels and, in its garden, Dickens's chalet, which once stood in the grounds of Gad's

LEFT *Dickens's chalet, now situated in the garden of the Dickens Centre in Rochester, once stood in the shrubbery of the writer's home at Gad's Hill. The chalet was a gift from a friend in Switzerland, and arrived at Higham station packed, in pieces, in 58 cases.*

RIGHT *A modern-day Magwitch, participating in Rochester's Dickens Festival, displays the fierceness that so terrified the young Pip in* Great Expectations.

RIGHT *Although he lived in London for several years, and travelled to the USA and Europe, Charles Dickens (1812–70) retained a love of Kent, his boyhood home, which is reflected in many of his novels.*

Hill, and in which he did much of his later writing. Opposite Eastgate House is the timber-framed mansion that Dickens used as Mr Pumblechook's house in *Great Expectations*, and Restoration House, which inspired Miss Havisham's Satis House, is just off the High Street. The magnificent Rochester Cathedral, which

features in *The Pickwick Papers* and plays a central role in *Edwin Drood*, is another of the many associations with Dickens. The city celebrates these twice a year, in winter and summer festivals, when participants parade through the streets dressed as characters from his much-loved novels.

Cellars, part of a wool warehouse and today the setting for temporary exhibitions, and the perfectly proportioned 18th-century Guildhall (*pictured left*). The Waterfront Museum, housed in an 18th-century warehouse, documents the town's maritime history. Poole Quay is the departure point for boat trips to Brownsea Island and, with its restaurants and other attractions, is popular among visitors.

Portsmouth E5

Flanked by two harbours, Portsmouth has been England's chief naval base since the time of the Tudors. Reminders of this history are to be found in the harbour, and include the Tudor warship *Mary Rose*, Lord Nelson's

flagship HMS *Victory*, and the world's first ironclad warship HMS *Warrior*, which was launched in 1860. The Royal Naval Museum is also located in the dockyard. Old Portsmouth is home to the City Museum and Art Gallery, the Cathedral of St Thomas of Canterbury, and The Camber, the city's original harbour, and landing place in 1585 of Sir Walter Raleigh, with England's first supplies of potatoes and tobacco from the New World. Portsmouth was also the birthplace of the engineer Isambard Kingdom Brunel in 1806, and of Charles Dickens in 1812; the latter's birthplace in Old Commercial Road is now a museum.

Rochester J2

Situated at the crossing of the Medway River on the route from Dover and Canterbury to London, Rochester has long been of strategic importance and was a settlement before Roman times. Its history is traced in the Guildhall Museum. Rochester's two most important landmarks are the Norman castle (*see page 159*), and the cathedral, built on the site of a Saxon building established in AD 604. The main body of the church dates from the period 1179–1240, and the wooden ceiling of the nave from the 15th century. The city has close connections with Charles Dickens, and features more often in his work than

CITIES, TOWNS AND VILLAGES (CONTINUED)

ABOVE *Shoppers meander along the Pantiles in Royal Tunbridge Wells, or simply sit and enjoy the sunshine. Some of the red tiles that originally paved the area can be seen in the town's Bath Square.*

any other place apart from London (*see feature on page 155 and also page 22*).

Royal Tunbridge Wells I3

Tunbridge Wells developed after its waters were found to be rich in iron early in the 17th century, reaching its heyday as a spa between 1735 and 1761, when Beau Nash presided as Master of Ceremonies, and becoming a royal borough in 1909. The spring still exists in the portico of the old Bath House, at the entrance to the Pantiles (*pictured above*), named for the square tiles with which it was originally paved but since replaced by Purbeck flagstones. The Pantiles, with its elegant colonnades and wrought-iron balconies, is now a shopping centre with antiques showrooms, popular among visitors.

Rye K4

This attractive medieval town was an important port, and one of the Cinque Ports (*see feature on page 106*), until the sea began to recede in the late 16th century. Its harbour is now two miles away. Best known among its steep streets is the cobbled Mermaid Street, home to the half-timbered Mermaid Inn (*see page 168*), once frequented by smugglers. The Church of St Mary dates from 1120 and is renowned for the cherubic 'quarterboys' that strike the quarter-hours. The 18th-century Lamb House was the home of the novelist

Henry James between 1897 and 1914. The town's history is traced in the Rye Heritage Centre on Strand Quay.

Sandwich M3

Sandwich was a leading port, and one of the original Cinque Ports (*see feature on page 106*), until the River Stour silted up in the 16th century, and later, after the arrival of Flemish clothworkers, became a thriving market town. Buildings such as Manwood Court, the White Friars in New Street, and the Dutch House in King Street are evidence of the Flemish influence, while exhibits from the town's days as a Cinque Port and other periods can be seen in the Guildhall Museum. The twin-turreted Barbican Gate, which guards the entrance to the town, was built by Henry VIII in 1539.

Southampton C5

Situated in a natural harbour at the head of Southampton Water, the estuary of the River Test, Southampton has been a port since Roman times and a passenger port since the 19th century. Among the famous ships to have set sail from here are the *Mayflower*, in 1620, commemorated by a memorial opposite the former pier, and the *Titanic*, in 1912, whose fateful journey is documented in the Maritime Museum. Also of interest are the Museum of Archaeology, and the Tudor House Museum

and Garden, which covers local history and Victorian and Edwardian life. At the city's southern end is the modern waterfront development of Ocean Village; on its western outskirts is the Lower Test Nature Reserve.

Whitstable L2

This seaside town was once the port for Canterbury, and still has a busy harbour, fringed with fishermen's cottages, and an active fishing fleet (*pictured below*). It has been known for its oysters since Roman times and today is famous for its seafood restaurants; the Oyster Fishery Exhibition, at the harbour, and the Whitstable Museum describe the industry, and an oyster festival is held each July.

Winchester D4

Winchester was created capital of Saxon England by Alfred the Great in the 9th century, but subsequently declined in importance, fulfilling a more modest role as a market centre. Many fine buildings from different periods survive, the crowning glory of which is the magnificent cathedral. Others include the 13th-century Castle Hall, Winchester College and Kingsgate, one of five medieval gates in the city wall, and the ruined Wolvesey Castle. The surviving wing of the Bishop's Palace, built by Christopher Wren in 1674, is also of interest. The City Museum documents Winchester's ancient history, and the Westgate Museum, situated on top of the 13th-century Westgate, covers later periods. Among the city's famous residents are Jane Austen (*see feature on page 50*) and Izaak Walton, author of *The Compleat Angler*, both are commemorated in the cathedral. (*See also page 23.*)

ABOVE *Small fishing boats cluster in Whitstable harbour, where the daily catch is sold from warehouses on the quayside.*

CASTLES AND STATELY HOMES

Arundel Castle F5

Seat of the Dukes of Norfolk and Earls of Arundel since it was built at the end of the 11th century, Arundel Castle, with its battlemented towers, is set in magnificent grounds overlooking the River Arun. The castle was badly damaged during the English Civil War, but was restored in the 18th and 19th centuries. It contains furniture dating from the 16th century, along with tapestries and paintings.

Bateman's Burwash I4

This Sussex sandstone manor house and gardens, built in 1634 in the Jacobean style, was the home of the writer and winner of the Nobel Prize for Literature, Rudyard Kipling (*see page 167*), from 1902 until his death. The house is set out as it was when he lived there, with Oriental carpets and artefacts revealing his links with India. The book-lined study is where he wrote *Puck of Pook's Hill* and other works, and is full of personal objects. Gardens sweep down to the River Dudwell, where Kipling installed one of the world's first water-driven turbines to provide electricity for the house.

Bodiam Castle near Robertsbridge J4

With its ramparts rising up out of a moat, Bodiam Castle is a dramatic sight. Built in 1385, it looks like a classic storybook castle, with castellated towers and a bridge across the moat. Visitors can walk up spiral staircases to explore the battlements and enjoy the spectacular views across the countryside. The romantic castle grounds extend to the River Rother.

Carisbrooke Castle near Newport D6

Standing about 150 feet above Carisbrooke village, the castle is built on the site of a Roman fort. The Norman keep is now the oldest part of the castle, which dates mainly from later periods. During the English Civil War, Charles I sought refuge in the castle, but he was imprisoned by the castle's governor and kept there until his trial and execution. Two of Charles's children were later imprisoned at the castle and one, Elizabeth, died there.

Chartwell near Westerham I3

See feature, right.

Dover Castle M3

This magnificent ancient fortress, set on a hill above the town, retains many elements from its long and varied past, including the Roman

CHURCHILL'S CHARTWELL

SET ON A HILLSIDE overlooking the Weald of Kent, Chartwell captivated Winston Churchill from the moment he first saw it in 1921. It was to become the country home of Churchill and his wife Clementine for over 40 years.

Churchill purchased the property in 1922 and commissioned extensive alterations, happily participating in much of the work—which included expanding the lake, constructing water gardens and, most famously, bricklaying. In the later 1920s and 1930s, Chartwell reached its heyday, when Churchill, active in politics, entertained politicians, writers and painters there. During the war, Chartwell was considered vulnerable to attack from the air, and closed, but the Churchills, based at Downing Street after Sir Winston became Prime Minister in 1940, visited the estate occasionally and received fruit and vegetables from its gardens every Monday.

After Sir Winston's postwar election defeat, the Churchills returned to Chartwell, where he found solace, walking in his garden or painting in his studio, his retreat at the bottom of the orchard. Another favourite place was the study, where he wrote many of his political speeches and the books that provided an often-necessary income.

ABOVE *Visitors stroll through the gardens at Chartwell. The rooms in the house remain as they were when the Churchills lived there.*

In 1946, the Churchills were rescued from financial difficulties by a group of friends and admirers who anonymously bought Chartwell, presenting it to the National Trust on condition that the Churchills could continue to live there. After Sir Winston's death in 1965, however, Lady Churchill relinquished it to the National Trust, and today the public can enjoy its elegant interiors and beautiful gardens, which are still imbued with the character of its famous owner.

BELOW *A photograph taken in the study at Chartwell depicts Churchill, who preferred to work standing up, reading at his lectern.*

CASTLES AND STATELY HOMES (CONTINUED)

lighthouse, which is one of the tallest Roman structures still standing in Britain. Tunnels built in medieval times were used during the Napoleonic Wars and the Second World War. There are re-creations of the visit by Henry VIII and his court in 1539, and of the treatment of a Second World War casualty in the underground hospital. Many special events are held at the castle.

Down House Downe H2

Down House was the home of Charles Darwin (*see page 167*) and his family for over 40 years. It was here that Darwin wrote his revolutionary book, *The Origin of the Species*. Visitors can see his study and displays about his theories.

Firle Place near Lewes H5

Firle Place (*pictured right*), the home of the Gage family for over 500 years, shelters in a cleft of the South Downs. The rambling house has some of its original Tudor buildings, but was remodelled in two stages in the 18th century, mainly using pale Caen stone. Firle Place is a family home but is open to the public and contains fine Old Master paintings, furniture, and Sèvres porcelain. The house is surrounded by an extensive park, set against a magnificent backdrop of woodland.

Goodwood House near Chichester F5

Home to the Dukes of Richmond since 1697, Goodwood House is still occupied by members of the family, the Earl and Countess of March. The 1st Duke's Jacobean house was extended in the Regency period and the building is a mixture of the two styles. The refurbished interior of Goodwood House provides an opulent setting for 18th-century paintings collected on the Grand Tour, family portraits, furniture and porcelain. The State Apartments, built for entertaining, are a venue for corporate and private functions.

Hever Castle near Edenbridge H3

The double-moated manor house of Hever Castle is set beside the River Eden. The medieval walls and gatehouse enclose a Tudor mansion built by the Boleyn family. It was here that Henry VIII courted Anne Boleyn, who became his second wife. The castle later fell into disrepair, remaining so until it was bought and renovated by the wealthy American William Waldorf Astor in 1903. He also built a 'village' of Tudor-style cottages in the grounds for guests, and added the gardens, including an Italian garden, and a lake.

ABOVE *Swans grace the tranquil waters of the Long Pond in the grounds of the magnificent Firle Place, which stands majestically in the background.*

BELOW *The entrance to Knole House, seen here from the park, has a splendid gabled front built by Thomas Sackville in 1605. Each gable is surmounted by a stone leopard, the family crest.*

Ightham Mote near Sevenoaks I3

This manor house has buildings dating chiefly from about 1340 until 1530, arranged round a courtyard and surrounded by a moat. It has been extensively renovated by the National Trust since 1988. The restored Tudor chapel has painted ceiling panels, Chinese wallpaper lines the drawing room, the billiard room has been restored to its appearance in the late 19th century, and the Robinson Library is as it was in the 1960s.

Knole House near Sevenoaks I3

Knole House (*pictured below*), known as one of the treasure houses of England, is home to the original Knole settee, among many other pieces of beautiful furniture, and tapestries, carpets and portraits. Built in the 15th century, Knole was enlarged in 1603 and has not been altered since. It is a 'calendar house', with 365 rooms, 52 staircases and seven courtyards. Many famous people have been connected with Knole, including the writer Vita Sackville-West, who was born there. It was the setting for *Orlando*, a novel by Virginia Woolf.

Leeds Castle near Maidstone J3

See feature on page 126.

Loseley Park near Guildford F3

Loseley Park has been the home of the same family since it was built by Sir William More from 1562 to 1568, at the request of Elizabeth I.

The total cost of the house, which replaced an earlier manor house, was £1,640 19s 7d. The building stone allegedly came from Waverley Abbey, following its dissolution, and some of the panelling was from Henry VIII's Nonsuch Palace. The house retains an Elizabethan style and contains many works of art. It is set in an estate of 1,400 acres of farmland and woodland, and a walled garden contains rose, herb, flower, fountain and vegetable gardens. This lovely house and its grounds are a popular venue for private events and for film and television productions.

Osborne House near Cowes D6
Famous as the country house of Queen Victoria, Osborne House was designed by Prince Albert and Thomas Cubitt as an Italianate villa and built between 1845 and 1851. It was a family home, and Victoria spent many of her 40 years of widowhood there. It was granted to the nation after her death and retains much of its Victorian style. In the First World War, a section was made into a convalescent home for officers, and patients included A. A. Milne and Robert Graves.

Parham Park near Pulborough F4
This lovely Elizabethan house was built by Sir Thomas Palmer in the late 16th century. It has many early features, such as a panelled Long Gallery with painted ceiling and a beautiful Great Hall. Many of the items in the house were collected by the Pearsons, who bought the house in 1922 and attempted to decorate it with objects that were in keeping with the interior. The grounds include a walled garden and 18th-century Pleasure Gardens with a brick and turf maze.

Penshurst Place Tonbridge I3
Built of local sandstone by successive owners, Penshurst Place has a medieval heart that features the magnificent Baron's Hall, dating from 1341. Later additions have made it a manor house with defences, and inside it holds a collection of tapestries, paintings, furniture and armour. The gardens retain the 16th-century walls and terraces, and the garden rooms date from the 19th century. A toy museum displays antique items, including toys used by generations of children from the Sidney family, who live at Penshurst Place.

Petworth House F4
Built in 1688 round the old manor house of the Percy family, Petworth House now contains one of the finest collections of paintings and sculpture in the care of the National Trust. The impressive mansion contains works by Turner, Van Dyke, Reynolds and Blake and limewood carvings by Grinling Gibbons. As well as the fine staterooms, the family rooms of Lord and Lady Egremont, who live there, are open on weekdays; the medieval chapel has been repaired and the old kitchens and servants' quarters are also open. Beyond the 30-acre woodland garden near the house is the 700-acre Petworth Park, designed by 'Capability' Brown and now home to a large herd of fallow deer.

Polesden Lacey near Dorking G3
This splendid Regency villa (*pictured below*) commands an enviable position on the North Downs. Built in the 1820s to designs by Thomas Cubitt, it was extensively refurbished in the early 20th century. Its last private owners, the Grevilles, bought the house in 1906 and designed most of the interiors in the Edwardian style, which has been retained. Mrs Greville was an heiress and society hostess, and her parties at Polesden Lacey were celebrated events. She even loaned the house to the future King George VI and Queen Elizabeth, now the Queen Mother, for their honeymoon in 1923. Her fine collection of porcelain and silver, as well as furniture and paintings, are displayed in Polesden Lacey, which evokes the era of country house parties. The extensive grounds include a rose garden and landscape walks.

Quebec House Westerham I3
Named after the place where he was mortally wounded in the war against the French, Quebec House was the childhood home of General Wolfe (1727–59). He lived in this gabled brick house until he was 11 years old, and despite changes after he left, it retains many original features, such as the panelled rooms, along with memorabilia relating to Wolfe. The Tudor stable block houses a display about the Battle of Quebec.

Rochester Castle J2
Commanding superb views across the River Medway and the town, Rochester Castle is a fine example of Norman architecture. It stands on high open ground, surrounded by medieval walls partly built on the foundations of the Roman city wall. The keep, built in 1127, is about 70 foot square and rises to over 100 feet. Its exterior is well preserved, although the floors and roof are missing.

Royal Pavilion Brighton H5
One of the most distinctive and exotic buildings in the country is the Royal Pavilion, with its Indian-style exterior and Chinese-inspired interior. It was built on the site of a farmhouse leased by the future George IV, who had it rebuilt as a classical villa in 1787. John Nash later altered the building, creating the celebrated building of minarets and domes seen today. One of the most spectacular rooms is the Banqueting Room, illuminated by a lamp weighing one ton and attached to the ceiling by a silvered dragon; the dining table is laid with Regency silver gilt. Queen Victoria's bedroom is dominated by a four-poster bed with six mattresses. (*See also pages 17–19 and entry on page 152.*)

Uppark near Petersfield E4
This late 17th-century house set high on the South Downs has magnificent views across the countryside to the sea. In 1989 a fire destroyed much of the interior, but an extensive restoration programme has re-created the elegant Georgian rooms, and restored paintings collected on the Grand Tour, and a famous doll's house. Below stairs, the servants' quarters have been set out as they would have looked in 1874, when H. G. Wells's mother was housekeeper here.

LEFT *The central section of the classical entrance to Polesden Lacey, shrouded in climbers. The villa replaced an earlier house, where the politician and playwright Richard Sheridan lived for a few years from the end of the 18th century.*

GARDENS

Emmetts Garden near Sevenoaks I3
Set on one of the highest spots in Kent, Emmetts Garden is an informal garden with spectacular views across the county. It was planted in the late 19th century and has something of interest throughout the year. There are daffodils and bluebells in spring, a rose garden in bloom in summer, and acer and cornus foliage in autumn. There are also exotic shrubs and a rock garden.

Great Dixter Northiam J4
The family home of the great garden designer Christopher Lloyd (*pictured below*), Great Dixter is surrounded by one of the most innovative and constantly changing gardens in Britain. The 15th-century house was enlarged by Sir Edwin Lutyens (*see feature on page 70*) from 1910. He also designed most of the gardens for Christopher Lloyd's father. Lutyens incorporated the outbuildings in his plans, such as the Barn Garden. Since then, Christopher has experimented to great effect with new plantings. The Long Border contains a range of plant combinations that change with the seasons, and the old rose garden has been replaced with a spectacular exotic planting of cannas, bananas and dahlias.

Mottisfont Abbey near Romsey C4
Set on the west bank of the River Test, Mottisfont Abbey is surrounded by sweeping lawns with ancient trees and walled gardens. A former Augustinian house, the abbey has been adapted over the centuries by a series of owners. The extensive gardens were remodelled gradually during the 20th century: Norah Lindsay designed a parterre, Geoffrey Jellicoe redesigned the north front with an avenue of limes and an octagon of yews, and the rose garden was designed in 1972 by Graham Stuart Thomas after the National Trust had taken over the property. The garden now contains the National Collection of Old Fashioned Roses, with over 300 varieties. A particular feature of the grounds are the old trees; one, the Great Plane, is thought to be the largest of its kind in the country.

Nymans Garden near Crawley H4
Situated in an Area of Outstanding Natural Beauty on the Sussex Weald, Nymans Garden reflects the taste of three generations of the Messel family, who had only three head gardeners in over 100 years. Its diverse collection of plants ranges from exotic species from distant locations to plants raised in the garden and named after the property or members of the Messel family. The surrounding estate includes a wild garden and woodland walks.

The Royal Horticultural Society Gardens Wisley F2
Wisley is the flagship garden of the Royal Horticultural Society and demonstrates a wide variety of gardening techniques and styles. Different designs are shown through a series of model gardens. Long borders show plant combinations, glasshouses include displays of orchids, vines and exotics, a 16-acre fruit field contains over 670 apple cultivars, and autumnal colour is a feature of the area known as Seven Acres. Wisley also contains the Society's laboratory, and horticultural trials are carried out on the Portsmouth Field.

Scotney Castle Garden Lamberhurst J4
Roses and wisteria ramble over the ruins of the 14th-century moated Scotney Castle, in one of the most romantic gardens in Britain. It was designed in the 19th-century picturesque style. The steeply sloping land is covered with rhododendrons and azaleas, and there is a Henry Moore sculpture on an isthmus on the lake, a memorial to Christopher Hussey, who gave Scotney to the National Trust in 1940. The extensive estate includes lovely parkland, meadows, woodland and hopfields.

Sheffield Park Garden near Uckfield I4
Arranged round four great lakes filled with water lilies and linked by cascades and waterfalls, Sheffield Park Garden was originally laid out by 'Capability' Brown, and then by Humphry Repton, in the 18th century. In the mid-19th century Sheffield Park became an important venue for cricket, and a pitch and pavilion were added. Trees reflected in the water, especially in their autumnal hues, are among the attractions of the gardens. Many colourful species were planted by Arthur Soames, who bought the estate in 1910. He was also responsible for extensive plantings of rhododendrons and roses. The gardens now contain the National Collection of Ghent azaleas.

The Sir Harold Hillier Gardens and Arboretum near Romsey C4
This 180-acre garden was established by the gardener Sir Harold Hillier in 1953. Hillier was a great plant collector, who travelled the world in search of new species, and his garden and arboretum now hold 11 National Plant Collections and a range of Champion Trees. There is always something of interest in the grounds, and for this reason it is known as a garden for all seasons. Particular features include the Gurkha Memorial Garden and the largest winter garden in Europe.

ABOVE *Roses clamber over an arch at Mottisfont Abbey, famous for its old rose collections. Many of the cultivars are derived from 19th-century French examples popularised by Josephine Bonaparte.*

Sissinghurst near Cranbrook J4
See feature, below.

Wakehurst Place Ardingly H4
Wakehurst Place, set round an Elizabethan mansion, is known as one of the most beautiful gardens in England. Maintained by the Royal Botanic Gardens at Kew, it has plants from around the world, and contains the Wellcome Trust Millennium Building, which houses a conservation project known as the Millennium Seed Bank. Wakehurst Place has a series of ornamental features, such as waterfalls and lakes, as well as exotic trees, lawns and woodland.

West Dean Gardens near Chichester F5
Classic 19th-century landscaping is evident at West Dean Gardens: a walk links 2½ acres of kitchen garden, 35 acres of ornamental grounds, 240 acres of landscaped park and 49 acres of arboretum. It has a variety of attractions, from a 300-foot-long Edwardian pergola to water and wild gardens, but the best known is the Victorian walled kitchen garden, where peppers, orchids and aubergines are among the delicate plants that grow in 16 glasshouses. In the beds outdoors are cabbages, carrots and other vegetables, as well as herbaceous borders; fruit trees are trained along the garden walls. West Dean College, set in the flint mansion house in the grounds, runs courses on many arts and crafts, and on subjects including gardening.

Winkworth Arboretum near Godalming F3
This hillside woodland has an award-winning collection of over 1,000 varieties of tree and shrub, including many rare species. The trees are planted round two lakes and stunning autumn colour is provided by specimens such as Japanese maples and the tupelo from Texas. In the spring, impressive displays of bluebells and azaleas bring added interest to the arboretum.

THE GARDENS AT SISSINGHURST

in 1937. The Nicolsons lived in the 15th-century South Cottage, where Harold wrote some of his biographies, including *King George V*, and the essay *The English Sense of Humour*.

Vita died in 1962, and Harold in 1968. Since 1967 the property has been run by the National Trust, and the gardens, where many of the Nicolsons' original features can still be seen, have become popular among lovers of gardens and literature alike.

LEFT *This view of Sissinghurst shows the famous rose garden and Yew Rondel.*

BELOW *The tower was built for the visit of Queen Elizabeth I, which took place in 1573.*

WHEN, IN 1930, the writer Vita Sackville-West first saw Sissinghurst, near Cranbrook in Kent, she described it as 'but a castle running away into sordidness and squalor, a garden crying out for rescue'. She and her husband, Harold Nicolson, bought the property and answered that cry.

The Nicolsons spent the following 30 years transforming Sissinghurst from a virtual ruin into a beautiful country home with one of the most beautiful gardens in all England. Parts of the Elizabethan manor house were restored, while others became features of the gardens, which were planted as a series of 'rooms', each with a different colour scheme or flowering season. Especially well known are the White Garden, its beds bejewelled with white flowers and grey foliage, and the rose garden, at its most splendid in June and July. At the centre of the rose garden is the Yew Rondel, a circular hedge with four openings offering tantalising glimpses of parts of the garden, which was designed by Nicolson.

In her study in Sissinghurst's Elizabethan tower, Vita Sackville-West did her writing, completing her novels *The Dark Island* there in 1934 and *Pepita*

MUSEUMS AND GALLERIES

The Booth Museum of Natural History
Brighton H5

Built by the ornithologist Edward Booth in 1874 to house his collection of stuffed birds, the museum has expanded to include over half a million other animals from across the globe. As well as examples of the taxidermist's art, there are skeletons ranging from the tiny pygmy shrew to the killer whale and about 50,000 fossils, minerals and rocks. Local natural history is also featured, including the bones of a Sussex dinosaur, dating from 140 million years ago.

Brooklands Museum Weybridge G2

The world's first purpose-built motor-racing track was built at Weybridge in 1907 by a wealthy landowner, Hugh Locke King, at a cost of about £150,000. The heyday of the racing circuit, the 1920s and 30s, is celebrated in displays; some of the buildings reflecting the Art Deco style have been used in filming period scenes. Brooklands also played an important role in the history of British aviation, and it was here that A. V. Roe flew the first British-built aeroplane in 1908. Tommy Sopwith learned to fly at Brooklands and built the Sopwith Pup and Camel there. The story of over 80 years of aviation at the site is told in the museum. Special events include car rallies and flying demonstrations.

Butser Ancient Farm
Waterlooville E5

Founded in 1972, this is an open-air laboratory for archaeology. Using evidence from excavations of prehistoric and Roman sites, archaeologists have re-created an Iron Age Farm (*pictured below*) and a Roman villa.

ABOVE *A section of the Overlord Embroidery shows some of the wartime leaders, including Dwight Eisenhower, Bernard Montgomery and Winston Churchill.*

The aim of the farm is to find out what life was really like 2,000 years ago: prehistoric and Roman crops are grown, early breeds of sheep and goats are kept, and ancient technologies are studied.

Canterbury Heritage Museum L3

The history of this ancient city is traced in this museum, in the restored medieval Poor Priests' Hospital. Displays cover periods from the Roman occupation, the founding of the cathedral by St Augustine, and the medieval period, when Canterbury was a destination for pilgrims. Local writers such as Joseph Conrad are also featured. A 'passport' covers entry to this museum and others in the city, including the Roman Museum, the West Gate Museum, the Royal Museum and Art Gallery, and the Regimental Museum.

Charles Dickens Centre Rochester J2
See feature on page 155.

D-Day Museum and Overlord Embroidery near Portsmouth E5

The Allied invasion of Normandy on D-Day, June 6, 1944, marked the beginning of the end of the Second World War. Displays and reconstructions evoke life in wartime Britain and the preparations for the invasion, which is re-created in detail with a landing craft, military vehicles and personal memorabilia. The centrepiece is a 272-foot-long embroidery depicting Operation Overlord (*pictured above*). Inspired by the Bayeux Tapestry, it took five years to make and is the largest work of its kind in the world.

Gilbert White's House and the Oates Museum Selborne E4
See feature on page 52.

Guildford Museum F3

Set in part of a 17th-century merchant's house, this museum focuses on local history, archaeology and needlework. The local history collection covers trades, industries, social life and memorabilia relating to local people such as Lewis Carroll, creator of *Alice in Wonderland*, and Gertrude Jekyll, the garden designer. The collection also contains Palaeolithic hand axes and 17th-century glass and pottery. The needlework collection includes samplers, patchwork, lace and dress accessories.

Jane Austen's House Chawton E3
See feature on page 50.

Maidstone Museum and Art Gallery J3

A wide range of collections is displayed in the museum, at Chillington Manor, an Elizabethan manor house. Exhibitions of fine and applied art include paintings, ceramics, glass, furniture, textiles and costume from the 17th to the 20th centuries. Archaeological finds cover the Roman to the medieval periods in Kent. The Ancient Egyptian collection features a mummy, while the Japanese collection has artefacts from the Edo period (1600–1868). The pieces gathered by Julius Brenchley, a 19th-century explorer from Maidstone, are in the ethnographic gallery. Victoriana, natural history and local military history are also featured.

The nearby Tyrwhitt-Drake Museum of Carriages is the most important collection of carriages in the country.

Museum of Kent Life near Maidstone J3

Located near the River Medway, this museum is housed in and around a collection of farm buildings. The museum describes various rural and agricultural activities: the hop-farming and processing system is demonstrated in a hop garden and an oast-house, agricultural machines are displayed in a barn, and produce is grown in a kitchen garden, orchard and herb garden. There is also an 18th-century farmhouse, a granary from the 19th century, a shepherd's hut and a forge, as well as a livestock centre and an aviary.

National Motor Museum Beaulieu C5

A high-level monorail takes the visitor through the roof of one of the finest motor museums in the world. The collection includes examples of the earliest vehicles, through the Golden Age of Motoring from 1919 to 1930, to classic cars of the later 20th century, such as the Volkswagen Beetle and the Austin Mini. Also shown are cars that have held the World Land Speed Record, racing cars, commercial vehicles and motorcycles. The museum is set in the grounds of Palace House and the 13th-century Beaulieu Abbey which, as well as the gardens, are open to visitors.

Powell-Cotton Museum, Quex House and Gardens Birchington M2

Major Powell-Cotton's dioramas, some measuring more that 70 feet, of exotic stuffed animals form the centrepiece of this unique museum. As a big-game hunter, Powell-Cotton collected and brought back animals from places all over the world, and displayed them in cases with painted backdrops depicting different environments, such as forests and swamps. He also collected artefacts, which form an ethnographic collection, expanded by other members of his family. Quex House, built as a Regency gentleman's residence and extended in the Victorian period, is also open, along with gardens and woodland.

Royal Armouries at Fort Nelson near Fareham D5

This fort, dating from the 1860s, is home to the Royal Armouries' artillery collection, which was transferred from the Tower of London. It is one of the most important collections of artillery in the world, with exhibits including sections of the Iraqi supergun of the 1980s. There are also French field guns from the Waterloo battlefield and fortress guns from India and China; some guns are still fired in demonstrations. Fort Nelson itself was built as part of the fortifications to protect the Royal Dockyard in Portsmouth, and visitors can explore the ramparts and tunnels in which ammunition was stored. The fort's living quarters have also been restored.

Tangmere Military Aviation Museum near Chichester F5

The general history of military flying and the history of the RAF station at Tangmere are told at this museum (*pictured right*). During the Second World War, the RAF at Tangmere played a vital role in the Battle of Britain and it was from Tangmere that Lysander planes flew to occupied Europe, carrying Special Operations Executive agents on their secret missions. After the war, Tangmere was the RAF's base for high speed flight.

Weald and Downland Open Air Museum near Chichester F5

As its name implies, this museum is situated outdoors. The exhibits are buildings displayed in 50 acres of countryside in a magnificent setting (*pictured below*). Over 45 historic buildings, ranging in period from medieval to Victorian times, have been rescued from certain destruction, rebuilt and restored at the

ABOVE *One of the four hangar-style halls at Tangmere shows a range of military aircraft.*

museum. Structures on view include a Tudor farmstead, a working 17th-century water mill and a Victorian school. Courses in building conservation and demonstrations of traditional rural crafts and skills are held at the museum.

World Naval Base Chatham J2

This museum documents over 400 years of naval history, its exhibits include HMS *Cavalier*, Britain's last Second World War destroyer and the spy submarine *Ocelot*. There is also a display of 15 full-size lifeboats, with related archive film and artefacts. The Wooden Walls section offers visitors the opportunity to join William Crockwell, an 18th-century carpenter's apprentice, for an animated display on the building of the warship *Valiant*.

BELOW *Cattle graze near one of the many historic houses in the idyllic rural surroundings of the Weald and Downland Open Air Museum.*

ARCHAEOLOGICAL SITES

EVER SINCE BRITAIN *broke away from the Continent and became an island, the south and east coasts have been a landing point for wave upon wave of peoples from mainland Europe, many of whom left traces of their presence. The coast and the adjacent interior are consequently rich in archaeological sites that tell the story of the island's long history of invasion, of which a small selection is provided below.*

Battle of Hastings Battlefield and Abbey Battle J5

The Battle of Hastings of 1066 was actually fought six miles inland, at Battle. Today, an impressive gatehouse, built in 1338, of a former Benedictine monastery dominates the town. The abbey was founded by William the Conqueror as a penance for those killed on the nearby battlefield. An audio-tour of the battlefield guides the visitor round the site, and displays describe the context of the battle, and abbey life.

Bignor Roman Villa F5

In 1811, a ploughman, while turning the soil, exposed a Roman mosaic pavement at Bignor, near the Sussex South Downs; subsequent excavations revealed it to be part of a Roman villa. Covering an area exceeding 4 acres and comprising 65 rooms, it is one of the largest in Britain. Its impressive mosaics, dating from the 4th century AD, include representations of the legendary characters Ganymede and Medusa, and fighting gladiators. An indoor marble fountain and underfloor central heating system are also of interest.

Cissbury Ring near Worthing G5

Cissbury Ring is typical of the grand Iron Age hill-forts built by warring tribes around 300–200 BC and, in its high, defensive position enhanced by a circular ditch and mile-long double ramparts, still looks defensible today. Even earlier human activity at the site has been indicated by hollows that are thought to have been the work of Neolithic miners, who dug pits and passageways some 4,000 years ago to extract flint nodules for use in the production of flint tools. In one of the mine-shafts archaeologists have found the remains of a Neolithic girl, possibly trapped by a rock fall and still holding a burnt torch in her outstretched hand.

RIGHT *A series of ditches mark the remains of the defences built in several phases at Richborough Castle between the 1st and 3rd centuries* AD.

Fishbourne Roman Palace and Museum near Chichester F5

Fishbourne, discovered by accident during the digging of a water-main trench in 1960, is the site of a magnificent Roman palace dating from about AD 75. It is thought to have been built for a Celtic king, Tiberius Claudius Togidubnus, who had supported the Roman invasion of AD 43. The impressive remains include 20 spectacular mosaic floors (*detail pictured left*), courtyards, corridors and a bath suite. In the museum, plans, photographs, artefacts, models and an audiovisual display tell the story of life at Fishbourne, and the garden has been replanted to its original plan.

The Long Man of Wilmington I5

This giant figure cut into the chalk hillside south of Wilmington, measuring some 235 feet in height, is of uncertain origin. The earliest reference to it dates from 1710, but local legend attributes it to the Iron Age, or even the Bronze Age; others explain it as a Roman creation, or that of a monk who lived some time between the 11th and the 15th centuries. Explanations as to the function of the figure describe him variously as a god, a fertility symbol and a folly.

Lullingstone Roman Villa near Eynsford I2

A house was first built at this site, on a narrow terrace cut into the hillside overlooking the River Darent, in about AD 80, early in the Roman period. In the 2nd century, baths and kitchens were added. The house was subsequently abandoned, but reoccupied late in the 3rd century, when the mosaic floors, a granary, a temple mausoleum and a circular shrine were built. The bath house was rebuilt and enlarged, and one room was converted into a Christian chapel, making this one of the earliest known places of Christian worship in Britain. Today, visitors can see Roman walls, mosaics and other finds from the site, housed under a permanent shelter. The remains of a small Saxon Christian church, built over the pagan temple mausoleum, are also of interest.

Richborough Castle near Sandwich M3

The Isle of Thanet in north Kent was once a true island, separated from the mainland by the Wantsum Channel, and the Romans constructed a fort at each entrance to the channel. Richborough Castle (*pictured below*), built on a peninsular at the southern end of the channel, dates from about AD 285. Richborough is reputed to have been the landing spot for the main Roman invasion in AD 43, after which it became an important base and the chief port on the east coast. The foundations of a triumphal arch built soon after the invasion survive, as does much of the outer wall of the castle, reaching a height of 25 feet in places. Remnants of Watling Street, the Roman road that ran, via Canterbury, to London, can also still be seen. Many of the utensils, ornaments, weapons and coins found during excavations beneath the walls of the fort can be seen in the museum.

THE GREAT OUTDOORS

IF THERE IS ONE FEATURE *that is characteristic of the geology of southern England, it is chalk, vast stretches of which underlie the region's rolling hills. This predominance is reflected in many of the beauty spots of the South, most spectacularly along the coast, where massive, craggy chalk cliffs stretch for miles.*

Beachy Head I6

This spectacular chalk cliff, rising sheer from the sea to a height of 534 feet, is still as impressive as it must have been when the Normans named it Beau Chef, meaning 'Beautiful Headland', which has since evolved into the present name. Magnificent views stretching as far as the Isle of Wight in the west and Dungeness in the east are to be had from its summit.

Box Hill G3

Box Hill, which takes its name from the dark-leaved box trees that grow there, is Surrey's best-known beauty spot. At a height of 564 feet, it offers splendid views of the surrounding countryside towards the South Downs, including Leith Hill, which, at 965 feet, is the highest point in Surrey. Box Hill's 1,200 acres of woods and chalk downs also make excellent walking. The Old Fort was built in the 1890s to provide protection from French invasion. Below the fort is the grave of Major Peter Labellière, a Dorking resident who died in 1800 and asked to be buried upside-down.

Dungeness L5

This bleak shingle promontory at the tip of Denge Marsh has seen many shipwrecks, and a lighthouse was first erected here in 1615. Today, two lighthouses stand on the shore, the current one dating from 1961 and a disused one, which offers spectacular views, from 1904. Looming out of the flat landscape are the two towers of Dungeness nuclear power station, where tours of the reactor hall and control room can be taken. Dungeness is also the southern terminus for miniature steam trains running to and from Hythe. Nearby is Dungeness RSPB Reserve, a wintering ground for many migratory birds, which has an information centre and offers a waymarked walk.

The Needles C6

The three 100-foot pinnacles that form the Isle of Wight's most famous landmark are part of a chalk ridge that once joined the island to the mainland. Today they are a major tourist

ABOVE *The Seven Sisters chalk cliffs reflect the glow of the sunlight on a winter's day. The gently undulating landscape and views along the coast make this a favourite place for walkers.*

attraction, and nearby is The Needles Pleasure Park at Alum Bay, where souvenirs of the multicoloured sands in the cliffs can be purchased. Alum Bay is also the site of the world's first wireless telegraph station, where Marconi conducted experiments between 1897 and 1900, commemorated by a monument in the car park. The grassy chalk ridge of Tennyson Down, named after the poet, who lived nearby, offers a tranquil walk to The Needles from Freshwater Bay.

The New Forest C5

Occupying some 145 square miles in the southwestern corner of Hampshire, the New Forest was formally established by William the Conqueror in about 1079, the term 'forest' meaning an area subject to forest law, where deer were safeguarded for the king's hunting. The area is now home to several varieties of deer, and wild donkeys and ponies. There are trees including beech, oak and birch, large heaths supporting a wealth of flora and fauna, and bogs containing rare plants, birds and insects. For the visitor, there are fine walking, riding and camping, as well as golf courses and football and cricket fields.

Old Winchester Hill D4

This area of chalk downland to the southeast of Winchester is a national nature reserve. It

is home to beech, yew and juniper trees and some rare wild flowers. The earthen ramparts of a 5,000-year-old hill-fort are to be found at the summit of the hill.

The Seven Sisters I6

A line of gracefully undulating chalk cliffs, the Seven Sisters (*pictured above*), in fact numbering eight, stretch along the coast between Cuckmere Haven and Birling Gap. The South Downs Way follows the clifftop, offering spectacular views and displays of wild flowers in summer.

The White Cliffs of Dover M3

The giant chalk cliffs that guard the town of Dover, for centuries the traditional gateway to the island from the Continent, have come to be seen as a symbol of England itself. Shakespeare Cliff, so named because it is mentioned in a scene in *King Lear*, is the largest, rising some 300 feet out of the sea. Separated from Shakespeare Cliff by a deep cleft are the Western Heights, occupied by fortifications of the Napoleonic War period. On the other side of the town is East Cliff, the summit of which is commanded by Dover Castle (*see pages 157–8*). A cliff path takes walkers to South Foreland and St Margaret's Bay beyond.

THE FAME OF SOUTHERN ENGLAND

SOUTHERN ENGLAND *has produced some world-famous achievers in a variety of fields. Many equally famous people originating from other parts, often in search of a rural retreat close to London, have also been drawn to the region over the centuries. Here we present a selection of those who at some time in their lives have made southern England their home.*

Will Adams
Navigator

(1564–1620, born in Gillingham) Adams began his seafaring life as a boy and later joined the navy. In 1598 he set sail for the Indies as pilot-major with a fleet of Dutch ships, reaching Japan in 1600. The first Englishman to visit Japan, he was thrown into prison on suspicion of piracy, but so impressed the Shogun with his knowledge of ships and shipbuilding that he was later freed and given an estate, a pension and the rank of samurai. He also served as the agent of the Dutch East India Company, helping to set up an English trading factory. His career in Japan inspired *Shogun*, James Clavell's novel of 1975.

H. E. Bates
Writer

(1905–74, born in Rushden) H. E. Bates, an exponent of the short-story form, started his working life as a country-town solicitor's clerk and journalist. These experiences developed his understanding of rural English life, which was to become a feature of his work. Bates, commissioned as a writer by the RAF in 1941, first became famous during the Second World War, with *The Greatest People in the World* and *How Sleep the Brave*, written under the name 'Flying Officer X'. Later works included *The Darling Buds of May* (1958), depicting farm life in Kent, which became a popular television series.

Vanessa Bell
Painter and decorative designer

(1879–1961, born in London) Vanessa Bell, elder sister of the famous writer Virginia Woolf, was a leading member of the Bloomsbury Group, whose members gathered to discuss aesthetic and philosophical questions. She studied at the Royal Academy Schools, and exhibited works in her decorative style, influenced by Matisse, in the second Post-Impressionist Exhibition in 1912. She left her husband, the critic Clive Bell, for the painter Duncan Grant, with whom she collaborated on interior design projects, and they lived periodically at Charleston, near Firle in Sussex, for several years.

William Cobbett
Writer and reformer

(1763–1835, born in Farnham) The son of a farmer and innkeeper, he left home at the age of 11 and walked to Kew Gardens to find a job. A self-educated man, he was, at times, sergeant-major, journalist, gardener, farmer, political agitator, Member of Parliament, English teacher, bookseller and publisher. He lived in France, Germany and America, eventually returning to England. He was both radical writer, serving a two-year sentence at Newgate for his comments on flogging in the army, and traditionalist, championing the ideal of a rural England resisting the ravages of the Industrial Revolution, a view propounded in his *Rural Rides*, published in 1830.

HILAIRE BELLOC

HILAIRE BELLOC, poet, historian and essayist, was born in France in 1870 and moved to England with his family during the Franco-Prussian war. His boyhood home, during the 1870s and 80s, was in Slindon, on the Sussex Downs, and he returned to the Downs in adulthood, buying a house called King's Land, near Shipley, where he was to live periodically until his death in 1953.

Sussex seems to have provided Belloc, whose life has often been described as restless and unsettled, with stability and continuity. It appeared in much of his work, and was the subject of *Sussex*, his highly personal account of the county. It also featured in *The Old Road*, published in 1904, where he described an ancient neolithic track between Winchester and Canterbury, which he believed had been revived

and followed by medieval pilgrims visiting the shrine of St Thomas Becket. He walked the route himself, timing his arrival at Canterbury to coincide with the day and hour of Becket's murder centuries earlier.

Belloc, a prolific and versatile writer, produced over 150 titles on many subjects, including theology—he was a devout Roman Catholic—and economics, as well as verse, biographies and satiric novels,

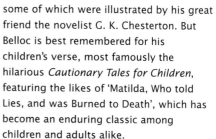

RIGHT *Hilaire Belloc, apart from being a prolific writer, also sat as Member of Parliament for Salford between 1906 and 1910, first as a Liberal and then as an Independent.*

some of which were illustrated by his great friend the novelist G. K. Chesterton. But Belloc is best remembered for his children's verse, most famously the hilarious *Cautionary Tales for Children*, featuring the likes of 'Matilda, Who told Lies, and was Burned to Death', which has become an enduring classic among children and adults alike.

LEFT *A scene from 'Matilda' shows people ignoring Matilda's cries for help in a real fire, because they had been tricked by her before.*

Colin Cowdrey
Cricketer

(Born 1932 in Bangalore, India) Displaying his talent at an early age, Cowdrey played for the Tonbridge School XI at 13, and later for Oxford University, becoming captain of the Oxford XI in 1954. He also played for Kent and for England, both of which he captained, taking part in a record 114 Tests for England. As chairman of the International Cricket Council between 1989 and 1993, he oversaw the return of South Africa to international cricket, and the agreement of the international code of conduct in 1992, the year in which he was knighted. His son Christopher has also captained Kent and England.

Charles Darwin
Naturalist

(1809–82, born in Shrewsbury) Most famous as the originator of the theory of evolution by natural selection, Darwin studied medicine at Edinburgh University, and botany, zoology and geology at Cambridge. From 1831 to 1836 he travelled as a naturalist on HMS *Beagle*, to places including Brazil, Chile, New Zealand and the Galápagos Islands, gathering information that would aid his future studies, chiefly carried out at Down House (*see page 158*). He constructed the principles of natural selection in the 1840s, and in 1859 published the controversial *The Origin of Species by Means of Natural Selection*, which eventually found general acceptance. Later works developed his ideas on evolution. After his death in 1882 he was buried at Westminster Abbey.

William Harvey
Physician and scientist

(1578–1657, born in Folkestone) Son of a prosperous merchant, Harvey was educated in Canterbury, at Cambridge, and later in Padua. His revolutionary discovery that the heart, acting as a pump, ensures the constant circulation of the blood through the human body, described in *An Anatomical Exercise on the Motion of the Heart and the Blood in Animals* (1628), was ridiculed by traditionalists. He was subsequently recognised and honoured, however, and went on to hold positions at St Bartholomew's Hospital and the Royal College of Physicians, becoming physician to both James I and Charles I, whom he attended at the Battle of Edgehill.

John Harvey-Jones
Industrial executive

(Born 1924 in Kent) After training at Dartmouth Naval College and serving in the navy, Harvey-Jones joined the large international chemicals company ICI in 1956. He rose to the position of chairman, a post he held between 1982 and 1987, and was instrumental in reshaping the company, before becoming chairman of Parallax Enterprises. More recently he has become well known to television audiences through *Troubleshooter*, a series in which he visited and advised businesses. He was knighted in 1985.

Rudyard Kipling
Writer

(1865–1936, born in Bombay, India) Rudyard Kipling, awarded the Nobel Prize for Literature in 1907, is chiefly remembered as a writer of short stories and poems, often depicting British soldiers in India, and of tales for children. *The Jungle Books*, the *Just So Stories* and *Kim* are among his most famous works. Kipling spent his childhood in India and at boarding school in England, and as a young man worked as a journalist in India. In 1902 he bought Bateman's, a house at Burwash in Sussex (*see page 157*), which remained his home until his death in 1936.

Bernard Montgomery (of Alamein)
Soldier

(1887–1976, born in London) Montgomery (*pictured below*), a veteran of the First World War, commanded the British 3rd Division in France early in the Second World War, and in 1942 was appointed commander of the demoralised 8th Army in North Africa. The German army in Africa under Rommel was seen as invincible, but Monty, as he became known, gave the British soldiers the will to win, which they did at the decisive Battle of El Alamein. He went on to lead the

British forces in the Normandy invasion in 1944, and received the German capitulation on May 4, 1945. After the war he was made a knight of the garter, and was created a viscount in 1946. He retired to Isington Mill near Binsted in Hampshire, where he wrote his *Memoirs* and kept mementos including his wartime caravan command centre.

Florence Nightingale
Nurse and hospital reformer

(1820–1910, born in Florence, Italy) Florence Nightingale is best known for her tireless work among injured soldiers during the Crimean War, when she drastically reduced mortality rates by imposing strict standards of cleanliness. She was also the founder of nursing training, and in 1860 established in London the Nightingale School for Nurses, the first such institution in the world. Having spent much of her life in Hampshire, where her family kept Embley Hall as a winter home, she chose to be buried at St Margaret's Church in nearby East Wellow.

Alfred, Lord Tennyson
Poet

(1809–92, born in Somersby) Tennyson's reputation as a poet was first established by the publication of *Poems* in 1842, and enhanced by *In Memoriam*, begun after the death of his friend Arthur Hallam, considered typical of Victorian poetry. He became Poet Laureate in 1850, and in 1853 moved to Farringford, on the Isle of Wight, which was to be his home for almost 40 years; he built a summer home in West Sussex in 1868. At Farringford Tennyson wrote such poems as 'The Charge of the Light Brigade', and loved to walk along the clifftops, to which the memorial on Tennyson Down above Freshwater Bay bears testimony today.

Virginia Wade
Tennis player

(Born 1945 in Bournemouth) Having spent much of her childhood in South Africa, Virginia Wade returned to England at the age of 15, later becoming a student at Sussex University. Highlights of her tennis career have included winning the US Open title in 1968, the Italian championship in 1971, the French championship in 1972, and the women's singles championship at Wimbledon in 1977. Today, she maintains her involvement with the sport through broadcasting.

HISTORIC HOTELS, INNS AND PUBS

The Dog and Bear Hotel Lenham K3

Hop bines are hung from oak beams in the restaurant and bar of this country inn and hotel in the picturesque village square of Lenham. One of the rooms in the Dog and Bear, Room 26, is allegedly haunted by a ghost who rearranges the furniture. Visitors who wish to avoid this supernatural activity can opt to stay in any of the other rooms in the hotel, which was built in 1602 and visited by Queen Anne in 1704.

The Falstaff Hotel Canterbury L3

Established in 1403, The Falstaff Hotel is situated just outside Canterbury's city walls. It is one of a number of lovely medieval, timbered buildings that line the street, many of which were built on the site of earlier hostelries that catered for pilgrims, especially those who arrived at Canterbury after curfew and were locked out of the city. The Falstaff Hotel has an internal courtyard that was once used by coaches and horses. Low ceilings, beams and panelling add to the hotel's atmosphere.

The George Hotel Yarmouth C6

Overlooking the Solent, the George Hotel on the Isle of Wight has lovely views across to Yarmouth Castle, built by Henry VIII, and the village of Yarmouth itself is home to the Royal Solent Yacht Club. The 17th-century building was constructed for the island's governor and Charles II is reputed to have stayed here in 1672. Renovations have retained many features such as the flagstone entrance hall and wood-panelled staircase. The hotel owns *The Master George*, a 36-foot motor yacht that can be chartered.

The Master Builder's House Hotel
Buckler's Hard, near Beaulieu C5

This hotel, in a scenic location on the banks of the Beaulieu River in the former shipbuilding centre of Buckler's Hard (*see page 14*), was once the home of the master shipbuilder Henry Adams, who lived there from 1749 until 1805. Located on the Beaulieu Estate at Buckler's Hard, the hotel has recently been renovated, and has a terrace and gardens. It is the sister hotel to The George Hotel, Yarmouth (*see above*).

The Mermaid Inn Rye K4

The Norman cellar and foundations of The Mermaid Inn (*pictured above, centre*) probably date from 1156, but the original building was destroyed by fire when the French raided the Cinque Port of Rye in 1377.

Rebuilt in about 1420 using Sussex oak, the inn prospered with the town in the 15th and 16th centuries, when Rye was an important port and Mermaid Street led directly to the sea. By the 17th century, smuggling had become a major activity in Rye and The Mermaid Inn was the haunt of notorious gangs. False panels in some rooms and a hidden stairway are indications of this infamous period. The inn gained a more reputable clientele in the early 20th century, when people such as the writer Henry James and the actress Ellen Terry lived nearby.

The Royal Hotel Winchester D4

Some sections of The Royal Hotel date from the 14th century, but the main building was the home of Lady West, who had it built in the 16th century. An ardent Catholic, she gave refuge to priests persecuted under Elizabeth I's Protestant rule. This connection continued in the 18th century, when the house provided a haven for nuns fleeing the anti-clerics of the French Revolution. A chapel built for the nuns survives as two bedrooms on the second floor of the hotel. An 18th-century 'silk manufactory' built in what was once a nearby building now forms the hotel's function rooms.

The Spread Eagle Hotel and Health Spa
Midhurst F4

Hilaire Belloc is reputed to have described this hotel as 'the oldest and most revered of all the prime inns of England'. Established in about 1430, the Spread Eagle Hotel has many early features, including a Tudor bread oven and Flemish stained-glass windows. There is also an oak-beamed lounge and many of the rooms are furnished with antiques. A health spa has been added.

The White Horse Shere G3

The building that is now The White Horse (*pictured below*) was originally a farmhouse, constructed in the 16th century, and probably became an inn in the 17th century. At this time, the inn had its own brewhouse and hops were grown in what was once the farmhouse garden. The area was known as being one of the most lawless parts of the county and The White Horse became part of the smuggling activity that was rife there. By the 19th century, Shere had become known as

an attractive village, and the writers and artists who visited it usually frequented The White Horse. The pub retains its intimate atmosphere, with tiny corridors linking a warren of rooms.

The White Horse Inn Chilham L3

This atmospheric inn in the historic village of Chilham dates from the 15th century, and has lovely beamed ceilings and an inglenook fireplace of 1460. It is reputed to be haunted by the benign ghost of a former vicar, Samson Hieron, who lived in Chilham during the English Civil War.

CALENDAR OF FESTIVALS AND EVENTS A SELECTION

THE SOUTHERN ENGLAND CALENDAR *reflects the broad spectrum of activities across this large and varied area. This calendar gives a flavour of some artistic, sporting and traditional events in the area, but details of many more, and precise dates, which may vary annually, may be obtained from the local tourist information offices (see* USEFUL INFORMATION *below).*

JANUARY

HASTINGS INTERNATIONAL CHESS CONFERENCE December–January

FEBRUARY/MARCH

FOLKESTONE AND DYMCHURCH EUROPEAN AND ALL ENGLAND SEA ANGLING CHAMPIONSHIP

APRIL

CANTERBURY CHAUCER FESTIVAL A celebration of Chaucer and *The Canterbury Tales*.

MAY

BRIGHTON INTERNATIONAL FESTIVAL An arts festival held during most of the month with events ranging from recitals and street theatre to fireworks and a circus.
EASTBOURNE INTERNATIONAL FOLK FESTIVAL Teams of folk dancers from around the world take part in this festival.
GUILDFORD SURREY COUNTY SHOW A one-day agricultural show, held at the end of May.
HASTINGS JACK-IN-THE-GREEN MORRIS DANCING FESTIVAL Festival of traditional dance with a procession during the May Day weekend and crowning of the May Queen.

JUNE

ARDINGLY SOUTH OF ENGLAND AGRICULTURAL SHOW A mixture of agricultural, horticultural, forestry and countryside activities.

ARUNDEL CORPUS CHRISTI CARPET OF FLOWERS AND FLORAL FESTIVAL A floral carpet extending for about 90 feet along the central aisle of the Roman Catholic Cathedral is a feature of this festival that culminates in a Mass and procession on the Feast of Corpus Christi from the cathedral to Arundel Castle for Benediction. Girls dressed in white scatter petals along the route.
EASTBOURNE INTERNATIONAL LADIES' TENNIS CHAMPIONSHIP Players compete on one of the finest grass courts in the world at Devonshire Park.
EPSOM RACECOURSE THE OAKS AND THE DERBY HORSERACING MEETINGS Two classic horse races that both date from the late 18th century, are held on the Epsom Downs.
GLYNDEBOURNE FESTIVAL OPERA This famous festival season of operas extends from May until August and attracts many world-class performers to this attractive venue.

JULY

CHICHESTER FESTIVITIES An arts festival of events including music, literature and fireworks held at venues in and around the town. The Chichester festival is a theatre season that lasts for most of the year.
GOODWOOD RACECOURSE GLORIOUS GOODWOOD A five-day race meeting on the Surrey Downs is held at the end of July or early August.
MAIDSTONE KENT COUNTY SHOW Agricultural county show held at Detling showground.
WINCHESTER HAT FAIR Festival with street entertainment and stalls.

AUGUST

COWES WEEK AND FESTIVAL Yacht races including the Round-the-Island Race, the largest sailing

race in the world *(above)*, and associated festivities held in late July and early August.
ROYAL TUNBRIDGE WELLS SCANDALS AT THE SPA Characters in Georgian costume re-create the town as it was 200 years ago for a few days at the end of July or early August.

SEPTEMBER

FAVERSHAM HOP FESTIVAL A celebration of the hop harvest, beer and brewing.
LEEDS CASTLE BALLOON AND VINTAGE CAR WEEKEND

OCTOBER

CANTERBURY FESTIVAL An arts festival of music, dance, drama, exhibitions and talks.

NOVEMBER

BRIGHTON LONDON TO BRIGHTON CAR RUN The famous annual veteran car run.

DECEMBER

ROCHESTER DICKENS WINTER FESTIVAL A parade through the town of people in Victorian dress, many as Dickensian characters, with a funfair and stalls. Summer festivals are held at Rochester and Broadstairs.

USEFUL INFORMATION

Listed below are the details of Tourist Information Centres for a selection of destinations. Please note that these details may be subject to change.

BRIGHTON AND HOVE
10 Bartholomew Square
Brighton, BN1 1JS
Tel. (0906) 7112255

BOURNEMOUTH
Westover Road
Bournemouth, BH1 3BU
Tel. (0906) 8020234

CANTERBURY
34 St Margaret's Street
Canterbury, CT1 2TG
Tel. (01227) 766567

GUILDFORD
14 Tunsgate
Guildford, GU1 3QT
Tel. (01483) 444333

NEW FOREST MUSEUM AND VISITOR CENTRE
Main Car Park
Lyndhurst, SO43 7NY
Tel. (023) 80282269

WINCHESTER
Guildhall, The Broadway
Winchester, SO23 9LJ
Tel. (01962) 840500

For general information, contact:

DORSET TOURISM
1st Floor, County Hall
Dorchester, DT1 1XJ
Tel. (01305) 221001

ISLE OF WIGHT TOURISM
Westridge, Brading Road
Ryde, PO33 1QS
Tel. (0983) 813800

SOUTH EAST ENGLAND TOURIST BOARD
The Old Brew House, Warwick Park,
Tunbridge Wells, TN2 5TU
Tel. (01892) 540766

SOUTHERN TOURIST BOARD
40 Chamberlayne Road,
Eastleigh, SO50 5JH
Tel. (023) 80620006

The following websites may also be of interest (NB website addresses can change):

Dorset Tourism:
http://www.dorset-cc.gov.uk

Isle of Wight Tourism:
http://www.islandbreaks.co.uk

South East England Tourist Board:
http://www.southeastengland.uk.com

Southern Tourist Board:
http://www.southerntb.co.uk

British Tourist Authority:
http://www.visitbritain.com/southern-england

The South of England:
http://www.gosouth.co.uk

INDEX

Note: page numbers in **bold** refer to captions for illustrations

ACKNOWLEDGMENTS

The editors gratefully acknowledge the use of information taken from the following publications during the preparation of this book:

AA Beautiful Britain, Southeast Britain, Reader's Digest Association Limited for the Automobile Association 1987

The Canterbury Tales: An Illustrated Edition by Geoffrey Chaucer translated by Nevill Coghill, Penguin Books Limited and Century Hutchinson Limited 1986

The Dictionary of National Biography, Oxford University Press

The Encyclopaedia Britannica

The Garden of England by Robin Whiteman and Rob Talbot, George Weidenfeld and Nicolson Limited 1995

A guide to The Pilgrims' Way and North Downs Way by Christopher John Wright, Constable & Company Ltd 1993

Kent by Nigel Nicolson, George Weidenfeld & Nicolson Limited 1988

National Trail Guide, The North Downs Way by Neil Curtis, Aurum Press Ltd in association with the Countryside Commission and the Ordnance Survey 1992

National Trail Guide, The South Downs Way by Paul Millmore, Aurum Press Ltd in association with the Countryside Commission and the Ordnance Survey 1990

The Old Road by Hilaire Belloc, Constable and Company Limited 1921

Pevsner Architectural Guides, Penguin Books

Philip's County Guide, East Sussex, general editor Keith Spence, George Philip 1993

Philip's County Guide, Hampshire, general editor Robin Dewhurst, George Philip 1993

Philip's County Guide, Surrey, general editor Keith Spence, George Philip 1993

Philip's County Guide, West Sussex, general editor David Arscott, George Philip 1993

The Pilgrims' Way by Sean Jennett, Cassell & Company Ltd 1971

Reader's Digest Illustrated Guide to Britain's Coast, Reader's Digest Association Limited 1996

South-East England by Oliver Mason, John Bartholomew & Son Ltd 1979

Thomas Becket by Frank Barlow, Weidenfeld and Nicolson 1986

Thomas Becket by David Knowles, Adam and Charles Black 1970

PICTURE ACKNOWLEDGMENTS

T = top; *C* = centre; *B* = bottom; *L* = left; *R* = right.

Front Cover The National Trust Photo Library **Back Cover** John Crook **2** Images Colour Library **4** Tetra **6–7** Gettyone Stone/Gary John Norman **10–11** John Bethell **12** John Crook **13** *B* Patrick Sutherland *R* Angus Taverner **14** NHPA **15** *L* NHPA *R* Michael Jenner *C* Angus Taverner **16** AF Kersting **17** Gatwick Airport Marketing **18** Gettyone Stone **19** Gettyone Stone **20** John Bethell **21** Gettyone Stone **22** John Bethell **23** Patrick Sutherland **24–25** Countryside Agency/Mike Williams **26** Shirley du Boulay **27** John Crook **28–29** Private Collection **29** The British Library, Roy 18, D.11, Folio 148 (detail) **30** *T* Tetra *C* Shirley du Boulay **32** John Crook **33** Museum of London **34** John Crook **36** *TL* Tetra *TR* Tetra *B* John Crook **37** John Crook **38–9** John Crook **40** The Dean and Chapter of Winchester **43** John Crook **44** *T* Tetra *B* Winchester Tourism Office **45** *TL* Winchester Tourism Office *TR* Diana Snow/Watercress Line *CR* Tetra *B* Tetra **46** AF Kersting **49** Countryside Agency/Mike Williams **50** *TC* John Crook *TR* John Crook *B* Chawton Jane Austen Museum **51** AF Kersting **52** Gilbert White Museum **54** Tetra **56** *T* Angus Taverner *B* Countryside Agency/Mike Williams **57** John Crook **59** AF Kersting **60** Tetra **61** AF Kersting **63** *T* John Crook *C* Tetra **64** *T* AF Kersting *B* Tetra **65** Tetra **66** Countryside Agency/Mike Williams **67** Tetra **69** AF Kersting **70** *TL* The Hulton Getty Print Collection *TR* Jonathan Buckley/Great Dixter *B* Country Life Picture Library **71** *T* KCC Tourism *B* AF Kersting **72** *TL* Tetra *TR* Michael Jenner *C* Michael Jenner **73** Loseley Park **74** *T* Southern Tourism/Chris Parker *B* AF Kersting **75** John Bethell **76** *T* Tetra *C* Countryside Agency/Mike Williams **77** Tetra **78** AF Kersting **80** Tetra **81** Tetra **82** Cephas/Mick Rock **83** Countryside Agency/Mike Williams **84** AF Kersting **86** *TL* NHPA/Dr Pott *TR* Dr Francis Rose *B* NHPA/Dr Pott **88** AF Kersting **90** Harry Smith Horticultural Photographic Collection **91** *BL* Tetra *CR* Angus Taverner *BR* Tetra **92** Countryside Agency/Mike Williams **94** Tetra **96** *TL* NHPA/ Stephen Dalton *TR* NHPA/Werner Zepf *C* NHPA/Stephen Dalton *B* NHPA/Stephen Dalton **98** QA Photos Ltd **99** Angus Taverner **100** AF Kersting **101** AF Kersting **102** Angelo Hornak Library **103** By kind permission of Dean and Chapter of Canterbury **104** The British Library, Add. 42130, Folio 208 (detail) **105** Sonia Halliday Photographs **106** *T* AF Kersting *BL* Dover Express *BR* Tetra **107** The British Library, BL Loan 88, Folio 4v/Paul Getty KBE/The Wormsley Library **109** The British Library, Harl. 5102, Folio 32 **110** Sonia Halliday Photographs **111** Courtesy of the Trustees of the V&A **113** AF Kersting **114** AF Kersting **115** Countryside Agency/Mike Williams **116** AF Kersting **117** *T* Kent Tourism *C* Tetra **118** Tetra **119** AF Kersting **121** Patrick Sutherland **122** John Bethell **123** British Paper Association **124** AF Kersting **126** *T* Kent Tourism *BL* Leeds Castle Enterprises Ltd *BR* Leeds Castle Enterprises Ltd **127** Leeds Castle Enterprises Ltd **128** Tetra **129** *T* Patrick Sutherland *B* Tetra **131** Tetra **132** Countryside Agency/Mike Williams **133** Countryside Agency/John Tylar **134** Countryside Agency/Mike Williams **136** John Crook **137** *TL* John Bethell *TR* Countryside Agency/Mike Williams **138** *TL* Kent Tourism *C* Kent Tourism **139** *TR* Countryside Agency/Mike Williams *C* Patrick Sutherland **140** AF Kersting **141** Countryside Agency/Mike Williams **142** John Bethell **143** Tetra **144** AF Kersting **145** *T* Angelo Hornak Library *C* Dean and Chapter of Canterbury **146** Dean and Chapter of Canterbury **148-49** Gettyone Stone/Paul Harris **150** *TL* Tetra *BL* The National Trust Photo Library *BR* John Crook **151** *BR* Museum of Rural Life *BL* The Royal Horticultural Society *C* John Crook **152** Angus Taverner **153** *T* English Heritage *B* John Bethell **154** John Bethell **155** *T* Private Collection *CL* Dickens Museum *CR* Tetra **156** *TL* Tunbridge Wells Tourism *BR* John Bethell **157** *T* Chartwell Museum *B* The Hulton Getty Picture Collection **158** *T* Firle Place Estates *B* Knole House **159** John Bethell **160** *CL* Great Dixter *BR* Mottisfont Abbey **161** *CL* John Bethell *BR* Patrick Sutherland **162** *T* D-Day Museum *BL* Butser Ancient Farm **163** *TR* Tangmere *B* Weald and Downland Open Air Museum **164** *T* Fishbourne Roman Palace and Museum *B* English Heritage **165** John Crook **166** *BL* Private Collection *BR* The Hulton Getty Picture Collection **167** The Hulton Getty Picture Collection **168** *T* AF Kersting *CR* Tetra **169** Angus Taverner

SEPARATIONS Studio One Origination Ltd, London

PAPER Périgord-Condat, France

PRINTING AND BINDING Printer Industria Gráfica SA, Barcelona, Spain